SOLOMON'S
BUILDERS

SOLOMON'S BUILDERS

FREEMASONS, FOUNDING FATHERS AND THE SECRETS OF WASHINGTON, D.C.

CHRISTOPHER HODAPP

Ulysses Press

Published by: ULYSSES PRESS
P.O. Box 3440
Berkeley, CA 94703
www.ulyssespress.com

ISBN-10: 1-56975-579-5
ISBN-13: 978-1-56975-579-2
Library of Congress Control Number: 2006907936

Printed in Canada by Transcontinental Printing

10 9 8 7 6 5 4 3

Acquisitions Editor: Nicholas Denton-Brown
Managing Editor: Claire Chun
Editor: Richard Harris
Copyeditor: Lily Chou
Editorial and production staff: Matt Orendorff, Lisa Kester,
    Elyce Petker, Steven Zah Schwartz, Stefanie Tamura
Index: Sayre Van Young
Cover design: DiAnna VanEycke, Christopher Hodapp

Distributed by Publishers Group West

For Alice, my own Sophia.

Table of Contents

✦✦✦

Acknowledgments

This book would not have been possible without the enduring excitement and tireless assistance of my wife, Alice. It is her love of history that has been the engine pushing me to completion.

I am indebted to Mark A. Tabbert of the George Washington Masonic National Memorial for his friendship and his assistance; to Daniel Thompson, secretary of Fredericksburg Lodge No. 4, for his kindness and generosity; and to the Grand Lodge Free and Accepted Masons of the District of Columbia for their warm welcome and kind hospitality with absolutely no prior notice.

To Michael Segall, Michel Singer, Philippe Benhamou and other French brethren who assisted in my quest for information about French Masonry before and after their own revolution.

To the incredible on-line resources of Paul M. Bessel, Gary Dryfoos, Phoenixmasonry, and especially the Grand Lodge of British Columbia and Yukon—Masonic brethren who labor long and tirelessly in obscurity and whose efforts are of incalculable value.

To Nathan Brindle, Stephen Dafoe, Eric Schmitz, Jeff Naylor, Jim Dillman and the other "Knights of the North" for their encouragement and their assistance. And to the brethren of Broad Ripple Lodge No. 643 and Lodge Vitruvian No. 767 for their friendship and their understanding during a very hectic year.

To Nick Denton-Brown, Richard Harris, Claire Chun and everyone at Ulysses Press who took part in proposing this project and working long, last-minute hours to get it to press. Thank you all for your support.

Finally, I must publicly thank Dan Brown. Consciously or not, it is his work that has kindled new interest in institutions the world had forgotten about for a long time, and given those of us who still believe in them a new chance to tell their story.

Author's Note

When Dan Brown published *The Da Vinci Code* in 2003, I suspect he had no idea that it would sell 61 million copies in three years and become a worldwide phenomenon. Sitting down at the computer to write the sequel to the eighth best-selling book in publishing history is, I am guessing, a daunting, if not terrifying, task.

Brown left clues on the dustjacket of *The Da Vinci Code* as to what his next book would be about. The biggest involved spotting certain letters in the book's inner flap that were printed darker than the others. Written out in order, they spelled a curious phrase: "Is there no help for the widow's son?" But one group around the world understood the message clearly—the ancient fraternity of Free and Accepted Masons. So it would seem the most eagerly anticipated sequel in modern history—believed to be titled *The Solomon Key*—is going to be about the Freemasons. Further, in an interview shortly after *The Da Vinci Code*'s publication, Brown himself said that the sequel would take place in Washington, D.C., and even held a contest on his website for fans to decipher other clues on the cover of the original book.

The world is still awaiting Brown's sequel, and several anticipated publishing dates have come and gone while Brown has dealt with a famous lawsuit and a big-budget movie. During the delay, the film *National Treasure* (2004) and novels like Brad Meltzer's *Book of Fate*, along with scores of books, articles and television shows seeking to out-think Brown's unpublished plot, have all touched on similar subjects.

In spite of the worldwide mania over topics Brown covered in his previous books, he is above all a novelist. The supposed facts that come from the mouths of his characters are frequently not true, in spite of his contention to the contrary. Brown's previous book *Angels and Demons* dealt with the Illuminati, a group that has often been erroneously tied to the Freemasons, ever since its short lifespan in Europe during the late 1700s. That's what writing fiction is all about, and Brown does spin a good yarn. But I suspect the Vatican, Opus Dei, and the National Organization for Albinism and Hypopigmentation are less than enthused by the liberties he has taken with facts. Similarly, Freemasons are nervous.

Solomon's Builders was not written to second-guess Brown's sequel, but to separate the truth from the fiction about the real Freemasons who were present at the birth of the United States, and the reality behind the building of Washington, D.C. Myths, legends and conspiracy theories have existed about the Masonic involvement in the history of the United States ever since the end of the American Revolution. This book is designed to give the reader the real story, before it gets lost in *Solomon Key* mania. There are no plot spoilers here, since no one knows what Brown has written until it lands in bookstores. But when you curl up in your comfy chair to read his undoubtedly exciting sequel, you will at least be armed with the truth ahead of time.

Christopher L. Hodapp
November 2006

Introduction

✦✦✦

Open your wallet and with any luck you'll find a $1 bill there. Take it out and look at it closely, maybe for the first time. You hold in your hand more than just a sheet of paper with limited buying power. It is a connection to more than two centuries of history. Look into the eyes of George Washington. His portrait is a commemoration of a decade of struggle and revolution; of the leadership of a man who was at one time venerated, in the words of Thomas Jefferson, as a "demigod"; of the founding of a great experiment in government in which the modern world of its day had neither experience nor confidence. And you hold a tiny connection with something else you have probably never thought of—the world's largest, oldest and most famous secret society, the fraternity of the Freemasons.

Turn the bill over and look at the many strange symbols on the back. Everyone knows that the pyramid and the all-seeing eye are Masonic symbols . . . right? It's all over the Internet. Entire books have been written about it. In the first two minutes of the 2004 film *National Treasure*, kindly, old Christopher Plummer tells his grandson that the Masons put it there as a clue to a vast and ancient treasure. The film is a work of fiction, but those curious clues remain, and even people who don't know what a Freemason is will tell you in solemn tones that they are Masonic symbols. But are they really?

There are other puzzles and clues in Washington, D.C. The plan of the city, designed by Pierre L'Enfant, is a tantalizing grid of horizontals, perpendiculars, diagonals and circles. Stare at them long enough, and patterns emerge. Five-pointed stars or pentacles. Right angles. Squares. Maybe even a compass. Just like the symbol of the Freemasons.

1

When you look at the monuments and buildings of Washington, D.C., and begin to dig deeper into the historical origins of the city and our nation, you find Freemasons everywhere. They are presidents, generals, builders, dreamers, diplomats, scientists, patriots and, occasionally, traitors.

Those of us who first got our childhood glimpses of science, logic and philosophy from watching *Star Trek* reruns know that history is a thing that should not be tinkered with. The past is an enormous, ongoing game of what scientists and sociologists like to stuffily call *domino causality*. That is, one thing leads to another. Go back in time and stomp on the wrong frog in the Mesozoic forest, and dinosaurs would still be roaming La Brea, California. Take the deadly, mind-altering lead out of the wrong emperor's cup in Rome, and we'd all still be speaking Latin and watching the Circus Maximus Extreme Games on ESPN-IV. Let Captain Kirk push Joan Collins out from in front of the wrong speeding milk truck in 1933, and the Nazis would have won World War II.

The creation of the United States is one of the most intricately woven and fascinating domino labyrinths ever set in motion. It happened at a precise moment in time, with an unusual cast of characters and an unlikely set of circumstances that has never been repeated. Historically, revolutions have been ugly affairs formed in the minds of a lofty few, touched off by someone's last straw, often leading to the murder of one despot with another—or worse, a whole committee of them. But the creation of the United States was different. It was unlike any other nation born from the fires of revolution, and there is a reason why.

In 1515, Sir Thomas More, the ill-fated chancellor to England's King Henry VIII, first imagined a unique, democratic society of the common people, free of monarchs and dedicated to the pleasurable aims of life, governed by a natural law upon whom all could agree. More called this paradise "Utopia," a Greek pun that meant both "good place" and "no place." Indeed, there existed no such good place. More had been moved to write *Utopia* upon hearing about

Columbus's discovery of the Americas. The notion of a New World set philosophers of Western Europe dreaming of an opportunity to start a new kind of society from scratch, benefiting from the collected knowledge and successes of history while learning from its failures.

A half-century later, Sir Francis Bacon concocted his own utopian tale. More's had been a place that set aside religious and economic differences to create a more perfect society. Bacon, in the spirit of the Age of Enlightenment, wrote of the "New Atlantis," a major metropolis that had every scientific advancement on an island called Bensalem in the South Pacific. It told of skyscrapers a mile-and-a-half high, manmade caverns three miles deep and submarines that plumbed the ocean depths. It spoke of a lavish college called *Salomon's House*, where scientific minds were nurtured and the new processes of the experimental method led to great invention and discovery. These utopian ideas would inspire generations of philosophers, dreamers and explorers. The discovery of the Americas was suddenly a blank slate upon which a new kind of world could be created.

It has been a common trait of patriotic Americans to lionize our founders, to treat them as though they'd sprung forth from their mothers' wombs not small, warm and pink, but fully grown and made of white marble or possibly cast in green patina bronze. In more recent times, it has been popular to rethink them and expose all of their baser traits, almost as a revisionist effort to blame our modern ills on the genetic code of fallibility embedded in our government by the founders' bad habits and prejudices. But they were not gods, or even "demigods." They were simply men trying to design something that had never been built before. A few of them had a plan, which they had first glimpsed in the lodges of Freemasonry.

The modern fraternity of Free and Accepted Masons, or the Freemasons, has existed officially since St. John's Day in London in June 1717, but its true origins are clouded in the obscurity of time, mystery and bad record-keeping. Their legendary beginnings date from the formation of the stonemasons' craft guilds in the Middle Ages. Their mythological origins descend from the great building projects of the Bible—the Tower of Babel, the Temple of Solomon and even Noah's Ark. The Freemasons are the world's largest and oldest fraternal organization, and their members can be found in almost every country of the world. These modern descendants of the builders of Solomon's Temple studied the utopian visions of More and Bacon. They were there at the dawn of the American Revolution, and before. They were there at its Declaration of Independence from its mother country and king. They were there at its victorious outcome and at the planning of its government. And they were there at the building of its new Federal City.

As a Freemason myself, I am well aware that the fraternity has often overstated the participation of Brothers in the formation of the United States. I once heard a Past Grand Master (who should have known better) tell a large group of new members (who *didn't* know better) that every lodge had a picture of George Washington hanging in it (not all do) because Washington had "started all of Freemasonry" (he didn't).

Richard Brookhiser, in his fascinating 1996 account of the life of George Washington, said, "Washington's Freemasonry is a difficult subject, not because everybody cares about it, but because hardly anybody does . . . almost everything written about it is either self-infatuated or loony. . . . "[1] He's right. Articles litter the Internet claiming that "most" U.S. presidents, along with most of the Founding Fathers, were Freemasons. Many Masons proudly, and incorrectly, claim this heritage. At the other end of the spectrum lies a whole subculture of conspiracy theorists who believe that the Freemasons and their fellow travelers, the "Illuminati," control everything from the U.S. government to international banking, including the press, all multinational corporations, and the decision on who gets to park in all the handicapped spaces. Depending on whose viewpoint is taken, they are either the shining heroes on horseback who created the United States single-handedly or the hobgoblins of Satan who are secretly bent on ruling an atheistic New World Order.

The truth lies somewhere between the two, as it usually does, and not exactly in ways that the conventional wisdom on either side of the fence believes. Freemasons were present and were influential in the creation of this new nation. Their membership numbers and the proportion of Masons in the general population have waned dramatically over the years, but at one time, they truly were the movers and shakers of society. They wielded tremendous influence, in ways even they did not fully realize at the time.

The ideology behind Freemasonry is that it is a brotherhood of the ancient craft masons who built the great cathedrals and cities of Europe. What the "operative" masons of the Middle Ages did was magic. They held the secret knowledge of geometry that enabled them to convert a small drawing into a massive bridge, castle or cathedral. They possessed architectural and engineering secrets that resulted in magnificent marvels of engineering that have stood the test of centuries. Their greatest achievements were the majestic medieval cathedrals, monuments to God built with the labor of hundreds of like-minded men united in a single vision.

The new Freemasonry of the eighteenth century would be speculative and theoretical—the principles of craft masonry applied to philosophy to build cathedrals in the hearts of men. Freemasonry was unique at the time of its modern, official birth in London in 1717, and its philosophy of equality, mutual responsibility, religious tolerance, personal freedoms and trust among men within its lodge rooms was a very new, and sometimes dangerous, concept. Life and society across Western Europe in the seventeenth and eighteenth centuries was very different than that found today. Outside the lodge, kings and religious leaders ruled with an iron whim. Civil wars were fought over whether there were five holy sacraments or just two, and even the smallest outcast Protestant denominations battled each other with bloodthirsty zeal. A large-scale democracy hadn't been around for almost two millennia, not since the Greeks and early Romans had dabbled in such nonsense, and Europe's monarchs found the notion of a democratic election to be more terrifying than any foe on the battlefield.

The building of a new capitol, Washington, D.C., would give the Masons a unique opportunity to combine the modern with the ancient styles of Freemasonry—the new speculative Freemasonry would now have the chance to actually work in stone, erecting its own city from the ground up. A New Atlantis would rise on the shores of Columbia, founded on the doctrines of their craft. And that is precisely what they did.

It was an idea without precedent and an omen of things to come from the new nation of upstart Americans. The Masons came to a miserable swamp where two scarcely navigable rivers met, near barely inhabited places known pompously by the names of Rome and Alexandria. They planted a stone in the ground and declared that their Federal City would rise from this place. Few capital cities of the past had been created from nothing, and those had been built by conquerors eager to leave their mark in the world and impress their neighbors with their power and riches. This new capital would be every bit as revolutionary and as carefully crafted as its founding documents. Unlike the old kingdoms they had rejected, the Federal City would not be a sprawling warren of accidental paths, alleys and goat trails, as the capitals of Europe were. Like Francis Bacon's imaginary utopia, this New Atlantis would be scientific, logical and planned. Everything, from the layout of her streets to the stylized motifs of her public buildings, would reflect, openly or secretly, Masonic and Enlightenment views and ideals.

Any Masonic researcher who sticks his toe in the water and starts proclaiming the Masonic membership of famous people does so at his own peril. Masonic, mainstream and pop historians have all made claims and counterclaims that famous figures were or were not Freemasons. It should be understood that no single source in the United States can definitively answer all such questions. Freemasonry in America before the Revolution was chaotic, and immediately after it, only slightly less so. Records were poorly kept, if they were kept at all, and many were lost during the war or other disasters in the centuries since. In many cases, researchers can only infer Masonic membership based on remarks in letters, appearances in public ceremonies with other known Masons, unsubstantiated claims of membership appearing in obituaries or family records, and other equally unreliable and unverifiable sources.

While Freemasonry has been characterized as a "secret society," its meetings are not secret, at least in the United States. Its lodges are clearly marked, and brothers have almost always proudly identified themselves as members of the fraternity. Apart from a tumultuous anti-Masonic period between the 1820s and the 1840s, Masons have not, as a rule, hidden their membership. Unfortunately, it is difficult to prove such membership when detailed archives do not always exist. Worse, false claims of Masonic affiliation can take on a life of their own once they appear in print, only to be reprinted and reasserted for years.

For that reason, you will find this book littered with qualifiers when Masonic membership is believed to be authentic but cannot be proved conclusively. I have endeavored to be as accurate as possible. To the many sharp-eyed Masonic researchers across the country who take exception with anyone I have included as a Brother in this book, I offer my advance thanks for your diligence and input, as well as my *mea culpa* for any errors.

I resisted writing this book at first, primarily because I wasn't certain that America was in a patriotic mood anymore. As I write this, the United States is involved in an unpopular war, and important issues about liberty and revolution, even in another country on the other side of the globe, are getting lost amidst a caterwaul of election politics, media gamesmanship and cynical sneering. But a simple event changed my mind.

I am a Freemason, and I was attending a gathering of a club for younger men who were members of the fraternity. Almost everyone in the room was under thirty-five with the exception of myself and the father of one of the other men. The older man came over to me and we began to chat. He was in his late sixties or early seventies and spoke with a very thick accent. The gentleman, an émigré from Transylvania in Romania, had come to America in 1965.

Romania in those days was a puppet state of the Soviet Union. Their king had been forced to abdicate by the Soviets in 1948, and the country had been bled dry economically to pay for Stalin's postwar debts. Between 1948 and the mid-1960s, almost two million Romanians had been arbitrarily thrown into prison for political, economic or other unspecified reasons. The Communists had the blood of at least 200,000 Romanian people on their hands, along with hundreds of thousands of incidents of torture and abuse of Romanian citizens. It was against this backdrop that this gentleman had secretly fled from his homeland as a young man and come to the United States.

Then he told me a curious thing. He had first read about the Freemasons in Leo Tolstoy's *War and Peace*, and like Tolstoy's Pierre, he wanted very much to become a Mason. But Freemasonry was outlawed at that time in Romania, just as it had been outlawed all across the Soviet bloc, Hitler's Germany, Mussolini's Italy, Khomeini's Iran and Hussein's Iraq.

When he came to America and became a citizen, he said, the first thing he did was to petition a Masonic lodge. Because it was a symbol of freedom to him. Because Freemasonry can only exist in a free country.

The issues of liberty and equality are intertwined with the fraternity of Freemasonry as much today as they were in 1776. Men living under fascist regimes have been persecuted or even executed for the "crime" of Masonic membership. Yet, Freemasonry survives and grows wherever men are free. One need only look as far as the former Soviet republics where Communism has died to see the rebirth of their Masonic lodges. Even in Romania.

The United States is a symbol of freedom the world over, but it's easy to forget that fact when the news is filled with stories of bomb plots, protesters and pessimistic national self-loathing. The flip side of anti-American terrorism is the unmanageable mob of immigrants beating down our doors, because the United States is still the destination for a globe filled with people who lie awake at night dreaming of liberties that Americans don't give a second, or sometimes even a first, thought. At least not until a little man from, say, Romania wakes us up and reminds us.

This, then, is the story of that brief moment in time when Freemasonry, the Enlightenment, revolution and fate came together to build what Abraham Lincoln would later call "a new nation, conceived in liberty, and dedicated to the proposition that all men are created equal." This was an incredibly revolutionary concept—one that Americans would bleed for again and again. It is the story of the new city that would become its capital. And it is the story of the members of the mysterious fraternity of Masonic brothers who helped to make Francis Bacon's New Atlantis a reality.

Solomon's Builders examines some of the myths and theories about the legends of Freemasonry in America, and the sometimes perplexing messages in stone that they left behind. But apart from the veiled messages, puzzles and monuments that Freemasons of old left to us, they gifted us with something of far more value than any treasure of gold—a constitution and a democratic republic.

CHAPTER I

A Knock at the Door

✦✦✦

Associate yourself with men of good quality
if you esteem your own reputation;
for 'tis better to be alone than in bad company.
—GEORGE WASHINGTON

November 4, 1752

The candidate reached out into the darkness and gave three distinct knocks on the door in front of him.

He could sense that the landing was darkened, even through the bandage wrapped around his eyes, but he could tell little else. The raucous noises of the tavern's public room drifted up the steps behind him, and the smell of roasting mutton, tobacco and hickory smoke from the cook fire permeated the air.[1] He knew the knot of anticipation that tightened in his chest before a session with his fencing master. The same sort of anxious grip had hold of him now, even though he tried to convince himself that this was a silly way to spend the evening. And frankly, he felt a bit silly as he reflected on the events of the last hour.

His friend had told him nothing of what was going to happen. The candidate had been told to dress as though he were going to church, and he'd done so with some care. He had worn his finest woolen coat, waistcoat and matching breeches, white shirt and stock. When he had arrived at Julian's Tavern, his friend had met him, then ushered him off to a small, darkened storeroom and closed and locked the door, leaving him in silence. After what had seemed like a small eternity, the door had opened abruptly, revealing two other men, known to him only slightly, who introduced themselves as the Stewards of the Lodge. The senior of the two solemnly asked if he had the vocation necessary to proceed, to which he had nervously replied, "Yes."

Then his friend had stepped forward and asked him, in a stiff and formal manner that the candidate had never heard him use before, "Do you seriously declare—*upon your honor*—before these gentlemen, that, unbiased by friends against your own inclination, and uninfluenced by mercenary motives, you freely offer yourself a candidate for the mysteries of Masonry?"

"I do," he responded.

"Do you seriously declare—*upon your honor*—before these gentlemen, that you are *solely* prompted to solicit the privileges of Masonry by a favorable opinion conceived of the institution, a desire of knowledge, and a sincere wish of being serviceable to your fellow creatures?"

He *did* have a favorable opinion of the society, and while he had heard of the new lodge being formed that year with several of the most important gentlemen in the county as its charter members, he hadn't sought membership just to hobnob with a few respected businessmen and planters. Clearly Freemasonry meant something important to them, something more than just gathering to eat, drink and trade gossip. These were men he admired, for their accomplishments but also for their intelligence and felicity of expression. His personal situation had changed dramatically in the last few months, and he felt decidedly underqualified for the new positions, both public and private, he would have to face now. To be brutally honest with himself, he wasn't sure he was up to the task. So perhaps the men in this lodge would provide the inspiration and the wisdom he felt he lacked.

"I do," he answered.

They asked him a third time. "Do you seriously declare—*upon your honor*—before these gentlemen, that you will cheerfully conform to the ancient and established usages and customs of the fraternity?"

"I will," he responded.

They asked his proper, full name and profession and collected his initiation fee of two pounds, three shillings. They then stripped him of his sword and coat, unwrapped his stock from his neck and spread open his shirt. They demanded that he hand over any metallic objects—buttons, rings, buckles, coins—and even ordered him to remove his left shoe and stocking. For a young man, he already possessed a profound sense of dignity and decorum, and this was decidedly undignified. They had covered his eyes with a cloth tied behind his head, and for the first time he was a little frightened as he felt a shank of rope slipped over his head and—was it a noose?—tightened around his throat. Then, without any further word from them, they left him in the silence of the room once more. Both comforting and frustrating, his friend sat silently with him, refusing to speak or answer him.

After nearly a half hour of sitting with nothing but his own thoughts, he heard the door open again, and a voice murmured that it was time. His friend carefully led the candidate, still blindfolded, down the hall. He wondered, as he heard shouts and laughter coming from the public room, if the entire tavern's collected regulars could see him being led around in this embarrassing and decidedly unkempt way for a gentleman to appear in public. Slowly and carefully, they led him up the stairs.

He stood waiting, penniless, defenseless, half undressed, blind, with a noose around his neck. The roaring fire downstairs should have generated enough heat to rise and chase them all out of the place, yet he was undeniably cold.

"Dear God," he thought, "what have I done?"

His friend stood next to him with his hand on his shoulder—both to guide him and to keep him from tumbling off the narrow landing and down the steps. It was a good thing too, for the door suddenly swung open, almost making him fall backwards in surprise, as a voice from inside roughly demanded, "Who comes here?"

"One who begs to have and receive part of the benefits of this Right Worshipful Lodge," his guide spoke for him, "dedicated to St. John, as many brothers and fellows have done before him."

"How does he expect to obtain it?" came the question, to which he did not remotely know the answer. His guide, blessedly, responded for him again.

"By being Free-born, and well reported."

He heard the door swing wide on its groaning hinges as the voice inside ordered him to enter. His guide whispered in his ear to always step off with his left foot, but just as they crossed the transom into the room, a sharp, cold point jabbed into his left breast, and the chill of fear shuddered through him. It was a sword or a spear of some kind, he was certain.

"Do you feel anything?" he was asked.

"I do!" he answered for himself this time.

"I receive you on the point of a sharp instrument against your naked left breast, to teach you that, as it is an instrument of torture to your flesh, so should the remembrance be to your conscience should you ever dare to reveal any of the secrets of Freemasonry unlawfully."

The candidate could feel that, though they were being deathly quiet, many other men were in the room, watching his every move. His senses were heightened by his temporary blindness. He no longer felt silly.

He was led forward and told to kneel. He groped forward in the darkness, searching for a rail or some other support, but his guide held him by the elbow and supported him as he dropped to his knees. Once he was kneeling, someone in the room began to pray.

"Vouchsafe thine aid, Almighty Father of the universe, to this our present convention, and grant that this candidate for Masonry may dedicate and devote his life to thy service, and become a true and faithful Brother among us! Endue him with a competence of thy divine wisdom that, by the secrets of our Art, he may be better enabled to display the beauties of godliness, to the honor of thy holy name. Amen."

"So mote it be," came the response from a strong chorus of unseen voices in the room. He was taken by the right hand and told to rise, follow his guide and fear no danger. His guide solemnly conducted him around the room, stopping behind each chair of the three principal officers. In a strange way, the words being spoken and their cadence almost reminded him of an Anglican mass. At last, they stopped behind the chair of the Master of the Lodge, who asked him, "My friend, do you have the desire to be made a Mason?"

"Yes," he answered.

"And is this of your own free will and accord?"

"Yes," he again answered.

He was instructed to advance by three distinct, special footsteps. When he stopped, the Master spoke again.

"My friend," he said, "you are now entering into a most respectable Society, which is more serious and important than you imagine. It admits nothing contrary to Law, Religion or Morality. Nor does it allow anything inconsistent with the allegiance due to his Majesty, the King."

Again, he was told to kneel, and he was assisted into a contorted position on his naked left knee, while his right formed a square. Into his left hand was placed a Bible, opened to the Gospel of St. John: *In the beginning was the Word, and the Word was with God, and the Word was God.*

A sense of solemnity mixed with unease settled over him. This was no mere initiation into one of the local drinking and dining clubs that had appeared in Fredericksburg. To a serious young man of faith and honor, this was a moment of great consequence. He laid his right hand upon the Holy Bible and swore that he would never reveal the secrets of the fraternity or his brothers. To do so risked an ancient penalty of the medieval church—his throat would be cut across, and his tongue torn out by its roots.

The obligation now completed, he was asked what he most desired, and his guide prompted him to answer, "To be brought to light."

"Then let him see the light!" the Master ordered.

He felt fingers fumbling with the blindfold, and suddenly the lodge room was revealed to him for the first time. Three tall candlesticks were spread out on the floor in a triangular configuration, and they cast a faint illumination in the otherwise darkened room. What he saw startled him, as all of the men—perhaps twenty or more—stood in a semicircle in front of him, with their swords drawn, each one pointing menacingly at his left breast.

Some of these men were known quite well to him. Many were his friends, and it alarmed him to see them threatening him at the point of steel. Every man there was dressed in a white leather apron, and some wore shining symbols, badges of their official lodge positions, on cords around their necks. The Master, Daniel Campbell, stood in front him, several feet away. On the floor, a curious

Introducing a new candidate into an eighteenth-century lodge, from Solomon in All His Glory *by Thomas Wilson (1777).*

pattern of an archway with a representation of three angled steps approaching it had been drawn with chalk. Behind them was a long table set with the preparations of dinner, and bottles of wine and ale. The men all returned their swords to their scabbards, and Master Campbell stepped forward, taking the new Freemason by the hand.[2]

✦ ✦ ✦

The place was the Lodge of Fredericksburg,[3] and the candidate seeking Masonic light that evening was twenty-year-old George Washington. The degree of Entered Apprentice, in which he and four other candidates were being initiated, was an ancient one, roughly similar in form to other Masonic lodges all over the world, with minor variations of language and style. But despite customary similarities in ritual, the initiation on this chilly November night was singular.

The young Washington was a wealthy plantation owner who dreamed of the military glory that had been achieved by many forebears in his old colonial family. The recent death of his step-brother Lawrence had made him a prominent figure in the colony, inheriting both the estate of Mount Vernon and an important position as adjutant for the militia. He was about to become Lieutenant Colonel George Washington, Commander of all of His Majesty's Militia forces for the colony of Virginia. He would soon make a name for himself in the Seven Year's War, better known to Americans as the French and Indian War, a struggle between Britain and France over vast territories in America. The struggle would nearly bankrupt both nations, and George Washington was one of the daring young British officers who would help to keep most of the territory in the hands of Great Britain.

Despite his love of farming and the peaceful plantation life at Mount Vernon, Washington's destiny was to lead an army. Like Napoleon and Wellington, he became known for riding along the front lines in front of his men, inspiring them simply with his presence, seemingly oblivious to passing bullets and cannonballs. King George himself had commented on the young man's gallantry after reading Washington's accounts of his exploits. Long before the Revolutionary War, young Washington was a famous man.

It is unquestionable today that George Washington is the proudest figure of Freemasonry in the United States. Statues and portraits of him are displayed not only in Grand Lodges and

*A popular nineteenth-century Masonic print of George Washington
dressed in lodge regalia, flanked by fellow Masons,
the Marquis de Lafayette and Andrew Jackson.*

Masonic museums but also in many neighborhood lodges, often showing him dressed in the regalia of the fraternity—a decorated white apron, a sash or collar with the badge of office of the Master of a lodge, and frequently holding a Mason's trowel. The George Washington Masonic National Memorial, thanks to its location atop Shooter's Hill in Alexandria, Virginia, stands nearly as high as the Washington Memorial across the Potomac in Washington,

D.C., and a portion of the fees of nearly every Freemason initiated today in the U.S. goes to support it. Statues and paintings of the first President appear in Grand Lodges and Masonic museums across the country.

Nearly as popular a figure of Masonic pride is Benjamin Franklin. Franklin's personal accomplishments as an author, scientist and statesman are unparalleled in early American history. He became a Freemason in 1731 and printed Reverend John Anderson's *Constitutions*, the first book on the subject of Freemasonry published in America. He would go on to become the Provincial Grand Master of Masons in Pennsylvania in 1753 and later become Master of Lodge of the Nine Muses in Paris during his long stay there, rubbing shoulders with Voltaire and other French philosophers and "freethinkers." In fact, Franklin so charmed the French court that he is still deeply revered there and is credited with eventually getting America the French military support that helped turn the tide of the American Revolution.

These pillars of American Freemasonry are just two of the many members of the fraternity who took the principles they learned in their lodge rooms and helped to found a new nation. It has been alleged both by Freemasons and anti-Masons alike, almost since the end of the revolution and the adoption of the U.S. Constitution, that "most" of the founders were Freemasons, that "most" of George Washington's generals were Masons, and that since that time, "most" of America's presidents have been members of the fraternity as well. Yet, one group makes this exaggerated claim and sees it as an admirable boast, while the other describes it as the nefarious plot of a cabal of evil conspirators. So just what is this strange organization that this particular group of men felt the need to join?

Freemasonry Defined

A real Freemason is distinguished from the rest of Mankind by the uniform unrestricted rectitude of his conduct. Other men are honest in fear of punishment which the law might inflict; they are religious in expectation of being rewarded, or in dread of the devil in the next world. A Freemason would be just if there were no laws, human or divine except those written in his heart by the finger of his Creator. In every climate, under every system of religion, he is the same. He kneels before the Universal Throne of God in gratitude for the blessing he has received and humble solicitation for his future protection. He venerates the good men of all religions. He gives no offense, because he does not choose to be offended. He contracts no debts which he is certain he cannot discharge, because he is honest upon principle. —*Farmer's Almanac, 1823*[4]

Freemasonry is the world's largest, oldest and best-known "secret society." Since its modern formation in London in 1717, literally millions of men the world over have knocked at the door of Masonic lodges, just as George Washington did. Its members have been presidents, kings and statesmen; shopkeepers, blacksmiths and dustmen; business leaders, ministers and common laborers. From the highest social strata to the lowest, within the confines of their Masonic lodges, men have met "on the level," to socialize, to perform their ceremonies, to freely discuss the issues of the day over a lively dinner, and to improve each other's lives—"to make good men better."

At its most basic level, Freemasonry is a fraternal organization that bases its initiations, ceremonies and symbolism on the tools, practices and vocabulary of the ancient and medieval stonemasons. It obligates its members to aid and assist each other and their families, to keep the secrets of its ceremonies and methods of identification, as well as the secrets of its members. The flipside of that secrecy is that it directs its members to remind each other of their faults, and to aid in their reformation.

Freemasonry's mythic legends originate in the great building projects of the Bible—the Tower of Babel, Noah's Ark and, most important, King Solomon's Temple in Jerusalem. The legends and rituals of modern Freemasonry use the allegories of the Temple of

Solomon and of the cathedral builders of medieval Europe to build a cathedral in the heart of each member—a strong, everlasting place for God to dwell, constructed over the course of a lifetime, and made more perfect with the aid of a group of fellow craftsmen. By encouraging its individual brethren to practice brotherly love, charity and the embracing of truth and honesty in the world around them, Freemasonry seeks to have a positive effect on society as a whole. Early American communities must have believed in its lofty mission. Between the end of the Revolution and the late 1820s, Freemasonry in the United States grew at a soaring rate, and nearly every town and village of any real size had its own Masonic lodge.

Freemasons generally claim their true origins to be in the 10th century, when England's King Athelstan, grandson of Alfred the Great, allegedly granted a royal charter officially creating the Guild of Stonemasons in the city of York.[5] The role of the guild was to act as a labor union, setting uniform wages, training workers, assuring a certain level of quality in their work, and caring for its members' welfare. The guild also protected the trade secrets that made stonemasons the most sought-after workers in Europe.

The stonemasons practiced the magical science of geometry. Using it, they could translate small drawings into massive structures. They could measure and carve giant stone blocks to fit together so carefully that they did not require mortar. Their understanding of physics allowed them to move these huge stones into the air and stack them at dizzying heights. And by the 1500s, the cathedrals had evolved into soaring works of art that defied gravity. Massive stone walls of the old Roman and Norman architecture disappeared, to be replaced by breathtaking stained glass that seemed to float with no visible means of support. The Gothic style transferred the crushing weight of the building and ceiling to amazing exterior supports called flying buttresses. Outside was a complex array of delicate stone archways that did the job of holding the building and preventing its collapse. Inside, the stone virtually vanished, and the stories told on thousands of intricate panels of colored-glass windows stretched upward, nearly to heaven.

The stonemasons, with their connection to these sacred monuments to God, quickly became legendary for their skills. Masons were taught never to reveal the secrets of their trade to outsiders, nor to write them down. Additionally, their members, once qualified, were given certain modes of recognition—grips or handshakes, signs or tokens, and passwords. These devices were developed so that guild members could travel to other worksites and prove their membership. The Master Mason was in possession of the "Master's Word," an equivalent of carrying a union card. Members gathered in *lodges*, temporary buildings at a jobsite where they ate, socialized, studied and perhaps even slept.

Over the years, ceremonies were developed to initiate boys into the guild as apprentices, and to "graduate" masters. Stories of the guild's origins were embellished, and the masons developed a code of conduct for their members. Geometry became venerated as a sacred science, and it became a popular Christian motif in art to represent God as an architect holding a pair of compasses in his hand while peering at the earth. Geometry could be used to design and construct buildings, circumnavigate the globe, predict the seasons, measure the heights of mountains and plot the movements of the constellations and planets. In short, geometry was a science descended from God, and so the masons must be divinely inspired. They certainly enjoyed a reputation that barrel makers, shoe cobblers and blacksmiths couldn't claim.

Solomon's Builders

At some point in the mid- to late 1600s, something changed in the lodges. Elias Ashmole became the first known non-stoneworking Mason to be made a member of a lodge in 1646. Ashmole was an important figure of the Age of Enlightenment in England. He was an alchemist, scientist, philosopher and member of London's Royal Society. Some records appear in Scotland and England of other "gentlemen" being accepted into lodges. Scholarship was becoming fashionable in the ranks of the nobility amongst men who before had only cared about their skill in war and court politics.

In 1717, four lodges met in London for the purpose of forming uniform, governing rules and holding an annual feast. This new Grand Lodge differed from the way the Stonemason Guilds had been organized in the past. The most important difference was that non-operative members—men who did not work in stones as their profession—predominated in the four lodges and in the future positions within the new Grand Lodge. Gentlemen, not laborers, took over the organization, which referred to its members as Free and Accepted Masons. Freemasonry after 1717 would ever after be known as *speculative*, building character instead of constructing buildings.

It has been suggested that today's Freemasonry really grew out of Scottish traditions that had been in place long before 1717.[6] Some claim that Freemasonry grew out of the mysterious legend of the Rosicrucians, a fictitious group of alchemists and mystics who supposedly traveled the world seeking hidden knowledge, and whose tales inspired the formation of imitation societies in the 1600s. Others believe that the ceremonies and traditions of the Freemasons descended from the Knights Templar after their excommunication and trials in the 1300s.[7] Still others have conjectured that Freemasonry's origins date back to the Mystery Schools of ancient Greece, or even Hermetic Egyptian sources.[8]

Masonic and academic scholars and historians have searched for the definitive connection between these or other, earlier sources and the Freemasonry that appeared in London in 1717, to no avail. The truth may simply be that a group of learned men saw in the stonemasons a chance to use their tools, terminology and teachings as an appealing allegory with which to encourage improvement in modern men. The new Freemasonry combined the best that the Age of Enlightenment embodied: philosophy, science, cosmopolitan equality and a search for truth both by the new methods of science and by the examination of ancient knowledge.

Whatever the real source of Freemasonry may have been, its popularity grew at lightening speed, and it literally spread around the world. It traveled on British and French ships to colonial ports in the Americas, the Mediterranean and Asia. It caught on among military men who were far from home for years at a time. Freemasonry was often spread by military lodges that conferred membership on soldiers and civilians alike. Their meetings were marked with drinking and toasting, a fine dinner, and friendship that crossed all lines of social, religious and economic status.

Eating and drinking clubs became popular in the early 1700s, and they often met in the same taverns as the Masons. But Freemasonry was different. Eating and drinking clubs taught little to their members, apart from the lessons of gluttony and intemperance on the painful morning after. But Freemasonry attempted to teach moral and intellectual lessons. And it taught something even more visionary, given the volatile times of religious and civil wars that had preceded it. It taught tolerance, manners and gentlemanly behavior. And it taught the value of learning.

Freemasonry still inducts its members in three different ritual ceremonies, called *degrees*. The new candidate is initiated in the Entered Apprentice degree, which teaches the importance of secrecy and honor among its members, as well as the tenets of morality, virtue, brotherly love, charity and truth. The second degree is the Fellow Craft, which strongly encourages Masons to study the liberal arts and sciences and seek moral truth in their lessons.

The third and final degree is the Master Mason. In the first portion of the degree, the obligations of the Mason are expanded to aid his brethren, their widows and orphans. But it is in the second half of the degree that Freemasons are connected with an ancient past. It tells the story of Hiram Abiff, a widow's son, who was sent by King Hiram of Tyre to Jerusalem to assist in the building of King Solomon's Temple around 1000 B.C.[9]

King Solomon built the temple as the centerpiece of his magnificent new city. It was constructed to hold the Ark of the Covenant, which contained the tablets of the Ten Commandments given to Moses, inscribed in stone by the finger of God himself. The Temple had an outer porch, called the *Ulam*, which faced the east to catch the rays of the rising son. Two bronze pillars, called *Boaz* and *Jachin*, flanked the Ulam and the doors entering the temple. The *Hekel*, or "Holy Place," was the Middle Chamber—a large, central hall with gold lamp stands, an altar with golden incense censers, and other ceremonial items. The third part of the temple was the *Debir*, the Sanctum Sanctorum or Holy of Holies, where the Ark was placed. Designed as a perfect cube, it was the dwelling place of God. Only the high priest could enter this windowless, sacred place. Many a war would erupt between Jews and their enemies over any real or perceived degradation of this inner sanctum.

The Masonic version of the story tells a fictionalized episode of the Temple's construction. Hiram Abiff is made the Grand Architect of the Temple, and only he knows the secret Master's Word. A promise is made to the workmen at the Temple that, when the job is completed, they shall receive the secret knowledge of the Master's Word. But a group of three impatient Fellow Crafts decide one day to accost Hiram and demand the knowledge they have not earned. The third craftsman strikes and kills Hiram, who dies without revealing the secrets of Masonry. When Hiram's body is discovered, a "substitute word" is created for Freemasons, until future generations can perhaps discover the true, secret knowledge that Hiram took to the grave.

The ongoing mission of the Freemason is to search for knowledge that has been lost and to build a spiritual Temple of Solomon in his own heart. This is the search for Masonic "light" that Washington and Franklin pursued, as did John Hancock, Paul Revere and James Otis, Revolutionary War officers, signers of the Declaration of Independence and the Constitution, and many other men in eighteenth-century America. Freemasonry is not a religion, despite its origins among Catholic cathedral builders and its subsequent adoption of an Old Testament episode about a Hebrew Temple, but it is religious. It doesn't teach any specific religious creed. It simply requires that its members express a belief in a Supreme Being. As a result, it is open to Christians, Jews and Muslims alike. Yet, in spite of its nonsectarian mission, no other institution apart from religion itself had a greater influence on these men who would build a new nation.

George Washington

In America's first century as a nation, an Anglican minister named Mason Locke Weems, who came to be known simply as Parson Weems, invented what America didn't possess—a detailed life story of the young George Washington. His book, *The Life and Memorable Actions of George Washington*, was an unparalleled bestseller, eventually propelling Weems out of the parson business and into the book business and the lecture circuit. It became a primer for generations of American schoolchildren. And the good parson was certainly in fine company historically, since the myths and legends of famous founders had been used to teach ethical lessons to the young since the days of ancient Rome. Unfortunately, to call stories like the young Washington cutting down the cherry tree "apocryphal" is a kindness. In other words, as a moral compass for American youth, Parson Weems's book was a great success. As biography, it's utter garbage.

Yet, no one should conclude that the honesty, honor and courage of Washington was an invention of moonstruck hero worshippers. That's a view borne out of twenty-first-century cynicism rather than eighteenth-century idealism. George Washington was everything that the most starry-eyed historian would have him be, and the love that Americans felt for him was not something manufactured.

What little we do know of Washington's authentic early life certainly confirms his later reputation for principled behavior. His was a proud family name, going seven generations back in the state of Virginia to the young royalist cavaliers on the run from Cromwell's victorious Puritan army after the English Civil War. But despite this proud and aristocratic heritage, his father Augustine, who died when Washington was eleven years old, had left no wealth to help propel the young man up the social ladder. He would have to make his own way, and he would remain just a little bitter throughout his life that his sharp intellect had not been fed by more years of formal education. Instead, by the age of sixteen, the steady and responsible teenager was already working as a surveyor to help support his household and his widowed mother. In the margin of one of his school papers that has survived, the youthful Washington reminded himself to "Labour to keep alive in your breast that little spark of celestial fire—conscience." It seems a far more poignant testament to the man he would become than any confession of having cut down the cherry tree.

Washington's dicey fortunes took a sudden about-face in 1752 when his older half-brother Lawrence died of tuberculosis. The death two months later of Lawrence's only child, a daughter named Sarah, left Washington the owner of one of the grandest plantations in Virginia, Mount Vernon on the Potomac River. Washington would build on this inheritance until it reached an impressive and prosperous 8,000 acres, spread out over five different farms. In fact, he was probably the wealthiest of America's Founding Fathers.

It could be argued that Washington, suddenly a young man of consequence, petitioned the Masonic lodge in Fredericksburg in order to continue to climb up the social ladder. Historian Samuel Eliot Morison's 1932 essay *The Young Man Washington* asserted that he was a "good joiner," implying that Washington was drawn to the lodge to make contacts to help him in this endeavor.[10] But this is a far too simplistic explanation for his love of Masonry and his association with it his whole life long.

There were doubtless other attractions for him in Freemasonry. From his stoic and serious boyhood, Washington was a great believer in dignified and proper boundaries in social behavior. There was also enough of the young British officer in him to breed a love of pomp, ceremony and, most importantly, tradition. His presidency was marked more than anything else by the extraordinary care that he took in all of his actions and conventions, knowing as he did that he was in the unusual position of establishing rather than simply following precedents. "I walk on untrodden ground," he said during his presidency. "There is scarcely any part of my conduct which may not hereafter be drawn into precedent."

Many historians have looked at the evidence that exists (and does *not* exist) concerning Washington's devotion to Freemasonry. When the French and Indian War was raging, Washington was sent with the militia into the wild lands of what are now West Virginia and Ohio, where he is known to have attended military Masonic lodges. A cave near Charles Town, West Virginia, is known as "Washington's Masonic Cave," with an area referred to as "The Lodge Room," in which it has long been said that Washington and other Masons held lodge meetings.[11]

After the French and Indian War ended, Washington returned to Mount Vernon, where he hoped to live out his life as a country gentleman and farmer. It was a busy life for him at Mount Vernon. His interests were wide, including horse breeding, racing, fox hunting and, most importantly, implementing new, scientific farming methods. There is no solid evidence that he attended a lodge between the end of the war and 1773, although it should be remembered that Mount Vernon was almost fifty miles, the better part of a full day's ride in good weather, from Fredericksburg Lodge. But in Washington's correspondence, he made it clear that he was quite happy to be a Mason and believed in its principles.

In later years, he became the Master of Alexandria Lodge when it applied for its charter from the Grand Lodge of Virginia. In the new nation's capital, the Federal City that would bear his name after his death, Washington encouraged and presided over the Masonic ceremonies at the laying of the cornerstone of the United States Capitol Building. And when he died, his wish was to be buried with a Masonic funeral. What cannot be found on paper was what Freemasonry taught him as a philosophy—lifelong self-improvement,

George Washington presiding over Alexandria Lodge.

complete religious tolerance, and the importance of being an example to his fellow men in both private and public life.

The young Washington had been denied a college education. While he may have been the richest of all of the Founding Fathers, when it came to schools and diplomas he was one of the least educated. His letters and speeches often reflected his humility over his lack of experience or education. And yet, when he died, Washington had one of the largest private libraries in the colonies, with over 900 books. Apart from his eight years with a tutor and in a country school, Washington was self-educated, and he spent his lifetime searching for knowledge.

Modern scholars have often tried to claim that Washington was a Deist, not a Christian. Indeed, it has long been alleged that Freemasonry taught Deism, an Enlightenment philosophy that had applied reason and the new scientific method to explaining faith. Deism was not a church or a religion, it was simply a new attitude about faith.

There is no question that Washington was influenced by Deism of the Enlightenment. But the fallacy in trying to pin down Washington's private beliefs is that they were, by definition, private. Making broad statements about what he did or did not believe presupposes that his personal faith could not change over the course of his lifetime. Washington attended the Anglican—later, the Episcopal—church throughout his life, including during his years of marriage with his wife Martha, although he did not receive communion. Perhaps he didn't believe in transubstantiation. Perhaps he was only going along to keep peace in the house. Or perhaps he considered himself too much of a sinner.

Deists were not atheists, but neither did they believe in miracles, saviors or virgin births. Their philosophy was that after creating the heavens and earth, God left mankind on its own, without interfering. Washington may have felt that it best explained his own rational belief in God as Creator, although he and other founders who are known to have been Deists—notably, Thomas Jefferson—filled their letters and speeches with appeals to God for strength, support and success in their battles and in their subsequent formation of a new country. There was an awful lot of public and private praying going on among them for a group of men who believed that God was some distant, uninvolved landlord.

What Freemasonry had taught Washington was tolerance for the beliefs of his Masonic brethren and, by extension, of every man. In their ceremonies, Freemasons refer to God as the "Grand Architect of the Universe"—not some bizarre, invented, pagan Masonic god, but a nonsectarian and nonjudgmental Creator who wouldn't prefer one member's beliefs over another. The lodge was not a place to proselytize. It was not a religious service, nor was it a replacement for religion. The lodge was a refuge from the world, a place where men of differing beliefs could escape the religious and political bickering of the outside world. Freemasonry encourages each member to worship God in his own manner, to attend his own church, mosque or temple, and to respect the private beliefs of others.

Washington carried this belief into his public life. He once wrote to a community of Jews in Savannah referring to Jehovah. To another Hebrew congregation in Newport, he wrote in 1790 that the United States "gives to bigotry no sanctions, to persecution no assistance," adding a quote from scripture, "every one shall sit in safety under his own vine and fig tree and there shall be none to make him afraid" (I Kings 4:25). Speaking to a delegation of Cherokees, he referred to the "Great Spirit," and he responded cheerfully to any religious congregation that wrote to him during his presidency, regardless of their beliefs.

For almost three centuries, Freemasons have had an extraordinary amount of trouble explaining the exact attraction of the organization. More than one Mason has cryptically said, "If you haven't experienced it, you just don't know." Washington can be provably placed at just nine lodge meetings in his lifetime, using direct evidence of rare record books or letters. But Masonry had a more lasting effect on Washington than moldy pages in any lodge record book can prove. The lessons he learned in the lodge that first night in 1752, and his other two degrees the next year, lasted a lifetime, and he applied them to his daily life in an ongoing search for Masonic light.

✦ ✦ ✦

The evening's festivities were coming to an end. Master Campbell stood and held his glass at arm's length. "Brethren," he said, "charge your glasses and toast with me!" They all stood, several refilling their empty glasses, and held them out in like manner.

"Brethren, with me, to the heart that conceals and the tongue that never reveals!"

All of the men raised their glasses and repeated the toast, drank, then slammed their glasses down on the table loudly in unison. One of the brothers broke into song, and he was joined by all but the new apprentices who didn't know the words yet.

> The World is in Pain,
> Our Secrets to gain,
> And still let them wonder and gaze on;
> They ne'er can divine,
> The Word or the Sign.
> Of a Free and an Accepted Mason.

'Tis this, and 'tis that,
They cannot tell what,
Why so many great Men of the Nation;
Should Aprons put on
To make themselves One.
With a Free and an Accepted Mason.

Great Kings, Dukes and Lords.
Have laid by their Swords,
Our Myst'ry to put a good Grace on;
And ne'er been ashamed,
To hear themselves nam'd.
With a Free and an Accepted Mason.[12]

CHAPTER 2

From Darkness to Light

✦ ✦ ✦

The worst thing of all is ignorance.
—KING ALFRED THE GREAT[1]

You can't have a light without a dark to put it in.
—ARLO GUTHRIE

The young George Washington's Entered Apprentice degree was his first step forward in his pursuit of Masonic light. The term "Masonic light" has often been a cause of misunderstanding and confusion. It sometimes leads people to conclude that Freemasonry is a cult or a church, when in fact it is neither. To appreciate what made Freemasonry so popular, so quickly, one must understand the very different world that existed before it.

It's more than mere coincidence that in the seventeenth- and eighteenth-century period called the Age of Enlightenment, the journey toward wisdom within Masonry was referred to as "attaining light." Masonry was the first-born son of the Enlightenment, an organization dedicated, even today, to the principles of illumination. But to comprehend the meaning of "light" in both cases calls for some understanding of the darkness that preceded it.

Many modern scholars disdain the use of the term "Dark Ages," as if such an ill-considered and politically incorrect phrase could hurt the feelings of Ethelred the Unready or the Venerable Bede at some imaginary cocktail party in the hereafter. But the fact remains that the age was dark indeed, as well as brutal, disease-ridden and unjust. And perhaps, more than any other factor, it was a dark age because it was an age of ignorance fed by two social forces, two sides of the same medieval coin—an immutable class system combined with the absolute control over the flow of information by the nobility and the clergy.

Generally speaking, the wisdom of ancient Greece and Rome had been lost with the fall of the Roman Empire around A.D. 410, when the city of Rome was sacked by the Visigoths. Franco-Germanic invaders kept coming for the next century, and the Goths, Visigoths and Huns who overran the empire were hardly men of a scholarly bent. Many books, plays and philosophical tracts were lost during this period. As the barbarians took hold of the West, piece by piece, learning slowly died with the empire. Of course, this loss of reading material was accompanied by a loss of the ability to read. By the sixth and seventh centuries, men of power who needed to communicate and to keep records generally kept a member of the clergy on staff to do this task for them, since priests and monks seemed to be the only ones left who knew how to read and write.

Even the book that was the most vital in the lives of both the nobility and the common run of humanity, the Bible, was a rarity. It is difficult for the modern mind to grasp just how important religion was in the lives of both the nobility and the peasantry in this period. It was more than church going on Sunday, more even than the cycle of feasts, fasts and festivals that bound communities together. The Church saturated every aspect of life, literally from the cradle to the grave. Yet during the Dark Ages, the average farmer, tradesman or petty noble, even if he could read, couldn't just pick up the Bible and dig in.

In the early Dark Ages, Bibles and other books were reprinted by hand, usually by monks, who protected both the remnants of Greek and Roman wisdom and the enormous number of tracts on history and Christian philosophy created by new thinkers. Early Bibles were glorious works of art, characterized by "illuminated" first letters on the pages as well as other lavish decorative touches. They were also rare and extremely expensive. Only the richest families could afford to actually own a Bible. In fact, it was something of a status symbol.

Apart from barriers to personal ownership, the Bible was written in a foreign language—not English, French or Spanish, but Latin. As with Judaism, in which the everyday language of Jews could be anything from Aramaic to Yiddish but the language of the Torah and the Holy Books was Hebrew, the holy tongue for a Christian was Latin. It was a language known only to priests and scholars, leaving it in the province of the Church to read and interpret the Bible for parishioners. Common people were never expected to read and reflect on it themselves, or to form their own conclusions about its contents.

As it became more and more entrenched, the Catholic bureaucracy would help to build the iron walls of class structure in feudal Europe. Many a cardinal or archbishop lived in the baronial style of a petty lord, unmoved by the threadbare existence of the average parish priest.

This dividing line between the classes, which the Church supported and reflected, was actually more like a brick wall, impossible for most people to breech. The essence of the feudal system was the structure of hierarchy in power. A knight errant, meaning a man who was a knight in rank but who owned no property, owed his arms and his loyalty to the warlord above him who owned a little land. This warlord owed his duty and fealty, meaning men in time of war and tribute in time of peace, to the baron who controlled the fief in which his land lay. And the richer and more powerful baron owed his fealty to the earl or duke above him, and so on and so forth, all the way up to the king. Every man, from serf to knight to lord, knew precisely who was above him and who was below.

The poor slob at the bottom of these heavy tiers of medieval society was the serf. He was not precisely a peasant, though he had no education and worked the land for his living. Serfdom was slavery by another name, for a serf and his family did not merely work the land. They belonged to the land. If a man won a fief in battle or inherited or purchased an estate, the serfs came with it. A serf had even fewer rights than a black sharecropper in the post–Civil War South and even less opportunity for education.[2]

Yet throughout the thousand-year Dark Age between the fall of Rome and the Renaissance, there were a few men who had a curious sort of independent status, although they were anything but noble. The seeds of a middle class were being sown in this period by wealthy tradesmen of one sort or another. But trade was not the only route to this socioeconomic middle ground. For example, as law courts became more common in Europe—nearly as common as they had been in ancient Rome—attorneys too achieved an odd status midway between the nobility and the peasantry, along with any sort of scholar or teacher, or high churchman.

None had a more unusual status than a stonemason, particularly a freemason, a man who had risen through the ranks of the Guild of Masons from apprentice to journeyman to full craft mason. "Free" in the sense that he was now a master of the required skills, he had the independence to go out from the guild in which he rose and look for work in other towns and cities, for other patrons.

A freemason was still a laborer, at most the head of a gang of laborers, but he possessed knowledge and skills that gave him a unique and elevated status. A noble usually treated a stonemason with respect, far more respect than he granted his foot soldiers or his serfs. Masons knew the secrets of geometry, a science that, like many other "sciences" of the Middle Ages, was considered akin to an occult or a holy art. They were masters of architecture, physics, engineering and aesthetics. Masons could carve massive stones into interlocking blocks, then send them spiraling upward to create a vaulted cathedral arch suspended in mid-air, literally reaching out to God in His heaven. He might be dirty, he might be poor, he might wear the simplest of clothing beneath a scarred leather apron, but a stonemason was far more important than a mere laborer.

As the Middle Ages drew to a close and the Renaissance rose like a new sun, knowledge of philosophy and the sciences became objects of interest to a nobility that had once held only skill in battle as a prowess worth attaining. For example, Lorenzo de Medici, "Lorenzo the Magnificent," the shining light of the Italian Renaissance, became a passionate collector of ancient texts. His library was said to be the finest private collection in the world, containing a copy of every book that had ever been printed in Europe. Owning and reading books was becoming something more than an eccentric indulgence, or even a necessity; it was becoming fashionable.

Eager to prove their intellects, these same nobles began to take an interest in what was going on inside the closed and secretive meetings of the Guild of Free Masons. Occasionally nobles, perhaps potential or past patrons, were invited to join the Guild as honorary members. It gave a blue-blooded sheen of aristocracy to the Guild, while gifting the noble with the luster of cryptic and mysterious knowledge. This would later give birth to the "speculative" Freemasonry that we know today. The sacred geometry of the stonemasons had reached a crossroads between the study of ancient mathematical knowledge, medieval esoterica and the modern scientific method, creating what is usually called "occult geometry." In this same fashion, medieval alchemy was developing into modern chemistry. For the Masons, certain shapes and angles, as well as certain mathematical quotients, were deemed to represent immutable forces of nature, either in harmony or in conflict. It was part of the "new learning" of the day.[3]

This new and fashionable pursuit of knowledge was not looked upon with favor by the Catholic Church. In fact, the powerful Church bureaucracy would hold to an ideal of control over the belief system of the faithful through the Renaissance, the Reformation and the Enlightenment, clinging fiercely to the authority they'd once had over the structure of belief in the West, down to the smallest details.

In its prime, the Catholic Church had powers and abilities far beyond those of mortal men. Its weapons were many and fearful. There was the Inquisition, which in its seven centuries of existence ran the gamut from a board of Catholic bishops, whose job it was to oversee the minutiae of regularity in Church doctrine, all the way to the madness in the Spanish Inquisition of the fourteenth and fifteenth centuries.

In the heyday of the Catholic Church, popes had far more power than kings. On paper, the pope was also a temporal king, ruling over the Papal States of central Italy from the fall of the Roman Empire until the unification of Italy in the late nineteenth century. A few popes, like Julius II during the Renaissance, took this temporal authority quite seriously. These warrior-popes not only led the mass but also led armies against encroaching powers. When the monarchs of Europe got out of line, popes drew their sharpest ecclesiastical swords—excommunication, or interdict. Popes could excommunicate a king who misbehaved, making of him a pariah to his own subjects. He was to be denied all sacraments of the Church, including a Christian burial if he should have the misfortune to drop dead. And if that didn't bring him to heel, then a papal interdict could be declared—an excommunication laid over an entire nation. This meant no marriages, no baptisms, no funerals and a very frightened public. The most powerful kings in history bent their knees to the pope, quite literally. As the centuries passed, it began to chafe.

A papal favorite was to force a king to stand before the Vatican, preferably in rain or snow, wearing sackcloth and ashes, holding a broom and a pair of shears, symbolizing his willingness to be whipped or shorn. This could go on literally for days, depending on just how put out His Holiness was. Eventually, the pope would appear to embrace his wayward son, and everything could go back to normal.[4]

Apart from all of these formidable weapons, the Church's absolute control over the minds and hearts of its parishioners was maintained through the most potent weapon of any tyranny—a carefully crafted and absolute domination of information. And Catholicism was about to go head-to-head with an enemy more dangerous than paganism or Protestantism—the birth of a new class that was in possession of a new and powerful weapon of its own.

The Engine of Change

One force brought about the death of the feudal system. A small event around the year 1450 set off several lawsuits in the small German city of Mainz but didn't attract much attention anywhere else. But, like the teenaged Bill Gates tinkering in his garage to create what seemed a useless and overblown widget to the average person, this forthcoming "gadget" would be far more important to mankind than all the battles or coronations or royal scandals that were the focus of people's attention at the time. A metalworker, gem cutter and all-around inventor with the unlikely moniker of Johann Gensfleisch zur Laden Zum Gutenberg was that rarest of birds, not just in the fifteenth century, but in any age—a man of vision. Literacy was on the rise, and people wanted books, which were incredibly expensive. Gutenberg dedicated himself to the task of bringing them the books they wanted, efficiently and inexpensively. Elegant in its simplicity, his printing press was brilliant. Don't print the whole page, just print the letter. His invention of moveable type, set up for each individual page, was an unprecedented breakthrough. Combined with a well-designed machine, featuring a pressure plate that kept pages from smearing, and an oil-based ink that actually worked better on cheap paper than it did on expensive velum, the result was a design so efficient that it remained relatively unchanged through the mid-1800s.[5]

Gutenberg would prove himself to be not only ingenious but audacious as well. His first few printings were short works, demonstrating to his investors that the contraption worked as promised. He then asked for enough money to create his masterpiece—the Gutenberg Bible. It was a bold move, considering that nothing he could have chosen to print was longer or more difficult. Hiring six employees and working for four years, Gutenberg completed his Bible in 1456, and it was the immediate smash hit that his backers had hoped for. But, like other technological innovations throughout history, the printing press couldn't be kept secret for very long.

Gutenberg and his assistants, from a mural on the history books in the Jefferson Building of the Library of Congress, painted by John W. Alexander (1896).

Within the next two decades, presses were appearing in England and all across Europe.

Now the Church, already under fire from idealistic reformers and breakaway Protestant sects, faced the most catastrophic disaster it had known since the reign of Nero. The prospect of a Bible in the hands of any person who wanted one was frightening enough; the thought of a Bible translated into the vernacular was absolutely appalling. Gutenberg's Bible was in Latin, but the Church knew that an English Bible would be the next step down the road to perdition. Of course, the logical question on the part of reformers was dangerous in itself. The Old Testament of the Bible was written principally in Hebrew and the New Testament principally in Greek, although Aramaic, the vernacular of the holy land in the time of Jesus, made brief appearances in both. The Latin Vulgate Bible, the Catholic Church's doctrinal text, was itself a translation, principally the work of St. Jerome in the very early fifth century.[6] So, if it was all right in the fifth century to translate the Bible from Hebrew and Greek into Latin, why wasn't it all right to translate the Latin Bible into English?

Before Vatican II, there was something comforting about being able to walk into a Catholic church in Richmond, England, Richemont, France, or Richmond, Virginia, and hear the same Latin mass. The very word *catholic* means "universal," and this aspect of reading the mass in Latin gave parishioners the feeling that this was so. Yet, it still left the question unanswered, for in the eyes of the reformers who were still devout Catholics, the miracle of the mass was not necessarily threatened because the faithful could go home and read the Book of Matthew in English.

Other nations had vernacular Bibles. The first German Bible, for example, was printed in 1466, and very soon after there were nine other versions in print in German alone. Yet England stood firm in her resolve that such a calamity would not occur on British soil. In fact, in the fifteenth century, to possess a Bible in English was an act of heresy punishable under the law. John Wycliffe, theologian, teacher and forerunner of the Protestant reformers to come, had, in the previous century, been the first to translate the Bible into English. He was charged with heresy for his trouble, but, though driven from his teaching post at Oxford, he was never brought to trial. But his activities caused so much trouble that more than forty years after his death, the Pope had his remains dug up and his bones burned to ashes.

But there was no way to stop controversial Reformation tracts by Wycliffe's followers and others from being smuggled into the country. Nor was it possible to stop printed copies of an English translation of the Bible put together by Wycliffe's disciples, Nicholas of Hereford and John Purvey, from being smuggled in from abroad. There was too much money to be made, and Wycliffe, Erasmus and other fiery radicals convinced too many people that every man had the right, and even the duty, to read and understand the word of God for himself.

Many visionary men of that period wanted to put their money into this new printing device. Men of the new, brazen capitalist class saw the immense potential profits in it. At the same time, Gutenberg's earth-shattering device brought on the same kinds of apocalyptic fears. Diaries, journals and royal edicts of the period reveal unease all over Europe. Political and theological rulers were unsettled by the possibilities for chaos in this new engine of ideas.

The mass of humanity in Western society had always gotten its news and information through the channels of power, carefully filtered through the proper authority. An English translation of the Bible in the hands of every man was a terrifying image for a typical bishop or cardinal of the period. Kings and electors were similarly unnerved by political tracts in the hands of the masses. At hand was the dawn of a new age, in which political authorities found themselves at war with a machine. Many a printer found himself in jail, his printing press confiscated or destroyed, as the civil authorities tried to cope with this new and powerful threat to their absolute sovereignty.

Gutenberg, by simply impressing words on paper, re-inking, reloading and repeating, unleashed upon the world the most awesome weapon of mass destruction mankind had ever known. Books that took dedicated monks and scribes ten and twenty years to painstakingly copy by hand, could now be cranked out, bound and sold for far fewer florins to far more buyers than ever before. More books meant more eyes looking at them, and more reasons for an uneducated public to learn to actually read. A book became something within the possibility of a man to actually own for a change. More readers meant more thinking and less listening to influential others. The age of critical thinking dawned.

The coming Enlightenment was arguably more important to the direction Western civilization headed than any other period. It came on the heels of centuries of religious war and political smugness that held a monopoly on monarchy and faith in every corner of Christendom. With the Enlightenment, an increasing number of political, religious and philosophical upstarts began asking "Why?" That one little word would topple kings from thrones and wrest half of a continent away from its previous landlords. The Enlightenment thinkers questioned the rights of kings to govern men, and clergy to govern souls. Promoting the concepts of liberty and inalienable rights was heretical and dangerous in the world at large, as blasphemous as spitting on the cross, and as punishable as treason.

The Bloodbath over Religion

With the organization of the premier Grand Lodge in London in 1717 and the adoption of Anderson's *Constitutions* for the governance of Masonic lodges in 1723, two vitally important tenets of Freemasonry were recognized. They had nothing to do with rituals or symbols, and they would become more entrenched as the century unfolded. The first was that there would be no discussion of religion within the confines of the lodge. The second was that there would be no discussion of politics within the confines of the lodge. Neither of these strictures grew out of a vacuum. Rather, they grew out of the experiences of the two previous centuries, and without them, Masonry could never have come to embody all that was noble in the ideals of the Enlightenment.

The Freemasons of the early 1700s were looking over their shoulders at a dark and sinister past that was still reaching out a bony hand to the present. They saw it when they looked around them and when they looked back. In Europe, the 1500s and 1600s were marked by a series of long and bloody wars of religion. Throughout the Middle Ages, the Catholic Church had been the ultimate arbiter over the faith of western Europe. But that absolute dominance was slipping, pulling the whole of the West into a quagmire of religious violence.

Of course, it could be argued that these wars of religion were political as well, since all monarchs were backing either the old or the new religion. Elizabeth I, who stands out as an exception to the rule, was willing to tolerate her Catholic subjects so long as they stopped trying to assassinate her. But for the most part, any concept of a separation of church and state was unthinkable. Monarchs did not back their religion of choice merely with speeches, or even with governmental sanctions against opposing faiths, but with swords and gunpowder.

Yet it all began not as a movement to split the Church, but simply to affect certain necessary reforms. The first outbreaks of scandal within the papacy came around the 10th century, confirming for Christians with an apocalyptic bent that evil had taken hold of the world, including the Church, and that it foreshadowed "the end of days," one thousand years after the birth of Christ.[7] Between 872 and 1012, more than a third of those on the papal throne died violent deaths, usually at the hands of their own successors. For example, Pope John XII, "the Christian Caligula," was murdered by a jealous husband while in bed with the man's wife, leaving behind overwhelming evidence that he had committed heresy, sodomy, rape and incest as well as adultery. And he wasn't the only one.[8] Many popes in this period had not one but a platoon of mistresses and a bevy of illegitimate children, who sometimes might even follow their fathers on the papal throne as if they were Tudors or Bourbons. Popes lived in outrageous opulence in the Lateran Palace. Simple Franciscan monks were persecuted and even sent to the stake for having the bad taste to point out that Christ and his apostles had lived in poverty.

For many reformers, the worst papal excesses were simony—the buying and selling of ecclesiastical offices—and the selling of indulgences, whereby sins were forgiven for a payment of money. In the beginning, these practices were somewhat rare, and the money was put to good uses, such as building the great cathedrals of Europe. Later, though, as the papacy fell into disrepute, the corruption became more brazen and more disgraceful. The money often went to support the pope's lavish lifestyle. These unsavory practices were Martin Luther's principal complaint about the Catholic Church.[9]

The advent of the printing press had a few advantages for the Church. Indulgences once painstakingly copied out by hand could now be printed and sold to the faithful by the thousands. But the advantage was to the reformers, who were able to publish and circulate tracts against the Church with voluminous efficiency.

By the time of Henry VIII's all-out war against the papacy in the 1530s, growing out of his desire to divorce his queen and to marry his mistress, kings and princes all over Europe were pulling away from the Church, taking it upon themselves to govern the religion of their own nations, as well as the conscience of each individual citizen. This was quite a radical idea, most common in some of the soon-to-be-Protestant German states of the Holy Roman Empire. When Henry VIII walked out on the pope and faced excommunication to form the Church of England, he demanded that the whole nation come along with him, and burned or beheaded anyone who said otherwise.

It was, in many respects, a terrifying time to be a Christian. "Heresy" was a word often heard. All these faiths, old and new, were marked by a fanatical certainty that all nonmembers of a particular sect were headed directly for the bowels of hell. Or at least they were headed for the stake. The Inquisition, though past its prime, still ruled through terror, while Protestantism began to splinter, fracturing into Puritans and Presbyterians, Anabaptists and Calvinists, Mennonites and Quakers. Men of tolerance and reason watched as western civilization ruptured into Catholic and Protestant camps. The bloodshed in the name of Christ was unbelievable and appalling.

In Britain, religious violence was becoming an epidemic. A man caught up in this changing of the guard could find himself being bounced back and forth from orthodoxy to heresy without ever changing a single opinion. It was like dancing without moving.

When Henry VIII died in 1547, having broken away from Rome, established the Church of England, sacked Catholic monasteries, married six times and brought unprecedented power to the English throne, he passed on to his reward, looking every bit as bloated and wrecked as might be supposed after such a turbulent thirty-eight-year reign. But for the English people, the drama was just beginning.

Henry was succeeded by his only son, Edward VI, a sickly child who died at the age of sixteen after a brief six-year reign. Edward's death brought chaos and civil war. His party within the British government, captained by the Dukes of Northumberland and Suffolk, tried to put Lady Jane Grey on the throne, asserting that as the daughter of Henry VIII's sister Margaret, she was the closest possible Protestant claimant. A pathetic figure, she ruled for only nine days. On the tenth day Mary, Henry's eldest daughter by his first wife Catherine of Aragon and the rightful heir to the throne by the Tudor bloodline, rode into London to a resounding chorus of hosannas. Lady Jane and her husband, Northumberland's son, were put to death.

The hosannas quickly died out. Mary had had a deeply troubled childhood, the result of her parents' divorce, her mother's death and her banishment from the court because of her Catholic faith. Living under constant pressure to conform to the new religion, she grew as fanatically Catholic as any prelate of the Church. Early in her reign, she set about earning her nickname "Bloody Mary." First she ignored the pleas of Parliament and her advisors and married a powerful Catholic, Phillip II of Spain, an act that put her at war with her Protestant subjects. She then proceeded to burn at the stake a series of beloved Protestant religious figures, setting in motion a chain of violent rebellions that would mark her interminable five-year reign.[10]

When Elizabeth I, a level-headed woman, finally came to the throne in 1558, her complete lack of fanaticism helped to close the wounds of religious strife within the country. But she would soon find herself at war with Catholic Spain, no matter how adroitly she tried to avoid it. Phillip of Spain was a rabid Catholic who had no intention of letting the island of Britain make these judgments for itself.

And so it went, right on into the next century. Elizabeth, the Virgin Queen, left no male heir, so the throne fell to James, the son of Elizabeth's old rival, Mary of Scots, since he had the strongest claim of anyone left alive. Crowned James I of England, as well as James VI of Scotland, he was the first Stuart king of England. This would hardly lay the thorny issue of religion to rest. James's son, Charles I, would reign over the first major civil war between Protestants, as the High Church Anglicans of the Church of England

and the king fought against the Puritans, who were led by Oliver Cromwell and Parliament. Riding on a sea of blood, Cromwell's New Model Army at last defeated the Royalists at the Battle of Naseby, and the king was beheaded at the order of Parliament in 1648. Cromwell ruled as Lord Protector, dictator in all but name, through eleven dreary years.

At last the life-loving English people got sick to death of no dancing, no drinking, no Christmas and very little joy of any sort, and invited the Stuarts to return to the throne, in the person of Charles II, a Catholic sympathizer. When he died without a legitimate heir, his brother James II, who was anything but quiet about his devout Catholicism, came to the throne, and it was like Bloody Mary all over again. Finally, these incessant civil wars ended in a refreshingly bloodless revolt as Parliament invited William of Orange and his wife the Princess Mary, daughter of James, to take the throne and bring a little sanity back to Great Britain.

What emerged from this tumultuous period of history was not atheism, as one might expect, but reason.

Utopia

The philosophers of the Enlightenment, enormously influential writers like Voltaire, Rousseau, Locke and Condorcet, had begun to preach a new dogma—that the fact of a man's faith being different from yours was not necessarily a good enough reason to kill him. This was only a part of their ideology of a rational God, a natural right to freedom and a brotherhood of man, an ideology that was storming the ramparts of the feudal system. The wedded bliss of the printing press and the idealists of the Enlightenment had given birth to a new class, the "thinking class," not limited to knights, nobles or serfs. It crossed the old lines, drawing in the wealthy middle class, the shopkeepers and tradesmen, some of the poor, and many of the petty nobility who dreamed of a better world for all men. It was their common bond of literacy, their joy in the exchange of the written word, that bound this new class together. The wildfire spread of Enlightenment principles, as well as Masonic ones, flew off the printing presses to a public hungry for ideas and debate.

Utopianism was the common thread that ran through most of the works of the Encyclopedists and Philosophes. Even strictly political writings of the period have the flavor of Utopianism about them, for they are treatises, not on the way things are, but on the way they could be. Rousseau's work *The Social Contract*, for example, is for the most part one long screed on the way the world and its governments should be, rather than the way they were. It is often cited as one of the works "to blame" for the French Revolution, which is as nonsensical as blaming it on the Freemasons.

There was nothing new about Utopianism. Long before Sir Thomas More coined the term in his 1516 work *Utopia*, Plato's *Republic* had laid out the principal elements of the form. Plato used a structure called "interlocution," which simply means two people talking, shooting the breeze about how to design the perfect city-state. Later utopian writers often used this literary form. Other visionary sociopolitical works used the narrative form of a journal or a story told by one character to another. For More, the word "utopia" was a play on words fashioned from the Greek words for "not," which is *ou*, and "good," *eu*, along with the word for "place," *topos*, so that the word *utopia* literally meant both "noplace" and "good place," a fitting enough name for a nonexistent fantasy state that was completely rational and free of greed, lust and selfishness.

Another work of utopian fiction in a similar vein that had enormous impact on Americans was *The New Atlantis* by Francis Bacon. Whether Bacon was making his own play on words in naming his ideal scientific edifice and secret society "Salomon's House" as a nod to the embryo of Masonry already in existence, or whether *The New Atlantis* was one more influence on the terminology and ritual of Freemasonry to come, is debatable. Historian Jean V. Matthews describes it as America's "cult of Francis Bacon" for the worship he received as the father (along with Isaac Newton) of the scientific method.[11] His vision of a New Atlantis would become a handbook for the founders and builders of America's new Federal City.

This utopianism of Bacon and his philosophical descendants was the same doctrine being preached in the Masonic lodges of London in the early eighteenth century. It was the principal reason that English Freemasonry was so quickly embraced all across Europe and the United States. A new world was at hand, in which anything was achievable for the new science and the new rationalism. The day of liberation from the religious and class tyranny of the past had arrived at last in every Masonic lodge. In London, this new "thinking class" had driven the birth of modern, speculative Freemasonry. Many of the most influential scientists, architects and philosophers in this new age were members of the Royal Society, founded by Charles II as a college and experimental center for all the branches of the new learning—the same purpose as Salomon's House in *The New Atlantis*. And many members of the Royal Society were also members of London's Masonic lodges.

Forbidding any discussion of religion in the lodge seemed the very essence of Enlightenment thinking, a wise, modern and supremely rational idea in light of the previous two centuries of bloodshed. All religions were equal in the hearts of their adherents, and all Masons were entitled to their own private beliefs. Or at least, it seemed a wise idea from a Masonic point of view. The nobility and the clergy had a different name for it.

When Louis XV of France sent his platoon of spies out to see what was going on in the Masonic lodges, he was appalled to discover that a Jew, a Catholic and a Protestant could sit side by side, along with a jeweler, an actor, a doctor, a tax collector, a Benedictine priest, several merchants, and even a black trumpeter from the King's guard—electing the best among them to the officer's line without consideration of religion or blood.[12] For the king, the very act of having elections was subversive. He would send an occasional raid on Masonic lodges as if they were gin joints during Prohibition. In its voluminous screeds against Freemasonry, the Church during the

Age of Enlightenment railed against the supposed diminution of faith in this sort of brotherhood. That much tolerance was simply not to be tolerated.

Napoleon once said, "The old nobility would have survived if it had known enough to become master of printing materials. The advent of cannon killed the feudal system; ink will kill the modern system." Having himself survived the period of the Terror under Robespierre by a hair's breadth, Napoleon understood more than most the potential for misuse in Gutenberg's gift to the modern age. Of course, his statement on the careful handling of the masses, however true, abrogates one of the most important of Masonic beliefs— the concept of *personal* enlightenment, combined with *personal* responsibility.[13]

While France's Masonic lodges were driven underground during their revolution, America's lodges flourished, and it was from the lodges of America that Enlightenment ideals—freedom, accountability, charity and the spread of literacy and opportunity to the least in society—poured forth over the new nation. By contrast, in France there would be no light of Freemasonry to lead them out of the primitive darkness of the Terror. For in the final analysis, the meaning of "Masonic light" was not merely the pursuit of knowledge, but the just and wise use of the power of knowledge. It was—and remains—a journey toward wisdom as well as tolerance, a road that mankind all over the world is still traveling.

CHAPTER 3

Freemasonry Before the Revolution

Flattering as it may be to the human mind, and truly
honorable as it is to receive from our fellow citizens
testimonies of approbation for exertions to promote
the public welfare, it is not less pleasing to know that
the milder virtues of the heart are highly respected by
a Society whose liberal principles must be founded in the
immutable laws of truth and justice. To enlarge the sphere
of social happiness is worthy of the benevolent design
of a Masonic institution; and it is most fervently to be
wished that the conduct of every member of the
Fraternity, as well as those publications that discover
the principles which actuate them, may tend to convince
mankind that the great object of Masonry is to promote
the happiness of the human race.
—GEORGE WASHINGTON[1]

In the statement above, directed to the Massachusetts Grand Lodge
in 1792, Washington speaks of "promoting happiness," a phrase so
similar to Jefferson's words in the Declaration of Independence. We
are, in fact, the first nation on earth to take a concept as personal and
ephemeral as "happiness" and insert it into a legal document, which
explains something of the American character. Americans want not
only to be happy themselves, but to spread happiness to every corner of the globe. Americans work more hours per week on average
than the citizens of any other industrialized Western nation, yet we

volunteer more hours per capita to charity than any nation on the planet. We even gave the world Disneyland.

And it must be understood that, in the Enlightenment world of the late eighteenth century, happiness was tied immutably to freedom. The most dangerously radical idea to come out of the Age of Reason was that the one was impossible to achieve without the other, since both were products of "natural law."

In understanding the history of the American Revolution, it helps to discover the degree to which these ideas flowed out of the Masonic lodges. The greatest difficulty facing the historian who attempts to answer that question is the lack of comprehensive, reliable documents available for study. Nor do these dusty, yellowing papers, membership lists and minutes of meetings have much to say on the subject of politicizing the lodges. That subject requires raising eyes away from documentary evidence long enough to look at the culture as a whole.

This chapter will begin by sketching out the information we have about the rapid growth of Freemasonry in the thirteen colonies in the eighteenth century. These facts are generally accepted without controversy, argued over only by Masonic historians, who rival the ancient Greek polemicists in their enthusiasm for debates about angels on pinheads. The long Masonic career of Ben Franklin seems a good example of the growing involvement of many influential Americans in Freemasonry.

The second question addressed in this chapter is a much tougher one: To what degree was the radicalization of American politics influenced by the Masonic lodges? Finding a definitive answer is a little like catching a will o' the wisp in a jar. So many historical complexities cloud the issue, such as the existence of "regular" and "irregular" lodges and the birth of groups patterned after Freemasonry that were nothing of the kind. But to a Freemason, it's important to at least attempt to answer the question because so many "nonfiction" books about Freemasonry that have been foisted on the public in the last decade have come at this particular subject with an axe to grind.

Freemasons are regularly accused in some circles of being a secret cabal of conspirators who plot the takeover of governments and the domination of the entire world. For the most part, such lurid accusations lack any factual foundation. However, there is one undeniable historical instance of this nightmarish Masonic conspiracy. A small group of influential Freemasons plotted the violent overthrow of their country's government. They met secretly, swore bloody oaths, helped to connive and foment an unpopular war that did not at first have the overwhelming support of the majority of the nation's citizens. And when it was over, this junta of prominent men infiltrated the legislative body of the new government and insinuated their Masonic schemes into its founding documents. Their devious plot unfolded as the American Revolution.

Yet these were the acts of individuals. They were certainly influenced by Masonry, but they were not cogs in some overarching plot hatched behind guarded lodge room doors. Before we lay the radicalization of colonial politics squarely at the feet of Masonry, another point about the culture of that time needs to be made. As the latter half of the eighteenth century unfolded, relations between Great Britain and her American colonies were deteriorating at a dizzying speed. The 1760s were marked by one protest or boycott after another, as the hard-working, ambitious colonists fought the reins of their colonial status with ever-increasing vigor. Consequently, quilting bees and Bible classes were becoming radicalized in this climate of dissent, as Americans increasingly demanded that their friends and neighbors climb on board with the campaign to win civil rights from the Crown. Certainly, at least some lodges were also egging this process on, whether they were forbidden from doing so by Masonic rules or not.

George Washington said that the great object of Masonry was to promote the happiness of the human race. Deist and Enlightenment philosophy said that the promotion of happiness was achieved by the promotion of freedom. Within that framework, it seems likely that lodges were a force behind the revolutionary politics of the period. But before wild-eyed conspiracy theorists gleefully leap to their feet in a chorus of "Ah-ha!" the issue needs a little more scrutiny.

Freemasonry in the American colonies had an enormous impact on society throughout the mid- to late 1700s. Its heritage stretched back to the Middle Ages, when the Freemasons' guilds operated tiny, democratic, government-like bodies within civil society for seven centuries. The lodges that had served the English stonemasons had performed judicial duties within their own membership. They had engaged in voluntary association and assembly, and they had performed as an independent unit of the local government.[2] As James Davis Carter wrote, "The Masons had not permitted the development of highly autocratic hierarchy with positions of privilege that could not be controlled by democratic means from below."[3] In other words, the Freemasons had figured out how to run a democratic society and make it work.

Freemasonry values freedom, not revolution. The term itself stems from the medieval practices that had required members to stay connected to a given guild or building project. Guilds were early forms of labor unions that sought to protect workers from scabs and interlopers, as well as train them and look after their common welfare. The term *freemason* meant that members were free to travel to different towns, and even different countries, to work, provided they had the proper skills and could prove themselves to be fully qualified members. In an age when a poorly constructed cathedral could— and sometimes did—collapse on the assembled congregation, professional qualification was a real and important issue. That's where the passwords and handshakes came in.

But freedom was a far cry from fomenting rebellion. John Anderson's *Constitutions* had said in 1723:

A Mason is a peaceable Subject to the Civil Powers, wherever
he resides or works, and is never to be concern'd with Plots
and Conspiracies against the Peace and Welfare of the Nation,
nor to behave himself undutifully to inferior Magistrates... So
that if a Brother should be a rebel against the State, he is not
to be countenanc'd in his Rebellion, however he may be pitied
as an unhappy Man.[4]

The lodges themselves were not hotbeds of Revolutionary
scheming; such discussions within their meetings would not have
been permitted. Although Freemasonry proudly claims some of the
most famous patriots of the Revolutionary War, the problem is that
they weren't supposed to be engaging in such matters in the first
place. And it isn't just in the United States that revolutionary thought
and the fraternity became entwined in both popular and Masonic legend. Freemason Simon Bolivar wrested the South American continent from Spain. Freemason Benito Juarez led Mexico's fight for independence. Freemason Giuseppe Garibaldi was the key figure in the
liberation of the Papal States from the ownership of the Vatican and
the creation of a unified Italy. Even in America, long after the revolution, Freemason John Brown led the raid on Harper's Ferry in 1859
for the cause of the abolition of slavery.

There was a loophole in Freemasonry's rules:

...If convicted of no other Crime, though the loyal Brotherhood must and ought to disown his Rebellion, and give no
Umbrage or Ground of political Jealousy to the Government
for the time being: they cannot expel him from the Lodge, and
his Relation to it remains indefeasible.[5]

One country's backstabbing, rebellious bomb-tossing traitor is
another's patriot. Freemasonry seemed to acknowledge that same
sentiment. While sedition wasn't talked about in lodge, brethren
who engaged in it weren't going to be expelled from the fraternity
when the dust settled. Freemasonry had no control over what was
said after the lodge closed and the ale started flowing.

American Freemasonry Wades Ashore

The search for the truth of Freemasonry's origins and influence in the New World is a tricky business. In 1827, Dr. Charles T. Jackson, a chemist and geologist from Boston, was performing a geological survey of Nova Scotia. On the shore of Goat Island, across from Annapolis, he and his assistant Francis Alger made an unusual find. Half-buried in the sand was a slab of rock, described as a gravestone, carved with the symbol of a square and compass and the date 1606. Masonic authors and wee-morning radio talk show callers have used the "Annapolis Stone" as "proof" that Masonry waded ashore in the Americas years before the Pilgrims got here. Never mind that carpenters and working stonemasons also used the square and compass as symbols of their craft guilds in those days. And never mind that the settlement in Nova Scotia was French, and that speculative Freemasonry wouldn't appear there for more than another century.[6]

Still, it is entirely credible that the men who settled in Jamestown, Virginia, in 1607 and elsewhere were inspired by the Enlightenment, including the utopian ideals of Bacon's *New Atlantis*, Rosicrucianism and other new philosophies, in their attempts to forge a New World in the Americas. The answer to whether modern Freemasonry was inspired by these movements, or whether Freemasonry itself inspired them, will probably never be known.

In 1682, a Freemason named John Skene arrived in America from Scotland. He had joined a lodge in Aberdeen in 1670, and he is generally credited as being the first speculative Freemason in North America. Unfortunately for Brother Skene, the colonies were a barren source of amusement for a Mason in search of fraternal association. He became the deputy governor of New Jersey shortly after arriving, but no record exists that he made any attempt to establish a lodge once he was here. Freemasonry back home in England was still primarily a guild for men who built with stone. But it was changing.

Although the problem with tracing Freemasonry's beginnings in the colonies always comes back to a lack of detailed record-keeping, it is generally accepted that one of the earliest Freemasons here was Jonathan Belcher. Born in Boston, Belcher became a Freemason while visiting London in 1704 in a "Guilde Lodge." It probably consisted mostly of operative stonemasons, along with a growing group of curious gentlemen who were slowly transforming Freemasonry into a philosophical fraternity.

The Grand Lodge of England was formed in 1717 in London with just four lodges, but it took the somewhat la-de-da position that it was to be the governing body for any expansion of the fraternity forever after. There would be schisms, disagreements and plenty of instances of just plain ignoring such claims of authority throughout the 1700s, and many of these occurred in the American colonies. The old, operative stonemasons' lodges had been closing all over England. New architecture favored bricks over giant, gothic blocks, and working in stone was a dying art. The change from operative Freemasonry to this new philosophical, speculative Freemasonry brought about by the new Grand Lodge resulted in renewed growth and interest. By 1723, there were at least twenty London lodges. Nine more were organized outside of the city.

Freemasonry arrived in France in 1725 and Spain in 1729. Over the next decade, it spread all across Europe. Both Scotland and Ireland formed their own Grand Lodges separately from England, and soon a competing Grand Lodge formed in England, referring to itself as the "Ancients" and proclaiming its practices to be more authentic than the first group in London, which became known as the "Moderns." The Ancients seem originally to have been made up of Irish and Scots Masons in London who either had been snubbed by their English brethren or preferred the company of more common folks. It seems to have been a city-slickers-versus-country-folks disagreement, but it lasted long enough to make waves in the colonies.

There has long been an ongoing debate as to which colony had the first "official" lodges and Provincial Grand Lodges, and Pennsylvania and Massachusetts have been duking it out with each other almost since the beginning. The first lodges appeared in Pennsylvania as early as 1730, Massachusetts in 1733, Georgia in 1734, South Carolina in 1735, New Hampshire in 1736, New York in 1737 and Virginia in 1743. By 1765, Freemasonry was firmly established in all of the thirteen colonies that would become the United States.

One of the biggest complaints that the Ancients had against the Moderns was their apparent love affair with the nobility. In spite of Masonic notions of equality and meeting "on the level," the Moderns courted members of the aristocracy to lend their Grand Lodge an extra gloss of classiness and legitimacy. The Ancients, on the other hand, felt that the presence of all of these nobs and toffs flew in the face of Freemasonry's ancient heritage as a guild for the workingman. The Ancients also believed that the Moderns had made too many innovations in the ritual ceremonies and had strayed too far from their origins.

The competition between the two groups, along with the growth of Scottish and Irish military lodges among British colonial troops stationed in the Americas, had the effect of creating chaos among the various lodges that were sprouting up across the landscape. The Grand Lodge of England was attempting to demand exclusive authority to issue charters for the creation of new lodges, while the upstart Ancients, Scots and Irish were chartering lodges themselves. And there were other lodges that seemed to germinate spontaneously, from out of nowhere. They were created by men who had become Masons in England or another colony, who then simply smacked a gavel on a table and declared themselves to be a new and independent lodge.[7]

The rivalry between the Ancients and Moderns in England would not be reconciled until 1813, when the two unified by mutual agreement as the United Grand Lodge of England. In the colonies, the situation was solved differently at the end of the Revolution, when each state formed its own governing Grand Lodge with control over all of the lodges in its jurisdiction.

Brother Franklin and Pennsylvania

In 1730, Benjamin Franklin was twenty-four years old. It was a big year for him. He was just back from visiting England, and had decided to settle down and marry Deborah Read, a Philadelphia girl whose husband had recently deserted her. Apart from the fact that another woman across town was carrying his illegitimate son, Franklin was turning over a new leaf and concentrating on his fledgling printing business. That same year, he formed the Junto, a scientific research and philosophy club that declared its love for all mankind and "truth for truth's sake."[8] The group immediately got to work on starting the first subscription library in Philadelphia, which would become the Philadelphia Public Library.

In the December 8, 1730, edition of the *Pennsylvania Gazette*, Benjamin Franklin published an exposé of the Masons' ritual. Franklin had probably encountered Freemasonry while visiting London, and it's entirely possible that he published the account as a way to get the Masons in Philadelphia to notice and contact him. It began with a supposed letter from a man in London who sought to ridicule them:

> The World has long Admir'd, that in such a numerous
> Company... there has been no one found, that in his Cups,
> or in any other Circumstances, would discover their Mysteries:
> But the whole appears so childish and ridiculous that this is
> probably the case, their Grand Secret is that they have no
> Secret at all.

What he had said was true. For all of its ritual, for all of the characterization of Freemasonry as a "secret society," the ultimate point of the fraternity was never about the secrecy of its ceremonies. But Franklin clearly did not find it childish or ridiculous, because he became a Freemason the following year, joining St. John's Lodge, which met at Philadelphia's Tun Tavern. That same year, he published the first book on the subject of Freemasonry printed in America, Reverend John Anderson's *Constitutions*, which he had received from

London. Franklin didn't print things just for the practice. He wouldn't have gone to the expense of publishing such a book if he didn't think it would sell.

Franklin became very active in his lodge, as well as in the Provincial Grand Lodge. He was elected as Junior Grand Warden in 1732 and became Grand Master in Pennsylvania in 1734. Due to the organizational chaos that prevailed during Masonry's formative years in the colonies, the Grand Lodge of Pennsylvania was not legally formed under the rules of the Grand Lodge of England. So in 1734, Franklin contacted Henry Price, the Grand Lodge of England's Provincial Grand Master in Massachusetts, looking to hawk some books and nosing around for Price's official blessing of Pennsylvania's Grand Lodge.

Franklin was appointed as Provincial Grand Master for the colonies in 1749, and in 1755 he took a prominent role in the dedication of the first Masonic building constructed for that purpose in America. He and the brothers of St. John's Lodge would also take part in the Masonic cornerstone-laying ceremony of the statehouse in Philadelphia, a building that would later be known as Independence Hall.

Freemasons were not free of controversy, even at this early period. It's a curious thing to think of our Founding Fathers with parents who fretted over the activities of their children. In 1737, a young man named Daniel Rees was killed when a group of non-Masonic pranksters pretended to initiate him into the Masons in a series of humiliating episodes. They tried to scare him at one point by igniting pans of brandy and underlighting their faces like campers holding flashlights under their chins as they tell ghost stories. When Rees failed to be suitably impressed by their face-making, one of them—accidentally or on purpose—threw a pan of the flaming liquor into his face. The burns were so severe that he died three days later. The event set off a storm of anti-Masonic furor in Philadelphia, and Franklin's mother was especially upset about his involvement with the fraternity. In a letter to his father, Franklin replied,

As to the Freemasons, I know of no way of giving my mother a better account of them than she seems to have at present, since it is not allowed that women should be admitted into that secret society. She has, I must confess on that account, some reason to be displeased with it; but for anything else, I must entreat her to suspend her judgment till she is better informed, unless she will believe me, when I assure her that they are in general a very harmless sort of people, and have no principles or practices that are inconsistent with religion and good manners.[9]

In 1748, Franklin retired and spent the rest of his life in public service. Unlike George Washington, who rarely attended lodge, Franklin continued to participate and visit lodges wherever he went.

In 1759, he sat in a lodge in Edinburgh, Scotland, and the next year, he was received at the Grand Lodge of England meeting at the Crown and Anchor Tavern in London.

Much of Franklin's later life was spent in France as a diplomat. While there as ambassador of the United States, he joined the *Lodge des Neuf Soeurs* (Lodge of the Nine Muses), where he assisted in making the French philosopher Voltaire a Mason. He was elected Master of the lodge in 1779. In 1782 he became a member of *Lodge de Saint Jean de Jerusalem* (St. John of Jerusalem), and that same year he was made an honorary member of *Lodge des Bons Amis* (Good Friends) in Rouen.

Benjamin Franklin, Provincial Grand Master for the Colonies, 1749.

The philosophy of Freemasonry influenced nearly everything Franklin did in his adult life. His dedication to science and learning became legendary in his own time, although it's often overlooked in ours. His personal charm at the French court was responsible for bringing France into the American Revolution on the side of the colonies and turning the tide of the war. His easy manner in difficult and trying moments of political impasse clearly exemplifies a man who learned skills of diplomacy at the helm of a volunteer group made up of fractious members in a volatile time. His public religious statements are synonymous with the Masonic views of belief in a Supreme Being, yet unbiased by any creed. Tolerance was almost always Franklin's public policy.

The Military Lodges

The life of a British soldier in the New World was a busy one. The North American continent may have been a backwater half a world away, but it was becoming a battleground for the eternal smack-downs between England and France. In the New World, fights, skirmishes and wars were breaking out with wearying regularity. "King William's War," in 1690 in Quebec and Nova Scotia, was the first chapter in what would become an ongoing war with France in the American colonies. "Queen Anne's War" raged between 1702 and 1713, with the Spanish entering the conflict on the side of France. England faced a two-front battle to the north in Canada and to the south in the Carolinas, the Caribbean and what is now Florida. Wars broke out in the West Indies and Jamaica in the 1720s and 1730s. "King George's War" lasted from 1844 until 1848, fighting the French to another standoff. At last the final grudge match—the French and Indian War—broke out seven years later and lasted until 1763.

The years leading up to the beginning of the American Revolution had their share of pesky police actions with an antagonistic citizenry. As a result, the common soldier didn't make it home to England very frequently. There was a sense that America was the boondocks, a footnote to the ongoing battles being waged across Europe. Troop strength in the colonies was usually quite small, and they often had to rely on the assistance of local militias and other irregulars.

Certainly, life in the military created long-lasting friendships between men. But the introduction of Freemasonry among both officers and soldiers forged something deeper. Regimental lodges first appeared in the British Army around 1732, and by 1755 there were at least twenty-nine of them. To the frustration of the Grand Lodge of England, these military lodges were generally chartered by the Irish and Scottish Grand Lodges. Unlike the lodges in cities and towns that met in taverns or private homes, these were mobile, carrying their officers' jewels, candlesticks and other regalia in trunks, along with the military accoutrements of the regiment. They met in tents, caves, isolated sections of woods or private rooms when they could be procured.

Military rank in the British Army prior to this period had developed much like civilian life. Officers generally came from the nobility, and the have-nots commonly remained at the bottom of the pecking order. But Freemasonry began to change the social order within the regiments. Officers and enlisted men sat side by side. In the lodge, the democratic nature of the Masonic officer's line was the opposite of what existed in the outside world. A private who presided as Master of his lodge outranked a major when the doors were closed and the gavel got whacked. Suddenly, lowly soldiers were no longer nameless, faceless cannon fodder to their commanders. For the first time, the foot soldier could speak openly and on the level with his superior officers. Civilians who were already Freemasons would occasionally visit the military lodges, and it was not unusual for non-military men to join military fraternities in these mobile lodges.

America's population had swelled in the 1740s and 1750s. When the French and Indian War broke out in 1755, it was the desire of King George that the American colonists get involved in fighting for

England in defense of their land. Unlike previous skirmishes in the New World, the French and Indian War would be a major conflict, and massive troop movements on both sides of the war brought an unprecedented number of well-trained soldiers ashore. The British Army set to work training colonists in military tactics, which meant that the colonial civilians worked closely with officers and soldiers. Colonials were always starved for news, culture and stories from the Mother Country, and the growing popularity of Freemasonry in England spread quickly in America.

As the war progressed, a growing number of non-aristocratic officers rose in rank throughout the Army and the colonial militias. Simultaneously, these men who were lower in social class were granted not only military titles but Masonic ones as well. Grand Lodges overseas needed to administer their rules, dues collection and other increasingly complex organizational duties by long distance through the appointment of Provincial Grand Lodge officers, inspectors, secretaries and Grand Masters. Suddenly, unschooled men from the countryside were learning about morals, manners, religious tolerance and social equality. They were learning leadership skills, public speaking, democratic elections and bureaucratic administration—all through their association with brother Freemasons.

More important than the influence on Freemasons themselves was the influence the fraternity had on the society around it. The goal of Masonry is to make good men better, and to make the world a better place by encouraging its members to become more responsible fathers, sons and citizens, and thereby becoming better examples to others. This is precisely what was going on in colonial America. Men who had no formal education were being introduced to the ideas of the Enlightenment, either directly as Masons themselves, or simply by association with Freemasons. As Michael Baigent and Richard Leigh point out in *The Temple and the Lodge*,

> Most colonists did not actually read Locke, Hume, Voltaire and Diderot or Rousseau, any more than most British soldiers did. Through the lodges, however, the currents of thoughts asso-

ciated with such philosophers became universally accessible. It was largely through the lodges that 'ordinary' colonists learned of that lofty premise called the 'rights of man.' It was through the lodges that they learned the concept of the perfectibility of society. And the New World seemed to offer a species of blank slate, a species of laboratory in which social experiment was possible and the principles enshrined by Freemasonry could be applied in practice.[10]

In the mid-1700s, it took three weeks to ride from Boston to Georgia. Each colony was very different, with its own laws and customs. Every region also had its own profound social and religious differences. There was no national sense of unity as there was back home in England. Yet the growth of Freemasonry meant that a stranger riding down the Atlantic coast could find friendship and assistance in almost every city. Freemasonry, by attracting the men who were most successful and admired in any given town, created an extended network of brethren all across colonial America. More than that, it was creating a sense of unity among the colonists, based not on political views, religious beliefs or economic status but on the relationships in the lodge fostered by tolerance, benevolence and common experience which existed in no other institution at that time.

To understand the degree to which Freemasonry pervaded colonial society, consider that before the Revolutionary War, the city of Boston had a total population of twenty-five thousand men, women and children. At the same time, there were six Masonic lodges with a combined membership of almost one thousand—a substantial portion of the adult men in the city. And it was in Boston that the seeds of revolution were planted.

Boston's Belligerent Brethren

Massachusetts was unique. The Massachusetts Bay Colony had been established with one of the few colonial charters that physically existed on this side of the Atlantic, instead of in some bureaucrat's office in London. The colony had been self-governed from the very start. It had a longstanding history of independent living and didn't take well to being pestered by the king.

Freemasonry officially moved into Massachusetts in 1733, when Henry Price was authorized by the Grand Lodge of England to form lodges in the colony. In July of that year, a group met at the Bunch of Grapes Tavern in Boston and formed what was appropriately named First Lodge No. 126. It was, in fact, the first lodge in America that the Grand Lodge had authorized (unlike earlier lodges that existed in Pennsylvania), and Price's position as Provincial Grand Master gave him the sole right to charter new lodges in the colonies. Not that such a pronouncement stopped the growth of *un*authorized lodges, or lodges chartered by other groups.

Such an upstart group gathered in Boston in 1752 at the Green Dragon Tavern and proclaimed a new lodge without anyone's authority, much to the annoyance of the Moderns in town. Worse, they declared themselves to be their own Grand Lodge and started to charter new lodges without any authority whatsoever. Eventually, they got around to applying to the Grand Lodge of Scotland for a charter, and in 1756 they became known as St. Andrew's Lodge.

St. Andrew's Lodge became popular for a variety of reasons, not the least of which was the fact that they began conferring different Masonic degrees than most other lodges. In addition to the Entered Apprentice, Fellow Craft and Master Mason degrees that all other lodges in America and England were conferring on their members, St. Andrew's Lodge also presented additional degrees that had developed in Europe (France, Scotland or both). These were the degrees of the Royal Arch, and they were called the Excellent Master, Super-Excellent Master, Royal Arch and finally, the Knights Templar degree. They described other parts of history having to do with King Solomon's Temple, and concerned the further search for knowledge and wisdom, in relation to this sacred site in the Holy Land.

The Knights Templar degree—or *order*, as it would become known—was something new in the colonies. Based upon the legend of the medieval Knights Templar, the famous order of crusading warrior monks, the new degrees had migrated to Boston from Europe in 1769, possibly from the military lodge attached to the 29th Foot, later the 1st Battalion of the Worcestershire Regiment, whose Masonic charter had come from the Grand Lodge of Ireland.[11] What was exciting about the new Templar degree was that decidedly lowborn men with no chance of ever becoming a knight anywhere else could suddenly have a noble title, at least within the confines of the lodge room.

In spite of its unorthodox and irregular origins, in the coming years St. Andrew's would have as members men whose names became synonymous with the cause of the Revolution: Paul Revere, John Hancock, Dr. Joseph Warren and James Otis. Paul Revere, a well-known silversmith, would become immortalized for his nighttime ride as the messenger proclaiming the approach of British troops at Lexington and Concord in April of 1775, when he and fellow Freemason William Dawes succeeded in warning the local militias. John Hancock would go on to become president of the Congress at the signing of the Declaration of Independence in 1776, forever after known for signing his name large enough so King George could see it without his spectacles. And Dr. Joseph Warren would become one of the leading revolutionary figures in Massachusetts. He was a respected physician, author and orator. In 1775, he became a major general in the Continental Army and died at the Battle of Bunker Hill.

The Green Dragon Tavern, the meeting place of St. Andrews, was named after a copper dragon hanging over the door that had turned green with age. It would later become known simply as the Freemason Arms. The lodge would actually purchase the tavern in 1764. It was a popular public house with the largest private meeting room in town, and many organizations connected with the early days of the revolution made use of its facilities. The North End Caucus, the Selectmen, the Long Room Club, the Loyal Nine, the Committees of Correspondence, and the Sons of Liberty were all groups engaged in various subversive activities in and around Boston. It was in this tavern that the Boston Tea Party was undoubtedly planned by men who shared membership in St. Andrew's Lodge. In fact, it would be St. Andrew's Lodge member James Otis who would throw down the first gauntlet in the break with England.

The colonies had been forced by the Navigation Acts of 1661 and 1663 to trade exclusively with England. This was more serious than it sounds, because it allowed a small group of merchants in England to set the prices of natural resources and crops shipped out of America, as well as the price of all finished goods that Americans were forced to import. They made a great wad of loot by setting the value of exports very low, while keeping the cost of imports very high. Not that the colonists paid a whole lot of attention to such pesky laws. Smuggling was endemic to the whole system. There weren't enough British revenue ships to patrol the coast of Maine, let alone the other three thousand miles of colonial coastline.

Historians generally date the beginning of the revolutionary period in 1761, when George III became King of England. George and England had a whopping problem. The ceaseless wars of the last hundred and fifty years or so needed to be paid for by somebody, and the British treasury was tapped out. The government had borrowed heavily from private Dutch and English banks, which sent the national debt soaring from £75 million in 1754 to £133 million just nine years later. The king and Parliament decided that the colonies were prospering quite nicely with their rich exports of goods and natural resources, and it was about time that they started paying for the expense of their own defense from the French and the Spanish. And the government was losing its patience with the now-open defiance of the old Navigation Acts as well. Why waste good money and the blood of English troops to kill the French if the Americans were going to keep buying French goods? The British had a point.

One of the first laws passed under George III's new reign had been the Writs of Assistance. In spite of the helpful and harmless sounding name, the writs were actually blanket search warrants giving British agents the right to barge into homes and shops to hunt for non-British products, without notice and without due process. Unfortunately, the first place the Crown tried to test out this oppressive new law was in radical Massachusetts, home of the upstarts in St. Andrews Lodge.

James Otis was a member of First Lodge in Boston, a Moderns lodge warranted by the Grand Lodge of England. He also joined St. Andrew's Lodge on January 4, 1754. Oddly enough, he held the position of Senior Warden in both lodges that same year, proving himself adroit enough to have a foot in both camps.[12] In 1760, Otis was appointed as Advocate General of the Admiralty Court, a prestigious position for a young lawyer. But the following year, he was called upon to argue the Crown's side in a case brought against the colonists under the Writs of Assistance. To the astonishment of both sides, instead of acting as an obedient servant of the court, Otis resigned his position and immediately offered instead to defend the accused colonists *pro bono.*

The Court met in Boston's Faneuil Hall. The Crown Advocate was now Jeremey Gridley, who was also a member of First Lodge, and Otis's old law school tutor. Otis vehemently denounced the new law, urging his fellow colonists to defy it and to "breast any storm of ministerial vengeance that their resistance might cause." Sitting with the spectators, the young attorney John Adams, who sensed a historic moment at hand, began at once to take notes on the eloquent three-hour speech that followed. It would be the nucleus of all further colonial appeals concerning unwarranted searches and seizures, which Otis denounced as being unconstitutional even under British common law.

He finished with the words that became the opening salvo of the American Revolution: "To my dying day, I will oppose with all the power and faculties God has given me, all such instruments of slavery on the one hand, and villainy on the other."[13]

Freemason James Otis's stirring denouncement of the Writs of Assistance is the reason Boston's Faneuil Hall is considered to be the Cradle of Liberty. Otis would go on to coin the phrase, "Taxation without representation is tyranny." But history would deny him his proper place amongst the Founding Fathers of the United States. In 1769, his politics led to a tavern brawl with a British customs agent, who beat him so severely about the head that he was later adjudged insane. He would experience only brief periods of mental clarity until his death in 1783.

But the pro-revolutionary sentiments that pervaded the membership of St. Andrew's Lodge was not the philosophy Freemasonry taught to its members. And lest you believe that all Freemasons sided with his sentiments, it is worth pointing out that most of King George's representatives in court on the day of James Otis's rousing oration were fellow Masons.[14]

"Independency"

It's tempting for both Masons and non-Masons to claim that revolution was the stuff that lodge meetings were made of, but it's not accurate. St. Andrew's Lodge was the exception rather than the rule regarding Freemasonry in revolutionary America. Out of more than one hundred lodges across the American colonies, only St. Andrew's Lodge in Boston can point to an overwhelmingly radical membership acting in a concerted manner to overthrow British rule. Independence was a controversial subject, and there were plenty of colonists who were just fine with being Englishmen. Indeed, the Masonic lodges that had been chartered by the Moderns, the Grand Lodge of England, were overwhelmingly Loyalist in their membership. This made sense in certain parts of the colonies, as the Moderns' lodges tended to have among their members provincial governors, mayors, importers and exporters and many others who derived their offices from royal appointments and business contracts with Britain. The Ancients' lodges, along with those chartered by the Scottish, Irish and the spontaneously formed irregular lodges, were more of the "working men's" lodges. The Ancients had not been enamored with courting aristocrats for members—it had been one of the biggest complaints they had with the Moderns to begin with.

St. Andrew's was in the lower-class North End of Boston, and its membership was made up primarily of laborers, sailors, merchants and artists from the dock area near the harbor. First Lodge and St. John's Lodge, on the other hand, were both chartered by the Grand Lodge of England and were Moderns lodges. Their membership was largely Loyalist, made up of some of the richest and most influential businessmen and members of government in town. So it is interesting to note that John Hancock, one of the richest men in Massachusetts, chose to join the more plebeian St. Andrew's.

With the chaotic state of Masonic jurisdictions during this period, it is curious that two competing Grand Masters for North America were both based in Boston. Dr. Joseph Warren of St. Andrew's Lodge was made Provincial Grand Master of Masons within one hundred miles of Boston by the Grand Lodge of Scotland in 1769. Three years later, his commission was extended to include all of North America, as far as the Grand Lodge of Scotland was concerned. Warren formed the Provincial Grand Lodge of Massachusetts for the Ancients in 1769, and it would eventually become the first independent state Grand Lodge in the United States after the revolution.

His counterpart in the Moderns was named John Rowe, who happened to be the uncle of his namesake, St. Andrew's member John Rowe. While having the same name, they were of completely incompatible politics and self-interests. Uncle John was Grand Master of St. John's Grand Lodge, a group of Moderns, and the Provincial Grand Master of North America for the Grand Lodge of England. Grand Master Rowe and his brethren were decidedly more loyal to king and country than their St. Andrew's counterparts.

The Boston Massacre

In the years leading up to the Revolution, England enacted a series of taxes, at first designed to stop colonial smuggling of non-British goods and then to raise government tax revenue. The American

colonies went into a major economic recession after the French and
Indian War, importing far more finished goods than the raw materials they were exporting, and sinking ever deeper into debt. Of
course, their English creditors were glad to keep raising their credit
limit. But the British didn't count on American anger over the new
taxes and duties.

In response to the Stamp Act of 1765, colonists boycotted the
import of British goods. The act also prompted a wave of political
activism and reactionary thought, including the argument that
Parliament had no right to tax the colonies if America had no one in
Parliament to represent them. In America, every colony had been
governed by its own representative government, each with its own
rules, laws and customs. Parliament had essentially left the colonies
alone for more than a hundred years, and the sudden attempt to tax
and rule from across the sea went over like a raving aunt moving into
the spare bedroom. England was literally annoying America into
rebellion. Of course, new rules, an uncooperative populace, and the
elimination of a hundred years of doing things their own way meant
that Britain's military commander in Boston, General Thomas Gage,
needed to move in an unprecedented hoard of troops to show the
folks there was a new sheriff in town.

By 1770 British troops stationed in Boston were uniformly
resented by the public, and the 29th and 64th Regiments were in for
special scorn. Street fights were common, and the city was in an ugly
mood. The most notorious fracas began when one teenager taunted
and insulted a young British soldier on guard duty before the Custom
House on the snowy night of March 5, 1770. He got his ears boxed
for his trouble, but instead of taking his medicine, the boy screamed
through the streets that he'd been "attacked" by the vicious British soldiers. A mob of at least four hundred people materialized with alarm-
ing speed, many of them fresh from the tavern.

It was obvious to the uneasy soldiers on duty that things were
coming to a head. Later, the Sons of Liberty would try to paint a
picture of the crowd as hundreds of helpless victims terrorized by six

British soldiers and their commanding officer, but the truth wasn't hard to fathom, even for radical Americans. The armed underground of the Sons of Liberty outnumbered the city's garrison troops by roughly five to one. Boston had been spoiling for a fight, and it got one.

Samuel Adams helped to put the torch to the riot, goading the onlookers to get up into the soldiers faces, to stop shouting insults and to start throwing things—first snowballs, then rocks and, finally, clubs. By the time the officer on duty, Captain Thomas Preston, arrived on the scene, the six soldiers were justifiably terrified. Then one rioter struck a British soldier with a heavy club, and before he could rise, he was struck again in the head by another club thrown from the crowd. The soldiers panicked and opened fire. Five men were killed, and another six were wounded.

A completely fictitious engraving of the riot, created by a revolutionary named Paul Revere of St. Andrew's Lodge, along with wide press coverage that was anything but even-handed, insured that the Boston Massacre would go down in history as a great revolutionary episode. One of its victims, Crispus Attucks, the first man killed, would become not only America's first martyr, but her first African-American hero. The killing of five rioters in self-defense does not a massacre make, but Paul Revere certainly turned it into one.

And yet, curiously enough, Revere's Masonic lodge itself was neutral territory. The records of St. Andrew's, ground-zero for the most notorious of Boston's rabble-rousers, show that they rented their meeting room to military lodges from both the hated 29th and 64th Regiments of the British Army, and even cooperated with the Masonic troops when they applied to the Grand Lodge of Scotland for a charter.[15]

A Consignment of Tea

For years, the saying was that if you were in the Green Dragon Tavern and ordered tea, you were a Tory. If you ordered coffee, you were a patriot. This was a tougher sacrifice than it sounds. The colonists loved their tea, as syrupy sweet as they could make it, and it was hard to give it up for a mere political principle.

In 1770, the Crown finally responded to the shrieking from British merchants who were losing their shirts from the trade boycott in the colonies and repealed all but the tea tax. Tea ranked fourth among all of Britain's exports to the colonies, in spite of the fact that three-fourths of the 1.2 million pounds per year of it Americans drank were illegally smuggled in from the Dutch. The tax on tea was a piddling one, but when Parliament had reluctantly repealed the rest of the taxes on the colonies, King George III had insisted the tea tax remain as proof that the Crown still had the right to tax its colonial citizens. Americans didn't happen to agree. Benjamin Franklin, in London to plead the case for the colonies, made no headway.

On November 29, 1773, the tea ship *Dartmouth* arrived in Boston. Attendees at a town meeting declared that they would never allow the tea to come ashore, but the admiral of the British Navy announced he'd sink any ship loaded with tea that tried to leave the harbor without unloading it first. The Sons of Liberty sent guards to stand on the wharf to make sure the tea stayed on the ships. In response, the governor called out his cadet corps and gave their colonel orders to keep peace at the wharf. Unfortunately for the governor and the customs office, the colonel of the cadet corps was St. Andrew's member John Hancock, so there probably wasn't going to be a lot of peacekeeping. But the Sons of Liberty were in a bind, and the clock was ticking. The rules were that cargo had to be cleared by customs within twenty days, or it could be confiscated by the British revenue officers and distributed.

On the 15th of December, Grand Master of North America for the Moderns, John Rowe, and Grand Master of North America for the Ancients, Dr. Joseph Warren, met to discuss something other than a disagreement over Masonic rituals. Rowe owned one of the tea ships in the harbor, and Warren was a powerful ringleader in several revolutionary organizations. Both men agreed that the governor needed to act fast to avoid the potential danger to ships, cargo or people. Warren knew what was coming, even if Rowe did not.

On the last day of the customs deadline, Brother John Hancock and Grand Master Rowe, along with the owner of the tea ship *Dartmouth*, met to convince the governor to step in and find some kind of compromise, but to no avail. The ships were not going to leave Boston Harbor without unloading the tea and paying the tax.

Brother Rowe's nephew John attended the Boston town meeting that night and wondered aloud, to the amusement of the crowd, whether tea would mix properly in salt water. The *Dartmouth's* owner arrived and reported the results of the day's meeting with the governor. Seven thousand Bostonians surrounded the Old South Meeting House to hear the news. At the same time, almost one hundred badly disguised Mohawk Indian imposters gathered at St. Andrew's member Johnathan Edes's print shop, waiting for Samuel Adams's signal to come from the town meeting.

At last, Adams stood and said, "This meeting can do nothing further to save the country." The word was passed to the street, and the "Indians" made for the harbor. Thousands of spectators made their way to the wharf and watched quietly as the raiders boarded three ships and sent 342 boxes of tea into the sea. The crews of the ships stayed below decks and did not put up a fight, and Governor Hutchinson's Cadet Corps moved away from the wharf. The British ships did nothing to stop the raid—a sixty-gun warship was within easy range—but its commanding officer, Admiral John Montague, watched the whole operation from his nearby home.

When the task was completed, the men shook their shoes out over the side of the ships to dump out any possible incriminating tea leaves. They then swept off the decks, and made each ship's first mate attest that only tea had been destroyed. As the weary "Indians" marched up the street, they passed the open window of Admiral Montague, who yelled down at them, "Well, boys, you have had a fine, pleasant evening for your Indian caper, haven't you? But mind, you have got to pay the fiddler yet!"[16]

Three months later, Parliament passed the Boston Port Bill, closing the harbor until somebody paid back the value of the destroyed tea, £9,659 and 6 shillings, just to be irritatingly precise, plus the lost duty on it. Not everyone was pleased with the actions of the Sons of Liberty. In London, Ben Franklin recommended Boston pay for the cargo, but he got little support. It is said he even offered to pay for it himself.

The Final Straw

Parliament decided to teach Massachusetts—and the colonies—an even bigger lesson and enacted what would become known as the Coercive Acts. The laws of the Massachusetts Bay Colony going back to 1691 were dismantled, and dramatic new powers were given to the Royal Governor. Town meetings could only be held with his permission. Judges, and even juries, were to be picked by the governor or his agents. Soldiers accused of murder were to be sent back to England instead of tried locally.

As for the rest of the colonies, westward expansion was to stop. The Quebec Act altered the boundaries of the Canadian territories, and suddenly Quebec was given land as far south as the Ohio River and west to the Mississippi. The area had been won from the French nearly a century before, yet the Crown was willing to let French-speaking Catholics move in to deter Protestant Englishmen from getting past the Alleghany Mountains. American colonists were going to stay snug along the Atlantic coast, where English ships and troops could more easily get at them if they dared to get out of hand. And as the final slap, the king appointed General Thomas Gage, the British commander of troops in Massachusetts, as the colony's new Royal Governor. There really was a new sheriff in town now.

◆ ◆ ◆

Simply because Freemasons have secrets that they promise not to reveal to the outside world is no proof of any sort of secret Masonic conspiracy to overthrow governments, to become the controlling "gray eminences" behind the throne, or to do anything else revolutionary. A Masonic lodge itself is frankly a lousy place to try to organize a revolution. Lodge members are proposed by other Masons, and questions of their politics or religion have always been improper subjects of discussion. That is true in the lodge room, as well as during the investigation and interviewing of a new member. The activities of St. Andrew's Lodge prove the exception to the rule.

Documentary evidence of important moments in history can often be a limp record of world-changing events. The night of the Boston Tea Party was to have been the traditional meeting for the election of officers in St. Andrew's Lodge, being the last regular business meeting before the Feast of St. John on December 27. The minutes for the evening simply noted that, "Lodge closed (on account of the few members present) until to Morrow Evening."[17] Yet, as a result of the Boston Tea Party, the lodge picked up twelve new members who wanted to associate with its revolutionary membership.

However, even in their tavern filled with radical extremists, they had to form different groups to carry out their activities. The raid on Boston's tea ships, the vigilante patrols, and the acts of outright treason were never planned in the lodge itself. In spite of the romantic allure of heroic revolutionary exploits and a connection to Freemasonry, it was not Freemasonry itself that sent tea to the bottom of Boston Harbor.

CHAPTER 4

War among Brothers

A rebellion is always legal in the first person, such
as "our rebellion." It is only in the third person—"their
rebellion"—that it becomes illegal.
—BENJAMIN FRANKLIN IN THE MUSICAL *1776*

The battle of wits that was about to turn bloody was not really about trying to balance King George's national debt by taxing the Americans into the Stone Age. His tea tax was remarkably minuscule, and certainly not worth getting people killed over. In fact, the king had written a letter to Prime Minister Lord North that, once the colonies submitted to the notion that Britain had the right to tax them and force them to submit, he was willing to tell them "that there is no inclination for the present to lay fresh taxes upon them."[1] England was facing possible rebellion much closer to home in Ireland, and the new empire stretched around the globe. If the Crown rolled over and took snotty insubordination from the American colonies, such a show of weakness would undoubtedly give its subjects elsewhere equally rebellious ideas. To say nothing of its foreign enemies.

Freemasons on both sides of the Atlantic would take opposing sides in the battle over American independence at many of the major turning points before and after shots were fired. This chapter presents a few of the Freemasons who impacted America in her struggle.

Edmund Burke

Not every member of Parliament was out to exact revenge against the colonies. Edmund Burke, an Anglo-Irish member of the House of

Commons, achieved his greatest fame by taking the side of America during the debates over the taxation of the colonies.

> Reflect how you are to govern a people, who think they ought to be free, and think they are not. Your scheme yields no revenue; it yields nothing but discontent, disorder, disobedience; and such is the state of America, that after wading up to your eyes in blood, you could only end just where you begun.

Burke, a Freemason in Jerusalem Lodge No. 44 in London, was a passionate speaker and author. He spoke eloquently on the abolition of England's slave trade, denounced the use of Indians against the Americans during the revolution, and fought for greater freedoms in Ireland, including the removal of restrictions against basic rights for Catholics.

The most famous quote attributed to Burke is arguably appropriate to explain the involvement of so many Masons in the revolution, in opposition to Masonry's charge to its members to be peaceable citizens: *The only thing necessary for the triumph [of evil] is for good men to do nothing.*

James Galloway and the Continental Congress

The twelve colonies outside of Massachusetts had done something that the king, the prime minister and Parliament had not counted on. They supported Massachusetts after Lexington and Concord. Up came the boycotts on goods imported from England again. With Boston Harbor socked in by the British Navy, food and supplies came in overland from the sympathetic colonies. They could be fractious with one another, but they were suddenly standing together.

On June 1, 1774, George Washington, then a member of the House of Burgesses, Virginia's legislature, voted in favor of a resolution declaring a colony-wide day of fasting and prayer in solidarity with Massachusetts. The king's newly appointed Royal Governor of Virginia shut down the meeting. Washington, along with brother

Masons Peyton Randolph and Richard Henry Lee, was selected as one of the seven delegates from Virginia to attend the Continental Congress that was to meet in Philadelphia in September of 1774.

The Congress was top-heavy with lawyers, and legal points turned the session into a debating society. The faction that wanted nothing less than independence from Britain cooled their rhetoric publicly because it was clear that not everyone agreed with them. Bostonians weren't the most beloved people in America, and there was no shortage of colonists who saw them as nasty troublemakers. The colonies were united in wanting to resist the squeeze play Massachusetts was getting, but breaking with England was something else entirely. Leading the pro-Revolutionary side were Massachusetts delegates Patrick Henry and cousins John and Samuel Adams, none of whom were Masons. But there were Masons on both sides of the fence.

Debates became endless, and delegates began to tire of it. After several days of ceaseless discussion, Freemason James Galloway had a proposal. At the time, Galloway, one of Ben Franklin's most trusted friends, was a member of Philadelphia Lodge No. 2. He was well respected and had served as speaker of Pennsylvania's Assembly for seven years. He was also a devout Loyalist.

Galloway put forth a Plan of Union that might very well have stopped the drive for independence and prevented the war, and he had a reasonable amount of support for it. He proposed that a president-general be appointed by the king, with a colonial legislature called the Grand Council to be made up of members appointed by each colony's assemblies. The council would agree that Britain had the right to tax the colonies, but the colonies would have the right to regulate their own internal affairs. Any laws passed by the English Parliament would be approved or disapproved by the council.

Galloway's plan was a stroke of diplomatic genius remarkably similar to a plan for uniting the colonies that Franklin had tried to promote in Albany twenty years earlier. Lest anyone think that Freemasons were all anti-British revolutionaries, the first and loudest supporters of this plan were fellow Freemasons John Dickinson of Pennsylvania,[2] and New York's John Jay.[3] The plan garnered enough supporters that those in favor of revolt became concerned and mustered enough votes to postpone its discussion indefinitely. When Galloway's plan was tabled, the die was cast for eventual revolution.

When the reports reached Congress from Boston that General Gage's three thousand troops had arrived and confiscated local stores of gunpowder, any plan for serious reconciliation with Britain was effectively killed. Little did Congress know that Gage was more than a little startled when his troops were met by almost twenty thousand armed, angry men from all across the colony. St. Andrew's Brother Joseph Warren's powers of persuasion were potent enough to talk them into going home and waiting for the proper time and place, but the new Royal Governor realized that he was woefully outnumbered. Gage had mouthed off to the king just months before that four regiments of troops would be plenty to show Boston the error of its ways. Now he was eating those rather poorly chosen words.

When Franklin finally returned from Britain, he was not exactly in the exalted position we hold him today. His son William, the Royal Governor of New Jersey, refused to resign his position or take the side of the revolutionaries. Because Franklin had been unable to change the minds of either his son or his best friend James Galloway, some in Congress (like his brother Mason, Richard Henry Lee) thought he might be a spy. Then too, Franklin was old. He was considered by many to be a relic of the previous generation.

Brother Galloway would remain a lifelong Loyalist, during and after the war, in spite of his friend Franklin's attempts to sway him. In 1776, he would join up with the British troops when General Howe took Philadelphia and be named as the superintendent of police, essentially the head of the civil government. When the city fell to the revolutionary forces, he fled to England, never to return. In 1788, the Pennsylvania assembly would find him guilty of treason in absentia and confiscate his lands.

Paul Revere's Ride

Historically, Paul Revere's role in the revolution has been reduced to a town crier on horseback, albeit a romantic one. Author David Hackett Fischer's book *Paul Revere's Ride* has gone a long way to place him in a much more important position than just Brown Beauty's screaming jockey. He was a large, burly man, and hardly had the appearance of an artisan skilled in silversmithing and engraving. He was a central figure in all of the many groups that met at the Green Dragon Tavern. Revere would serve the cause throughout the war and afterward engraved the first Great Seal of the United States.

Revere was the Senior Grand Deacon in the St. Andrew's Grand Lodge officer's line and Dr. Joseph Warren's right-hand man. When the word came in from all over Boston that the British troops were assembling a small fleet of longboats on April 18, 1775, Warren, the Sons of Liberty and the St. Andrew's members all knew Gage's troops would be on the move.

The events of April 18th and 19th are the shared folklore of America. Revere and fellow Mason William Dawes were dispatched to alert Lexington to the impending arrival of the British regulars and warn Sam Adams and Brother John Hancock that they were being hunted. The "one if by land" lantern that was hung in the steeple of the Old North Church was placed there by Sexton Robert Newman, who would go on to join St. John's Lodge in 1783 and then St. Andrew's Royal Arch Chapter in 1794.[4]

Revere was stopped briefly by a patrol of British soldiers. Some say he talked his way out of being arrested or shot, but Masonic folklore claims that he gave a Masonic sign and was released by soldiers who were brethren.

Paul Revere would try his hand as a military commander with mixed results. Later in the war, he would be the artillery commander at the humiliating Penobscot Expedition, which would go down in history as the greatest naval disaster in American history until Pearl Harbor. But he would continue to serve as a cannon maker and gunpowder manufacturer until the war's end, and even made anchors, spikes, sheathing and pumps for warships like the U.S.S. *Constitution.* He survived the war, and in later years he would serve as the Grand Master of Masons in Massachusetts.

Dr. Joseph Warren

A pamphlet circulated in the summer of 1770, written by a Tory, said of Dr. Joseph Warren, "One of our most bawling demagogues and voluminous writers is a crazy doctor." Warren became a physician in 1768, but a year later he was writing against the English import duties enacted by the Townshend Acts in the *Boston Gazette* under the anonymous byline, "A True Patriot."

As Grand Master of Masons in North America for the Ancients, Warren had a network of spies throughout Boston and Massachusetts, including many of St. Andrew's members and, amazingly, even General Thomas Gage's own American-born wife. Many have speculated that his spy network grew through the Masonic lodges. It's hard to say with spies.

When compatriot (and non-Mason) Samuel Adams went to Philadelphia as part of the first Continental Congress in 1774, Warren became the top figure in Massachusetts' revolutionary political movement. During the congress, Warren wrote a series of denouncements of King George and Parliament, declaring that a king who violated the rights of his subjects and their colonial charter had forfeited their allegiance. His writings became known as the *Suffolk Resolves*, and their arrival in Philadelphia was greeted with unanimous approval of the congress.

Warren was made major general of the Massachusetts Militia when hostilities broke out at the Battle of Bunker Hill. His body was identified on the battlefield by Paul Revere's extensive dental work. He was buried where he fell, but his body was later disinterred and moved to several different locations over the years before finally being laid to rest in Forrest Hills Cemetery, with an appropriate monument to his role in the revolution.

The Military Lodges of the Revolution

There were at least ten military lodges at work in the American forces. Washington encouraged membership in the lodges, believing it brought a greater bond between the men, especially his close officers. They were a typically American melting pot. Quakers, Anglicans, Virginia plantation owners, Connecticut shopkeepers, Germans, Frenchmen, Scots and Americans—all could find common ground in the military lodges.

Master's Lodge at Albany, New York, received eighty-three new members in 1776. St. George's Lodge at Schenectady, New York, where many Revolutionary officers were made Masons, used their lodge's funds for the support of the families of its members who had been taken prisoner.[5]

American Union Lodge at Morristown, New Jersey, was the most famous, attached to the Connecticut Line of the army. Washington was certainly a regular attendee, and for almost two centuries it was believed that General Lafayette was made a Mason in American Union. He certainly attended its meetings. After the war ended, the lodge settled in Marietta, Ohio, in 1790 and became one of five lodges that formed the Grand Lodge of Ohio.

There were also more than thirty British military lodges in America during the revolution.[6] One of the most peculiar developments in American Freemasonry occurred in 1777, when the Provincial Grand Lodge of Pennsylvania (Moderns) issued a warrant for a military lodge in the British Army fighting against American troops—Unity Lodge No. 18 in His Britannic Majesty's 17th Regiment of Foot. If you think that Pennsylvania's Freemasons actively participated in treason, that depends on whose side you were on.

In 1777, British troops were in control of the city of Philadelphia, and the rebellious Americans had fled into the countryside. The Tories were in charge, and as far as they were concerned, it was the so-called patriots who were behaving treasonously. The Loyalists were also in control of the local lodges, and the Provincial Grand

Master was on the king's side. As a result, when the 17th Regiment of Foot lost its original Scottish charter issued in 1771, they applied for a new one from the Grand Lodge of England through its Provincial Grand Lodge in Philadelphia.

In July of 1779, the 17th Regiment was captured at Stony Point, and its warrant and lodge regalia fell into the hands of American troops. The U.S. commander, General Samuel H. Parsons, was a member of American Union Lodge, and instantly recognized what his troops had in their possession. He immediately returned it to the 17th Regiment, with a letter that explains the mystic tie between Masonic brethren so well.

> When the ambitions of monarchs or jarring interest of contending States call forth their subjects to war, as Masons we are disarmed of that resentment which stimulates to undistinguished desolation; and however our political sentiments may impel us in the public dispute, we are still brethren, and (our professional duty apart) ought to promote the happiness and advance the weal of each other. Accept, therefore, at the hands of a brother, the Constitution of [your lodge]. . . which your late misfortunes have put in my power to restore to you.[7]

A common claim has been made over the years that all, or certainly most, of George Washington's generals were Freemasons. Careful scholarship has tempered this claim—33 out of 74 commissioned generals of the Continental Army between 1775 and 1783 were provably Masons.[8] They included: Major General John Stark, the independent-minded New Hampshire hero who coined the phrase "Live free or die"; Major General Israel Putnam, one of the first four major generals appointed by Washington and the only one to serve the duration of the Revolutionary War; Major General Henry Knox, who would later in life become commander in chief of the Army and secretary of war; and Brigadier General Mordecai Gist, who would later be Grand Master of Masons in South Carolina. Gist was president of a convention of military lodges at the end of the war that proposed a national Grand Lodge for the United States and nominated George Washington to be its first Grand Master. Washington appreciated the honor, but turned it down.

Two of Washington's generals in particular enjoyed great fame after the war, achieving worldwide recognition for their achievements. One became famous, the other, infamous. Both were Masons.

Major General Gilbert Lafayette

Today in Washington, D.C., near the White House, there is a little park known as Lafayette Square. In the center stands a statue of Freemason Andrew Jackson, seventh president of the United States. But at each corner of the park stand statues dedicated to four foreign generals who served on the side of America during the Revolution. All four were Freemasons. General Thaddeus Kosciusko was a Polish statesman who served as one of Washington's generals and was a member of a lodge in Soleure, Switzerland. Major General Baron Frederick W.A. von Steuben became a Mason in Europe and a member of Trinity Lodge No. 10 (later No. 12) in New York City. Jean Baptiste, baron de Vimeur de Rochambeau, who served as a general in America, later became Marshal of France, and was a Mason there. But the park itself is named after a most remarkable man and Mason. Marie-Joseph-Paul-Yves-Roch-Gilbert du Motier, Marquis de La Fayette, was born in 1757 in Auvergne, France. Many Americans have heard of General Lafayette and his role in the American Revolution, but few know of just how dedicated he was to the cause of liberty even before he arrived here, and after he returned home.

Gilbert was just two years old when his father was killed at the Battle of Minden during the Seven Years' War in the American colonies. His mother and grandfather died when he was eleven years old, which left him a very rich orphan with the title Marquis de Lafayette. His father had been a military man, and young Gilbert desired to follow in his footsteps. He entered the French Army at fourteen and became a part of the King's Musketeers. At sixteen, a marriage was arranged between Gilbert and Marie-Adrienne-Françoise de

Noailles, daughter of Jean-Paul-François, fifth duc de Noailles, and one of the wealthiest families in France. The marriage took place in 1774, when the bride was just fourteen. Lafayette was immediately promoted to the rank of captain. Although the marriage was arranged, Lafayette and Adrienne remained devoted to each other all their lives and had a son and two daughters.

For many years, it was commonly believed that Lafayette became a Freemason in the military lodge, American Union No. 1, either at Valley Forge or at Morristown, New Jersey. Many accounts written long after the war say that he made this claim himself. But French records claim that he became a Mason in France before the war, in Saint-Jean d'Ecosse du Contrat Social Lodge on December 15, 1775, with the encouragement of his commanding general, Charles-François, comte de Broglie.[9] He desperately sought revenge against Great Britain, both for the death of his father during the French and Indian War and for the humiliating loss of French possessions in America. In 1775 Lafayette spoke of his bitterness to the Comte de Broglie, who introduced him to a German mercenary in the French Army, John Baron de Kalb.

Lafayette was nineteen years old when the war broke out in America, and he and his friend de Kalb enthusiastically arranged through diplomatic channels to be allowed to leave French service and join the Continental Army. Like Lafayette, hundreds of French officers were lining up to leave for America, and Lafayette was assured by American agents that he would be given the rank of major general when he arrived in Philadelphia. The war was not going well for the colonists, and though the French king Louis XVI had approved at first, he began to reconsider the idea of French soldiers winding up on the losing side of a war with the British. The French and Indian War had been an expensive enough defeat on American soil.

Lafayette had already purchased a ship, and he and fellow French officers and friends were outfitting it with provisions for the voyage. He ignored an order from the king to stop his preparations. With the added noisy objections of the British ambassador at Marseilles,

Lafayette was arrested. Donning a disguise, he made a daring escape and set sail with de Kalb and several others. In spite of being pursued by British ships, he landed two months later in South Carolina and made his way to Philadelphia.

His prearranged entry into the Continental Army as a major general was at first rejected by Congress, who felt that commissioning a foreigner with no battlefield experience would be an insult to American officers who had proved their mettle. He had not been the first foreign officer who showed up in Philadelphia demanding a commission and other enticements. Lafayette countered the objection by offering to take the position for no pay, and that he should be regarded as a volunteer. His startling offer, combined with his enthusiasm and his family connections and personal fortune, convinced them to honor his negotiated rank.

Honorary Congressional appointment or not, it was up

The Marquis de Lafayette.

to Washington to assign the young man. They met on August 1, 1777, and the general took to him at once. He quickly became part of Washington's inner circle, and the two men became lifelong friends. Lafayette was wounded almost immediately at the Battle of Brandywine in Pennsylvania, just a month after joining up with Washington. But what he lacked in experience, he made up for in passion for the American cause. And Washington saw in the teenaged officer an important role model for the young American soldiers he was commanding.

Lafayette would go home briefly to intercede with King Louis to assist the American cause once Britain had declared war on

France. When he returned to America in 1781, he was placed in command of forces charged with defending all of Virginia, and he spent his own fortune to outfit his troops when the Congress could not. He played an important part in the battle of Yorktown and the capture of the British commander Cornwallis.

After the American Revolution, he returned to France and freed the slaves on his estate. He established an estate for them in Cayenne, French Guiana, which he also offered as a haven for Washington's slaves. There, he prohibited the sale of slaves, set up schools for the children, paid workers a fair wage, and enforced plantation rules that applied equally to blacks and whites.

As a French patriot, he joined the National Assembly, where he was instrumental in the adoption of the French red, white and blue flag. He fought for the formation of a constitutional monarchy, and in 1789, he proposed a Declaration of the Rights of Man and the Citizen, patterned after America's example and written with the help of Thomas Jefferson.

It is a tragic irony that the debt incurred by Louis XVI in assisting America in its revolution helped bring financial ruin to France. This, along with crop failure and crushing inflation, led to the bloody French Revolution in 1789. Lafayette had been placed in command of the National Guard of Paris, where he helped protect both commoners and aristocrats, including the royal family. Yet, he himself helped lead the storming of the Bastille—in later years he would send a key from the prison to his friend Washington. He straddled the line between the radical philosophy that fueled the revolution and his own more moderate politics, while doing what he could to prevent the madness and murder that would place even his own life in danger. He eventually denounced the Jacobins when it became clear that their goal was to behead the king and queen. In 1792, the Jacobin-controlled National Assembly declared him to be a traitor.

He fled to Belgium, but as one of the early revolutionaries, he was captured and imprisoned by the Holy Roman Empire in Austria. Meanwhile at home, The Terror was killing every aristocrat it could find. Lafayette's son fled to New York, but Adrienne and their two daughters were imprisoned, eventually securing their release only because of pressure from the American government. The rest of her aristocratic family was executed just five days before the Terror collapsed with the death of Robespierre.

Immediately, Adrienne went to Austria with her children to beg for Lafayette's release. When the Holy Roman Emperor refused, she and the girls joined him in his prison cell for the next two years. New York Representative Gouverneur Morris finally negotiated the release of the entire family in 1797.

Throughout his life, Lafayette's popularity in France came and went with the waves of political unrest. He would be hated one year as the head of the National Guard for putting down a riot and killing fifty protesters. He would be offered as a candidate for mayor the next. His commissions would come and go. Yet he survived both the American Revolution and the worst period in France's history, and like his father figure Washington, in the end he would retire to his plantation, La Grange, with his wife. Adrienne's health never fully recovered after the many years of confinement in France and Austria. She died in 1807 at the age of forty-eight. Lafayette, heartbroken, would never remarry.

In 1824, he visited America at the invitation of Thomas Jefferson and spent a year traveling the country. The American Revolution's fiftieth anniversary was approaching, and Lafayette was one of the few heroes of the period who was still alive. He spoke in many places, including several Masonic lodges, where he was treated with the same sort of adoration that had been reserved for Washington, which never ceased to astonish him. Everywhere he went, adoring crowds followed him through the streets. It was during that visit that the park north of the White House was renamed to honor him. Literally hundreds of other parks, towns and counties in the United States are named after him.

Lafayette knew and dined with the first seven presidents of the United States—Washington, John Adams, Thomas Jefferson, James

Madison, James Monroe, John Quincy Adams and the future president Andrew Jackson. During his trip across the United States, he stopped at Bunker Hill in Massachusetts and took a small amount of American soil from the base of the monument there back to France with him. He died in 1834, and was buried next to his wife in the tiny Picpus Cemetery in Paris. Since his death, the American flag has flown over his grave, undisturbed even during the Nazi occupation of Paris in World War II.

According to his last wish, when his body was laid to rest next to Adrienne, the little bit of soil that he had brought home from America was sprinkled over his grave.

Benedict Arnold

The story of Benedict Arnold is a tragic one. Arnold was a hero in the American Revolution, and his military accomplishments turned the tide of the war in favor of the colonists at least twice. He was brave and quick-witted on the battlefield and showed great cunning as a military strategist. And in the end, he became America's most notorious traitor.

Benedict Arnold came from a wealthy family that had fallen on hard times. His father's business failures forced Benedict to leave school at fourteen. He briefly apprenticed in his cousins' apothecary, but at fifteen he joined the Connecticut Militia to fight in the French and Indian War. Because of his young age, he was released before he saw action, but one event of the war angered and haunted him as an adult. The commander of French troops at the battle of Fort William Henry (1757) had promised Indian allies guns and booty when the battle ended but instead offered mild surrender terms to the British, which left the Indians with few spoils. Outraged, the Indians massacred as many as 180 British men, women and children while French officers looked on helplessly.[10] Even though young Benedict was well on his way home at the time, he would never forgive the French for the rest of his life.

While still a young man, he went into business as a bookseller and apothecary in New Haven, Connecticut. His business expanded, and through several shrewd real estate deals he made enough money to buy three ships and start a successful trade with the West Indies. He often took command of his own ship, and while on a voyage in the islands, he became a Freemason in a local lodge. He went home and affiliated with Hiram Lodge No. 1 in New Haven, Connecticut, in 1765.

When the British passed the Stamp Act to enforce a protectionist trade policy, Arnold did what most American sea merchants did. He became a smuggler. But the new taxation by Britain soon drove him severely into debt. When he received news of the so-called Boston Massacre in 1775, he became outraged and joined the Connecticut Guards. And when the war began at Lexington and Concord, as their captain, he led a march of the militia, fresh with new recruits from Yale University, to join the Revolution in Massachusetts.

He successfully convinced Massachusetts' military officials to mount an expedition to take Fort Ticonderoga, steal its many cannons and use them to break the British siege of Boston. Arnold was made a colonel in the Massachusetts militia and led his Connecticut troops in the raid, one of the early successes of the war. He had believed himself to be in command of the mission, but Colonel Ethan Allen was the local officer favored by the Massachusetts troops. Arnold and Allen jointly commanded the raid, which was accomplished with just one shot fired. Arnold went on with fifty volunteers to raid more supplies from Fort Saint Johns, farther up the river. But instead of being given command of the forts when the battle ended, Arnold was passed over. In disgust, he resigned his British commission.

After he proposed a part of a plan to attack and capture Quebec City and Montreal, Arnold was commissioned as a colonel in the Continental Army and given command of the forces headed for Quebec. Just before he set out on the Quebec mission, his wife tragically died in New Haven. The Canadian campaign failed, and Arnold was wounded in the leg. But he managed to assemble 350 volunteers to continue a siege of the city until reinforcements arrived. For his bravery, he was promoted to brigadier general.

The next year he successfully repelled an attempted invasion from Lake Champlain, and in 1777 he quickly assembled volunteer forces to turn away a surprise attack by the British in Danbury, Connecticut. He went on to Philadelphia, where he briefly became the ranking officer in the city. But command of the forces there was given to a newer, less experienced officer. Again, Arnold had been snubbed for promotion, and again he resigned. Washington still had faith in him and deplored Congress's treatment of the talented general. He had Arnold reassigned to Massachusetts and the area around Fort Ticonderoga.

Arnold performed yet another daring maneuver at Saratoga when his forces successfully cut off the retreat of General Burgoyne's British troops and forced his surrender. Arnold's strategy was better, yet he was snubbed by his own superior, General Horatio Gates, who left him out of the battle plans and refused to acknowledge Arnold's role in defeating Burgoyne. Arnold's leg was shot again at Saratoga, this time rendering it useless, but, while convalescing in Albany, he refused to have it amputated.

When the British were finally chased from Philadelphia, Washington placed him in command of troops there. But when word came that America had sought an alliance with France, Arnold became enraged. Ironically, it was his own success at Saratoga that convinced Louis XVI to openly ally with the rebels and make a large financial commitment to the American side. Arnold had hated the French for all of his adult life, and their entry into the war changed his outlook. He had believed the revolution was merely to fight the repressive policies of the Crown, not to declare independence. But the entry of the French made it clear to him that complete separation from England was the American goal. Undoubtedly this was a naive position, or perhaps it was simply his justification for his subsequent treachery, but whatever the reason, he became a Loyalist.

The British troops had just been driven out of Philadelphia, but there was a large Tory population in the city. Arnold began seeing Peggy Shippen, the eighteen-year-old daughter of a local judge whose loyalties were unclear, and they married after just one month. But Arnold's lavish new lifestyle drew the suspicion of Congress, which court-martialed him over financial improprieties with military money. Arnold finally had enough humiliation at the hands of both Congress and the military command.

In July of 1780, he was placed in command of the fort at West Point. He was secretly corresponding with the British general in New York City, using his new wife's former paramour, British Major John André, as his courier. In his messages, he offered to hand the strategic fort at West Point over to the British in return for £20,000 and a commission as a brigadier general. The plot was revealed when André was intercepted by American troops and hanged, while Arnold fled to the protection of the British.

Although the British never fully trusted Arnold, they did place him in command of sixteen hundred troops on a mission to burn Richmond, Virginia, and in 1781 he was part of a diversionary force in Connecticut to draw American attention from Lord Cornwallis's invasion. But after the British defeat at Yorktown, he moved to London and tried unsuccessfully to convince King George III to keep fighting. Over the years, he moved to Canada, then back to London in 1792. He died in 1801, destitute, and his wife Peggy and their four children returned to Philadelphia in disgrace.

Arnold was an enigmatic character. Brother Mason Dr. Joseph Warren had been widowed in 1773, leaving four children who were orphaned by Warren's death at Bunker Hill. True to his Masonic obligation, Benedict Arnold came to their relief. Having become friends with Brother Warren while in Massachusetts, in April 1778, Arnold contributed $500 toward their education. He also persuaded Congress for a pension to support them from the date of the father's death until the youngest child reached the age of consent.

During the time he spent in Canada after the war, he went broke lending money to Loyalists and Masons who he knew would never repay him. Nevertheless, the bonds of Freemasonry are dissolved by the treachery of treason. His name was removed from the record books of Hiram Lodge No. 1 in New Haven where he was a member. Even his signature from a visit to Solomon Lodge No. 1 in Poughkeepsie, New York was marked out and labeled "traitor" by order of its members in 1781.

As Arnold was on his deathbed, he asked to be buried in the uniform of the American Continental Army and prayed to God for forgiveness of his betraying the cause of liberty. A captured American soldier had once told Arnold that if he were caught, they would cut off his patriotic right leg, bury it with full military honors, and then hang the rest of his traitorous body on a gibbet. There is no denying his part in victories like the battle of Saratoga. On that battlefield, there stands a curious monument to his bravery. It depicts a single boot, draped over an upturned cannon barrel, with the inscription,

> In memory of the most brilliant soldier of the Continental Army who was desperately wounded on this spot the sally port of BORGOYNES GREAT WESTERN REDOUBT 7th October, 1777 winning for his countrymen the decisive battle of the American Revolution and for himself the rank of Major General.

That most brilliant soldier's name is not inscribed.

Society of the Cincinnati

> The officers of the American army, having generally been taken from the citizens of America, possess high veneration for the character of that illustrious Roman, Lucius Quintius Cincinnatus, and being resolved to follow his example, by returning to their citizenship, they think they may with propriety denominate themselves the Society of the Cincinnati. —*First meeting of the Society of the Cincinnati, 1783*

In ancient Rome, former consul Lucius Quinctius Cincinnatus was working on his farm when word was delivered to him that he had been appointed dictator in order to repel an invasion. The sitting consul, Minucius, was under siege by the Volscians and the Aequi. Cincinnatus put down his plow and took up the sword. In just sixteen days, he took control of the army, freed Minucius and repelled Rome's enemies. He then went home and again took up the plow.

George Washington was often referred to as the American Cincinnatus, because as soon as the British surrendered at Yorktown, he went home to his farm. At every turn, factions across the country offered him every kind of honor and position. These included the Freemasons, who wanted him to become the first Grand Master for a new Grand Lodge of the United States. Had he the desire to become America's first Caesar, the dictatorship might very well have been handed to him. But Washington preferred to take up the plow.

As the war came to an end, he faced a crisis from within the military. He had commanded the Continental Army for eight tortuous years. But in 1782, his men received word that Congress, powerless to raise money itself and ignored by the states, was broke and could not pay the soldiers, many of whom had fought six years with no pay. Disgruntled officers now planned a military coup to take over the new nation's government and make Washington their king. The fledgling democracy's fate was about to be decided.

On March 15, 1783, the officers involved met in a church in Newburgh, New York, to discuss their scheme. Washington had broken up such meetings before, but not this one. They were there to make the decision to proceed with a coup, with or without their general. Quite unexpectedly, in strolled Washington, who was not exactly a welcome sight.

"Gentlemen," he began. "As I was among the first who embarked in the cause of our common Country; as I never left your side one moment, but when called from you on public duty; as I have been the constant companion and witness of your Distresses, and not among the last to keel, and acknowledge your Merits . . . it can scarcely be supposed . . . that I am indifferent to [your] interests. But . . . this dreadful alternative, of either deserting our Country in the extremest hour of her distress, or turning our Arms against it, . . . has something so shocking in it that humanity revolts from the idea . . . . I spurn it, as every Man who regards liberty . . . undoubtedly must . . . . As you value your own sacred honor, as you respect the rights of humanity, and as you regard the Military and National character of America . . . [do not] open the flood Gates of Civil discord, and deluge our rising Empire in Blood."

His speech was not well received. The men grumbled and grew restless as he pulled a letter from his coat. It was from Congress, to address their grievances. He stumbled over it at first, squinting, unable to read it, and then stopped. The room grew quiet as he reached into a coat for a pair of glasses. Most never knew that he needed glasses to read, and to see this man they had followed for eight years suddenly so vulnerable made them pause.

"Gentlemen, you will permit me to put on my spectacles," he said, "for I have not only grown gray but almost blind in the service of my country."

By that simple, humble, quiet gesture, Washington shamed them. They had all grown older together. They had lost much and seen many friends perish on the battlefield. But what they were planning was dishonorable and would destroy the very ideas they had fought for. Many of the men began to weep as they gazed upon this man they loved who suddenly seemed so weary. Washington read the letter, which explained the financial straits Congress found itself in. With that, he slowly left the room without another word. After he left, the assembled men voted unanimously to agree to the control of the military by the civilian government.

When Washington voluntarily gave up his position of power after the revolution and returned home to Mount Vernon, King George was said to have remarked, "If true, then he is the greatest man in the world." Washington's example created the rules, customs and protocol for American generals and presidents who followed him. He believed that government service was a noble profession, but that too much power in the hands of government would destroy a democracy.

Following the incident, several of Washington's officers who were Masons conceived of a new organization called the *Society of the Cincinnati,* named after the legendary Roman consul. Two Masons, Major Generals Henry Knox and Baron von Steuben, conceived of the group, and membership was limited only to officers in the Continental or French military and their descendants. Enlisted men and officers of the state militias were not eligible. Its aims were to assist its members in need, along with their widows and orphans, similar to the Freemasons. But it also was the first organization in the United States, like so many that existed in aristocratic circles in Europe, which was designed to be a hereditary elite group.

Of the 5,500 officers eligible, perhaps 2,150 of them joined.[11] Washington was made the first president general of the society, and he served until his death in 1799. His successor was Alexander Hamilton. But despite the presence of such honorable men and Washington's enthusiasm for the group, other founders were not so enamored of it.

Freemason Ben Franklin and non-Mason Jefferson both objected to its obvious pretensions to nobility and primogeniture. Such inherited honors, passed from one generation to the next through its members' eldest sons, reeked of monarchy. And Franklin in particular had a special dislike for the symbol used on its insignia. Fashioned as a lavish medal and designed by Pierre L'Enfant, it featured a prominent bald eagle, like the new nation's great seal. Franklin had long argued against the eagle's use on the seal, and was alarmed at its appearance in the Cincinnati's heraldry, believing it to be a bird of "bad moral character." And Freemason Eldridge Gerry, while admitting the high moral conduct of the men associated with the society, nevertheless distrusted such a group and feared that the mere presence of, or endorsement by, such men would unduly influence popular elections for political officials, based simply on the fame of its members.

Those members included twenty-three of the fifty-four signers of the U.S. Constitution, and several members went on to found major cities of the western expansion that followed the revolution— Pittsburgh, Fort Wayne and Cincinnati. The society lived on and still exists today, with chapters across the country and in France. With an approximate membership of 3,300, their national headquarters are at Anderson House in Du Pont Circle in Washington, D.C.

Similar groups based on family connections to the revolutionary period would arise, such as the Daughters of the American Revolution, but none would inspire such widespread nervousness as the Cincinnati. Undoubtedly, it was due to the military background of its members. In the political climate immediately after the revolution, the only thing scarier than a standing army was a tightly knit brotherhood of military officers.

It is interesting to note that in the Connecticut chapter, as an example, forty percent of the founding members of the society were, or would become, Masons.[12] Similar statistics held true in the other state chapters. Freemasonry became quite popular during the war among officers and enlisted men. But while Washington, Knox, Von Steuben and others had attempted to create a sort of Masonic organization for the men who had earned honor by bravely fighting in the war, its exclusivity kept it from growing. Freemasonry experienced a post-Revolution expansion because, while it was an exclusive society in that its membership was limited, its inclusiveness transcended social, religious or hereditary barriers. Freemasonry remained unlike any society that came before it.

Prince Hall and the Masons of African Lodge

The story of Freemason Prince Hall is a proud and yet ignoble episode in American Masonic history. Although Prince Hall's work to bring Freemasonry to the free black men of Boston was a labor of love and a story of pride and determination in the face of adversity, it is a shameful mark on the Freemasons of the day who refused to live by the tenets of the institution.

Prince Hall's early life is unknown.[13] William Grimshaw's 1903 book, *Official History of Freemasonry Among the Colored People in North America*, claimed that Hall was born in Barbados in 1748, but that has long been discredited as an invention.[14] Other sources say he was born in Africa, and Hall referred to himself as an African for most of his adult life. That was not uncommon—blacks during the period often referred to themselves as African, instead of the term Negro, which was preferred by whites. It is generally believed today that he was born in 1735 as a slave in the household of William Hall of Boston. His owner, a leather worker, taught the trade to Prince. Hall apparently manumitted him in 1770, at the age of twenty-one. Again, records are difficult to prove, as there were several men in Boston during the same period with the same name.

Hall's birth and early life would be of little interest to anyone but certain Freemasons. One of the requirements for Masonic membership since Anderson's *Constitutions* was that a man must be freeborn, meaning not born as a slave. The requirement was meant as an assurance that a new Mason was legally allowed to swear an oath on his own honor and volition—something that a slave or indentured servant could not do. Grimshaw's book was designed to invent a "freeborn" status for Hall in order to put a stop to questions raised in later years by white Masons who discounted the legitimacy of his Masonic membership. Sadly, this contention has caused one of the worst injustices perpetrated within the fraternity for more than two centuries.

Prince Hall and several other black Bostonians were interested in becoming Masons and forming a lodge for other free Negroes. On March 6, 1775, Prince Hall and fourteen other free black men were initiated into Lodge No. 441, an Irish military lodge attached to the 38th Regiment of Foot of the British Army garrisoned at Castle William (now Fort Independence) in Boston Harbor. The Master of the lodge was Sergeant John Batt, and he conferred the Entered

Apprentice, Fellow Craft and Master Mason degrees on Prince Hall, Peter Best, John Canton, Forten Horward, Cyrus Johnston, Peter Freeman, Prince Rayden, Prince Rees, Duff Ruform, Thomas Santerson, Bueston Slinger, Boston Smith, Cato Speain, Benjamin Tiler and Richard Titley. They became the first known black Masons in America.

Batt granted the new Masons a special dispensation to meet as African Lodge No. 1, U.D. (Under Dispensation), which allowed them to march in processions and perform funeral services but not to initiate new members. This was a standard practice for any new lodge. It had to prove over a certain period of time that its members could properly perform ritual and conform to the rules of its Grand Lodge before being given a charter. They couldn't make new Masons yet, but if black men could somehow manage to receive Masonic degrees in other lodges, they could then join African Lodge. In Boston, this wasn't likely—certainly not in the Moderns' St. John's Lodge, and probably not in the Ancients' St. Andrew's Lodge, either.[15]

For any more men wanting to join through a British military lodge, it was also bad timing. The revolution broke out five weeks later, and right in their backyard. Masons or not, Hall and his brethren were now on opposing sides of the war with their "mother" lodge of British soldiers. It is believed by many that Prince Hall went on to enlist in the 2nd and 6th Regiments of the Massachusetts militia and is believed to have fought in the Battle of Bunker Hill. As a skilled leather worker, Hall provided drumheads to the Army. His son, Primus Hall, also fought in the war and received a pension from the Continental Army.

When the war ended, Hall campaigned for the creation of Negro schools in Boston and opened a school in his own home. He appears as a Boston property owner and voter on the tax rolls in 1787 and was an early leader in the abolitionist movement. He petitioned the Massachusetts legislature to abolish slavery in 1777 and succeeded in convincing them in 1788 to pass laws preventing the kidnapping and sale of free Negroes as slaves. In 1786, when Shay's

Rebellion broke out, Prince Hall wrote to Governor Bowdoin offering the services of the entire membership of his lodge. In all, he was a remarkable man.

American Freemasonry at this time was in an organizational turmoil. Most American lodges were Ancient or Modern lodges chartered by England's two competing Grand Lodges. There were also Irish and Scottish Grand Lodge warrants floating around, many having been issued for military lodges or their descendants, like African No. 1. One by one, the new states created new Grand Lodges to administer the lodges in their jurisdictions. Massachusetts was in such turmoil that it actually formed three opposing Grand Lodges for a time—the Moderns, the Ancients and a new Independent Grand Lodge of the Rising States, before settling down in 1783 to just one.[16] But when African Lodge sought a charter from the Grand Lodge of Massachusetts (Moderns), their white counterparts spurned them. Sympathetic Masons who understood the ins and outs of Grand Lodge politics and jurisprudence suggested they contact the Grand Orient of France for a new warrant, but Hall wanted to go straight to the source of the "fountain" of the fraternity in England. So in 1784 he petitioned the Grand Lodge of England for a new charter, listing nineteen Master Masons, four Fellow Crafts and eleven Entered Apprentices as members. While the Grand Lodge received their request, their payment was another question. Somehow the money had managed to disappear between Boston and London. Finally, three years later, Hall entrusted another payment and letter to John Hancock's brother-in-law, Captain John Scott, who made the delivery and finally returned with their warrant.

The Grand Master of England just happened to be the Duke of Cumberland, the brother of King George III. It remains unclear if issuing the warrant to the lodge was done out of brotherly love and affection or out of revenge for the rebellious Masons of Boston, who would undoubtedly be angry over England chartering *anything* in America, but especially a lodge of black Masons. Nevertheless, on May 6, 1787, African Lodge officially became Lodge No. 459 of the

Grand Lodge of England. The Prince Hall Grand Lodge in Boston today still has the original document, the only surviving warrant from the Grand Lodge of England authorizing a lodge in the United States of America.

African Lodge dutifully forwarded its annual dues payments to London each year, but repeated communications to the Grand Lodge after receiving the charter went ignored or unanswered. It is unknown if the money ever arrived. In 1791, African Lodge was visited by black Freemasons from Pennsylvania and Rhode Island. Using the authority granted by its English charter, African Lodge authorized the creation of a Lodge in each of those states. Hall by this time claimed the position of Provincial Grand Master, which arguably allowed him to do this. Whether he knowingly exceeded his authority or not, he was getting no communication from the Grand Lodge back in London, in spite of his letters and money sent to London. Prince Hall died in 1807.

As the War of 1812 raged between the United States and England, the Ancients and Moderns signed an agreement of Union in London and merged in 1813. With no notice to African Lodge, they were stricken from the record of the new United Grand Lodge of England. Eventually, like their white Grand Lodge counterparts, the Masons of African Lodge decided that, according to the manner in which the Grand Lodge of England had declared itself sovereign in 1717, three or more lodges could do the same in America. Ignored by England and denied by their American brethren, in 1827 they declared their independence from any other governing authority and formed the Prince Hall Grand Lodge.

Over the centuries, the predominantly white Grand Lodges have made various claims about the legitimacy of Prince Hall's "freeborn" status, the origin of his membership, the history of African Lodge's charter and the authenticity of its documents, all in an effort to discredit or ignore the existence of Prince Hall Freemasonry. No such similar standards have been used to measure the origin of other Grand Lodges in the United States, but a "separate but equal" Masonic universe has grown and thrived in America almost since the nation's beginnings. Prince Hall Freemasonry has been a proud and vibrant part of the African-American social community since its beginnings and remains so today.

It was not until 1989 that mainstream and Prince Hall Grand Lodges across the United States began to officially recognize each other. Because state Grand Lodges are considered sovereign, and there is no national Masonic governing body, such recognition must be done on a state-by-state basis. There are black mainstream Masons and white Prince Hall Masons. The issue of recognition simply means that members of one group may or may not visit or "communicate Masonically" with the other, except by a treaty between the Grand Lodges. But the two sides have remained largely separated as a matter of choice, even after joint recognition has occurred.

Sadly, institutionalized segregation continues to exist in Freemasonry. As of 2006, the regularity of Prince Hall Masonry has been settled by all but eleven state Grand Lodges in the United States—and all of them except West Virginia are among the states of the old Confederacy: Alabama, Georgia, Mississippi, Texas, Florida, Kentucky, Tennessee, North Carolina, South Carolina, Louisiana and West Virginia. In Canada, Prince Hall recognition has not been extended in Ontario. The situation remains an embarrassment to the rest of the Masonic world.

Masonic State's Rights

In the aftermath of the revolution, Freemasonry was without a governing body in the United States. Several attempts were made to form a Grand Lodge of the United States, but all failed. The schism between the Ancients and Moderns raged on, both in England and America, until the two groups merged in London in 1813. By then, the Masons in the United States had fallen into the pattern of founding their own individual Grand Lodges. This continues to be true of Masonic governing bodies in the U.S. today, and every state, plus

Washington, D.C., has its own Grand Lodge. Most states have a Prince Hall Grand Lodge as well.

During the postwar period of the 1780s, Pennsylvania was one state whose Masonic affinity had switched. When Benjamin Franklin had been Grand Master of Masons in Pennsylvania in the 1730s, the Grand Lodge had been allied with the premier Grand Lodge of England. Over time, and especially during the war, when many Loyalists were members of Moderns lodges, the mood of the state's Freemasons changed. The Ancients had taken over. The new Grand Lodge of Pennsylvania became an unquestionably Ancients organization. This long-forgotten, seemingly trivial schism between the two sides had important and sad results.

When Benjamin Franklin, the most famous Mason in Pennsylvania and a member of the Lodge of Nine Muses in Paris, died in 1790, thousands lined the streets of Philadelphia for his funeral. But the Ancient Freemasons of Pennsylvania refused to bury him with Masonic honors.

CHAPTER 5

How the Freemasons Invented America

In 1722, an Englishman named Daniel Coxe wrote a book with the unwieldy title, *A Description of the English Province of Carolana, by the Spaniards Call'd Florida, and by the French, La Louisiane, and also of the Great and Famous River Meschacebe, or Missisipi* [sic]. His father, Dr. Daniel Coxe II, physician to both King Charles II and Queen Anne, had been given the largest royal land grant to an individual in America. It included everything between the 31st and 36th north latitudes, west all the way to the Pacific—almost one-eighth of the total landmass of the United States and Canada, comprising parts of what are now Virginia, Georgia, both Carolinas, Florida, Louisiana and everything on both sides of the Mississippi as far north as Kentucky. It is an unfortunate geopolitical law of survival that land is only yours if you can keep it. For almost a hundred years Coxe and his descendants tried without much success to interest their English countrymen in colonizing the region. The family finally gave up in 1769 and returned it to the king in exchange for a nice, manageable farm in New York. Most Americans have never heard of Daniel Coxe, once owner of the ground that about 95 million of us now water, mow and rake leaves off of every year—much less his book. That's a shame, because Daniel Coxe—a Freemason—invented the United States.

In *A Description of the English Province of Carolana,* Coxe described the terrain, flora and fauna of this massive landscape, as told to him by traders, trappers and other ambitious travelers. It was essentially a lengthy brochure to interest potential colonists in the Carolana project. As lavish and romantic descriptions of far-flung, exotic lands go, it's a masterpiece. Spain and France both had territorial claims to much of the same area, and in the preface to his book, Coxe admits that defending it against foreign claim jumpers would be a challenge, especially if it had no settlers. At one point, he recommends that everything west of the Mississippi be given to the Spanish and everything east of the river should be English land. Any French in the area, it was suggested, should just go home.

One of his greatest frustrations was that the other existing English colonies, stretching along the eastern coastline of America, were a fractious bunch. One thing was certain: If the Spanish or the French decided to flex their colonial muscles, it was a near total certainty that the individual English colonies would have no interest whatsoever in banding together to help defend the all-but-vacant land from foreign power, or even hostile Indian tribes. Isolated and stubborn, each of the various colonies had its own government, customs and attitudes. They were New York Dutch, Delaware Swedes, New Jersey Scots, Pennsylvania Quakers, Massachusetts Puritans and merchants and Virginia planters descended from fleeing English Cavaliers. Every colony had its own identity. Their neighbors were largely strangers and not to be entirely trusted. What Coxe proposed was the first plan for a Union of the Colonies, with an assembly made up of delegates from every colony, and a national executive who would unite the states for their mutual benefit and protection—an arrangement strikingly similar to the administrative system of Freemasonry's grand lodges.

Daniel Coxe himself was a Mason, a member of Lodge No. 8 at Devil's Tavern in London. In 1730, while he was back visiting in London, he was named Provincial Grand Master for New York, New Jersey and Pennsylvania, and in 1731, just before his return to America, he was toasted as the Provincial Grand Master of North America.

In 1754, in response to troubles in the West, the English recommended a union and federation of the colonies in defense against the French. Freemason Benjamin Franklin, a representative from Pennsylvania to the Albany Congress, proposed a Plan of Union remarkably similar to Coxe's. What makes the proposals of Brothers Coxe and Franklin interesting is that their plans were essentially the same system used by Provincial Grand Lodges to govern Masonic lodges in their jurisdictions. Franklin would later say that his Albany plan was not adopted because it gave the colonies too much democracy, which worried both the king (who didn't entirely trust his subjects) and the colonies (who didn't entirely trust their neighbors). His proposal would ultimately be voted down by the colonies, who had no desire to work together, much less be watched over by a chief executive "President-General." But Franklin's plan would be resurrected again and used as the framework for the Articles of Confederation that governed the states between the revolution and the adoption of the U.S. Constitution.

When the Continental Congress declared independence from Britain in 1776, it appointed a committee to formulate a plan for the union of the states. Freemasons on the committee included John Dickinson, Thomas McKean, Joseph Hewes, Robert R. Livingston and others.

How, one might ask, did Freemasonry become so intertwined with the formation of the United States and the system that governs it? And how is it that a supposedly "secret society" from London spread around the globe so quickly and influenced so many of the men who would ultimately transform the world?

Creating a Civil Society

Historian Margaret Jacob, in her book *Living the Enlightenment*, makes the incisive observation that what Freemasons were actually doing behind closed doors in their secret meetings, whether they realized it or not, was creating civil society. The lodges "sought to civilize, to teach manners and decorum, to augment the order and harmony of civil society. They taught men to speak in public, to keep records, to pay 'taxes,' to be tolerant, to debate freely, to vote, to moderate their feasting, and to give lifelong devotion to the other citizens of their order."[1]

It was precisely this enjoyment of private freedoms in the confines of the lodge that made Freemasonry's popularity explode around the world in an incredibly brief period of time. Within just sixty years of the first meeting of the Grand Lodge of England in London, Freemasonry had spread like wildfire across Europe and to nearly every colonial outpost. The ships of England, France, Denmark and others carried Masonic brothers to foreign lands, and they brought the fraternity everywhere they went. In a very brief span of time, the public came to know the reputation of Freemasons as a group. Stories of the Masons appeared increasingly in newspapers of the period. The elections of lodge and Grand Lodge officers were common items in the papers, and their cornerstone-laying ceremonies and formal processions were remarkably effective public relations events. As early as 1732, the Masons became vocal promoters of free, public schools in the colonies. Freemasonry was slowly laying the foundations of our American system.

Most popular scholars of the American Revolution completely ignore the contributions of Freemasonry to the actions and the thought processes of our Founding Fathers. When Masonry is addressed at all, it is generally glossed over with brief assertions about the "influence" of Masonry on this period, with no exact statement of how or why this might be so. Innumerable books about the revolution, the Continental Congress and the Constitutional Convention, from stalwarts like *The Ideological Origins of the American Revolution* by Bernard Bailyn to modern classics like *Decision in Philadelphia* by Christopher and James Lincoln Collier, *Miracle at Philadelphia* by Catherine Drinker Brown and *A Brilliant Solution: Inventing the American Constitution* by Carol Berkin, give Freemasons the same brush-off. Even books that supposedly address the broader cultural framework of the period, such as *Toward a New Society* by Jean Matthews or *After the Revolution* by Ray Raphael, reduce Masonry to a footnote. A few give Freemasonry's place in revolutionary history a little more than a thoughtless paragraph, notably Steven C. Bullock's *Revolutionary Brotherhood* and Margaret Jacob's *The Origins of Freemasonry* and *Living the Enlightenment*.

Several of these books mention Masonry only to remind the reader that George Washington took the first presidential oath of office on the Bible from a Masonic lodge. But in fact, the Declaration of Independence, the Constitution, and particularly the first ten amendments to the Constitution that we call the Bill of Rights, all are steeped in Masonic philosophy and principles. Scholars of the period seem to agree on some sort of vague affirmation that Freemasonry was important, *somehow*, and that it was inextricably tied to the founding of America, *somehow*. But they are vague about precisely how.

Masonic authors aren't flawless sources of information either. In the nineteenth and twentieth centuries, Masons were a little too enthusiastic and fanciful about claiming that "most of Washington's generals" and "nearly all of the signers of the Declaration" were Masonic brethren. Even they would make the same fuzzy claim that Freemasonry had shaped the founding of the United States, yet they never seem to be forthcoming with any details.

The Enlightenment was a period of experimentation and visionary thinking. Old rules were being broken every day, and the men who sat down to design a new government for this New Atlantis looked for inspiration in many places—the democracy of Athens, the republic of Rome and especially English common law. But there was one place where democracy was being exercised, religious and political tolerance was being practiced, and men from every walk of life and political persuasion were governing themselves without going for each others' throats: in the lodges of the Freemasons. Freemasonry was the firstborn son of the Enlightenment, and it was a greater single influence on our Founding Fathers than any other.

The principal authors of the founding documents of the United States were not provably Freemasons. James Madison, the author of record for the Bill of Rights, was thought to have been made a Mason in Hiram Lodge No. 59 in Westmoreland County, Virginia, but the records have long ago been lost, and it has never been proved. Loss of records happened fairly often in this period, whether by fire, flood, war, well-intentioned secrecy or just good old-fashioned incompetence. Madison's personal sponsor and mentor, Thomas Jefferson, author of the Declaration of Independence, was never a Mason. But it really doesn't matter whether either man was a member of a lodge. Neither were John Adams, Alexander Hamilton or Gouverneur Morris, all important figures in the creation of the new nation's legal structure.

It doesn't matter because Freemasonry surrounded these men, literally and figuratively, in politics, in society and in everyday life. Mr. Madison's protégé and close friend, future president James Monroe, was a Freemason. So, of course, were the two most revered, nearly worshipped figures of the period, George Washington and Benjamin Franklin. And so were a large percentage of the men Madison and Jefferson dealt with in their daily lives. Many of their most trusted friends and advisors were Freemasons: men like John Jay,[2] co-author with Madison of the *Federalist Papers* and first Supreme Court chief justice; Robert Livingston, the great statesman and diplomat who closed the deal on the Louisiana Purchase; the Marquis de Lafayette, beloved French hero of the American Revolution; and Jefferson's fellow Virginian and cousin John Marshall, soldier, diplomat, future chief justice of the Supreme Court and undisputed leader of the so-called Essex County "Junta" that controlled Richmond politics for decades.

Lodge parlance and principles can be found writ large in our national creed because, at this time more than any other in history, the language of the lodge was the language of the businessmen, landowners, politicians and military officers who were shaping the political dialogue of the colonial period. This saturation of Masonic ideals occurred not only in back-room politics but in American society as a whole. Before and during the revolution, military lodges had spread Freemasonry across the landscape, as officers and soldiers conferred Masonic degrees on new recruits and civilians alike. Masonic lodges had spread from every major city in the colonies into the smaller towns and villages, and they were meeting in taverns, coffeehouses or even private homes. And as Margaret Jacob pointed out, they were teaching their members how to behave like civilized gentlemen and how to govern themselves. The speech and appearance gap between the aristocracy and the rising middle class was closing fast. And the egalitarian ideals of the lodge were being spread all over the colonies in many ways besides contact between members.

It was fashionable during the Age of Enlightenment to keep a personal journal. It would become not just the habit of intellectual gentlemen but, like newspapers and broadsides, a source of information transmitted amazingly far and wide to an audience eager for any and all books, particularly political ones. Travel was difficult and dangerous, and so for fifty years any travelogue from a distant land, especially the wild new land of the American West, was likely to become a bestseller in the colonies as well as in Europe.

George Washington's first experience of public attention came in this manner, when he was only twenty-one. As a major in the Virginia militia, he had volunteered for a dangerous mission to the Ohio territory, to deliver a diplomatic ultimatum from the governor of Virginia ordering the French out of the area, which was claimed by the British crown. France and Great Britain were on the verge of the French and Indian War. Washington kept a diary of his experiences on this arduous trip, and on his return, he had them published. It was a smash hit. All things political were in even greater demand. Politics was becoming nearly an obsession for men and women, young and old.

This was the time of the literary or political salon, from the humblest to the most blue-blooded and gracious. Exchanging information sometimes began at the crack of dawn. Coffee, an exotic import from the Middle Eastern land of Yemen, had become extremely popular. Gentlemen, sometimes only half dressed, wandered from their rooms to the nearby coffee shop in the morning, savoring their daily caffeine while the newspapers were read aloud and loudly commented on. In the afternoons, in pubs and taverns from Portsmouth to Boston, middle-class men were enjoying political readings and discussions along with their gin and ale. And in the evenings, fashionable Paris and London salons read and discussed the poetry, novels and political writings of the day.

Even in the unfashionable corners of America, the backcountry of Maine or the coastal fishing villages of Massachusetts, plainspoken Americans were doing the same thing as the glitterati in the salons of Paris and London. Some of these small reading circles had started life as innocuous weekly Bible readings, but they evolved over the course of the revolutionary era into something far more politically charged. In our America of the twenty-first century, citizens tend to get their information in darkened solitude, staring into the mesmerizing blue light of their computers or 24-hour news channels. In the nineteenth century, the greatest joy of absorbing the news of the day was found in the communal aspect of it all—in the taverns, reading circles, salons and lodges, and in the lively discussions that followed.

Modern Freemasonry was born in the taverns of London, and when it spread to America, the traditions continued. The centerpiece of the typical Masonic meeting was the feast, complete with lively discussion and ceremonial toasts—to the king, each other and all "poor, distres'd Masons wheresoe'r dispers'd." Unlike other dining or drinking clubs of the period, the Masons crossed social and economic boundaries that usually kept men of different classes apart. They encouraged conversation on the topics of the day once the meeting was over and stressed the importance of education. A substantial portion of the second degree ceremony, the Fellow Craft Degree, amounted to a crash course in the liberal arts. Freemasonry was raising the bar on its initiates and members, embodying the central message of the Enlightenment: the wider spread of knowledge.

Benjamin Franklin's profession as a printer brings up another important connection with the spread of Masonry, as well as the literature of the Enlightenment and the Revolution. Franklin set up the first circulating library in Philadelphia in 1731, and in 1753 he was appointed as the deputy post master general of North America. As a Freemason, printer, librarian, scientist, postmaster and student of philosophy, Franklin's entire life was the trade in new, Enlightenment and Masonic ideas in the New World.

The increasingly efficient spread of knowledge and information at every level of society meant that Masonic ideas were being absorbed by people who were not members of a lodge. The men who were most admired in this period, the *philosophes*, the political thinkers and the revolutionaries, had amongst them a large number of Freemasons. This was a part of the Masonic influence on the culture of the late 1700s.

The Constitution of the Freemasons

The legal system that governed the colonies before the revolution was English common law. Many of the Founders were lawyers, including the brightest legal minds of the age, such as John Adams, Alexander Hamilton, John Jay and John Marshall, so of course they were thoroughly familiar with the common law,. It was a great influence on the development of our own judicial system. But the English legal system was—and is—very different from what was born in our Constitutional Convention.

England has no written constitution. It didn't in 1215, and it doesn't today. It certainly didn't in 1776. In conversation, Englishmen refer to their "constitution," but it is a misleading concept. England's governing system is based on written and unwritten rules, implied powers, judicial precedents, gentlemanly agreements and quaint customs. The queen still has the right to dissolve Parliament if she chooses to do so. Parliament has the power to declare or rescind laws, even laws that seem to limit its powers, and there is no "supreme court" or other constitutional watchdog to prevent it. In fact, most of Magna Carta's more than sixty different articles—the supposed bedrock of England's legal system—have been whittled away by Parliament over the years. In 1828, Parliament took the bold step of nullifying one of its articles. By 1969, only four remained in place. Most importantly, Magna Carta was not terribly concerned with human rights. It was very respectful of the rights of the Church in England and of the liberties of rich, powerful, land-owning, army-leading and potentially trouble-making nobles. But barrel-makers, blacksmiths and milkmaids were still out in the cold.

The Freemasons, however, *did* have a constitution. They had developed their own constitution for the governing of the stonemason Guilds. Their first written guidelines, known as the Regius Manuscript, was written in 1390. It was a poetic rendering of rules and guidelines for the conduct of its members, along with a brief telling of the mythical and Biblical origins of the building profession. It was a design for the organization of its lodges, a description of the responsibilities of its members and a rulebook for their conduct. It exhorted the stonemasons to be responsible citizens and churchgoers and served as a guide to etiquette and a plea for higher education in the liberal arts. But it was a written constitution, added to and subtracted from over the centuries.

In 1717, the Grand Lodge of England was formed. This was the first time a central governing body had attempted to bring several individual lodges together under one organization. Freemasonry had changed in the previous century from a guild of craftsmen, who worked in stone to build cathedrals, into a philosophical fraternity that used cathedral building as a metaphor for character-building. Five years after the formation of the Grand Lodge, Dr. James Anderson crafted what were known as the Ancient Charges, or more commonly as Anderson's *Constitutions*.

First published as a book in 1723, they contained a fanciful history of the Freemasons and the arts of geometry and architecture, plus a collection of songs for Masons to sing at their feasts and meetings. Most importantly, they laid down the specific duties of a Mason, along with a collection of general regulations. While the Regius Manuscript and its descendants spent lots of time discussing the proper conduct of a Mason in church (say your *Our Father*, don't cuss, keep your voice down), Anderson's document was very different. It was a true product of the new age of Enlightenment:

> A Mason is oblig'd by his Tenure, to obey the moral law…
> But though in ancient Times Masons were charged in every
> Country to be of the Religion of that Country or Nation, what-
> ever it was, yet it is now thought more expedient only to oblige
> them to that Religion in which all Men agree, leaving their par-
> ticular Opinions to themselves; that is, to be good Men and
> true, or Men of Honour and Honesty, by whatever
> Denominations or Persuasions they may be distinguish'd;
> whereby Masonry becomes the Center of Union, and the
> Means of conciliating true Friendship among Persons that must
> have remain'd at a perpetual Distance.[3]

In Freemasonry, this is essentially the definition of "meeting on the level." In other words—equality, freedom of religion, and sepa- ration of church and state. Freemasonry was unlike anything that had come before it. Here was what was conceived to be an *exclusive* organization that was designed to be *inclusive* in its rules and pre- cepts. The Masonic rules about religion are a good example. After centuries of religious and political strife that had caused excommu- nications, wars, torture, beheadings, burnings and untold other calamities, Freemasonry was determined to put a stop to intolerance, at least within its lodge rooms. The Freemasons placed no political or religious barriers on their membership, and their stated goal was to unite men, not divide them. If God and politics were the two biggest obstacles to civilized gatherings, there was a simple answer: eliminate them as topics of conversation.

Anderson's *Constitutions* laid out a design for the government of an organization that was based on tolerance, equality, good citizen- ship and benevolence. It was religious without being a religion. It had a centralized authority but made many provisions for self-governance of individual lodges. It provided mechanisms for admitting new local lodges into the Grand Lodge. It laid out procedures for administering and amending its rules and reprimanding rule breakers. It described its membership as men of "all Nations, Tongues, Kindreds and Languages."[4] It described proper behavior for its members in a civilized society, including the importance of adherence to the law of the land, as well as kindness and moral conduct. In short, it was a design for a utopian society, but one within practical reach. It was a federal system of government with a central authority and individual, subordinate lodges that were run under their own local sets of by-laws. It included terms of office for officials, a description of the rules for selecting officers, provisions for financial responsibility and checks and balances, a guarantee of freedom of speech and faith, and, most importantly, the right of every member to vote.[5]

The individual lodges retained control of strictly local lodge affairs under their own sets of bylaws while the Grand Lodge administered the general affairs of the order, much as state governments operate separately from the federal government. The Grand Lodge was obliged to meet once a year and was granted the right to make new laws, provided the original foundations of the organization, the *Ancient Landmarks*, were not changed. Article XXXIX of James Anderson's *Constitutions* states:

> Every Annual Grand Lodge has an inherent Power and Authority to make new Regulations, or to alter these, for the real Benefits of this ancient Fraternity: Provided always that the old Land Marks be carefully preservd, and that such Alterations and new Regulations be proposed and agreed to at the third Quarterly Communication preceding the Annual Grand Feast, and that they be offered also to the Perusal of all the Brethren before Dinner, in writing, even of the youngest Apprentice, the Approbation and Consent of the Majority of all the Brethren present being absolutely necessary to make the same binding and obligatory.[6]

Representative government and majority rule were expressed in Article X:

> The majority of every particular Lodge, when congregated, shall have the Privilege of giving Instructions to their Master and Wardens, before the three Quarterly Communications hereafter mentioned, and of Annual Grand Lodge too; because their Master and Wardens are their Representatives, and are supposed to speak their Mind.[7]

Article XXVIII Section 4 gives the lodges the right to change existing laws or propose new legislation by stating that Grand Lodge is:

> To receive and consider of any good Motion, or any momentous and important Affair, that shall be brought from the particular Lodges, by their Representatives, the several Masters and Wardens.[8]

Section 2 of Article XXIX established the idea that agents are responsible to the legislative body in financial matters:

> The Grand Wardens and the Stewards are to account for all money they receive or expend, to the Grand Lodge, after Dinner, or when the Grand Lodge shall see fit to receive their accounts.[9]

The concept of checks and balances on the executive branch appears in the power to impeach the chief executive officer in Article XIV:

> If the Grand Master should abuse his Power, and render himself unworthy of Obedience and Subjection of the Lodges, he shall be treated in a manner to be agreed upon in a new Regulation: because hitherto the ancient Fraternity have had no occasion for it, their former Grand Masters having all behaved themselves worthy of the honorable office.[10]

Article XXVIII constituted the Grand Lodge as a supreme court of appeals and arbitration, either by the body or by committee, in these words:

> All members of the Grand Lodge must be at the Place long
> before Dinner... in order to receive any appeals duly lodg'd
> that the Appellant may be heard and the Affair amicably decid-
> ed; but if it cannot, it must be referr'd to a particular Report to
> the next Quarterly Communication.[11]

Freemasonry was clearly a laboratory for creating a representative form of government that could be applied in a practical, real-
world manner.

Get out the Vote

While scholars of note usually ignore Freemasonry as an influence
on our early republic, they make much of the fact that all our
Founding Fathers were students of the past, particularly the Classical
past—Greece and Rome. And there is no question that the body of
knowledge from the Classical period had an enormous impact on
them as it did on every educated gentleman in Western civilization
since the Renaissance. The Greeks did invent the concept of democracy, while the Romans conceived an even higher political art form,
the delicate and complex series of checks and balances that was the
Roman Republic. But on the subject of civil rights, the notion that
the Founding Fathers drew up a government based on the Classical
forms begins to fall apart. It's easy to see that their architectural styles
were influenced by Classical civilization. It's not so easy to draw the
same conclusion about their politics.

This is certainly not to imply that there was no borrowing from
Greece and Rome. A solid Classical education was one thing most of
our Founding Fathers had in common. Even the ones, like Washington himself, who had a little less formal education still generally
knew Latin or Greek. They'd read Plato and Aristotle, Caesar and
Marcus Aurelius. The importance of Plato's *Republic* as part of a long
chain of Utopian thinking is accepted without question as an influence on the men of the Continental Congress. Besides, any child of
ten can look around at the architecture of America, from the Capitol

building to the bank or funeral home on their town's Main Street, and see the pervasive influence of Classical styles. But Classical influences leave a large, gaping hole in our understanding of the revolution that can't be filled with Plato and Aristotle. To look only at the Greeks and the Romans is to be blind to a far greater influence on the birth of the United States.

The city-state of Athens has always been given the historical laurels as the first democracy. But for the Athenians, democracy meant that the important men who would be called upon to fight for the city were also the ones who could vote on the issues of the day. Women were barred from voting. Slaves, of which the Athenians had many, also had no vote. Those who owned no property were denied the right to vote. And, perhaps the most snobbish edict of all, no foreign-born man could vote, no matter how long he had lived in Athens. Even Aristotle, arguably the greatest Athenian who ever lived, was turned away at the voting booth because he had been born in the small and relatively unimportant town of Stagirus in Macedonia. This may have annoyed the great old philosopher, but it wouldn't have surprised him much. Both Plato and Aristotle were oligarchists, proponents of a city-state in which only the cream of society, the noble, the educated and the elite, would control the government. It's estimated that, in reality, only about ten percent of the 300,000 inhabitants of the city of Athens actually had the right to vote. The idea for universal suffrage certainly did not come from Greece.

It didn't come from Rome, either. The Romans did create the world's first representative republic. But it was an incredibly cumbersome, top-heavy piece of work, and universal voting rights were not exactly at its center. Roman society was divided into two classes, the patricians and the plebeians, and it wasn't simply a division between the haves and the have-nots. "Patrician" did not necessarily mean noble-born. One could become a patrician simply by being the son of an elected consul. Plebeians had their own tribal assemblies that voted in a powerful bloc. The true nobility consisted of about a dozen major families whose names rang throughout the history of

Rome, all the way back to the early days of the Republic. This did give the nobility a certain amount of power, but it was more a matter of prestige.

In the days of the Republic, apart from the deliberating body of the Senate, there were all sorts of assemblies: tribal assemblies, Centuriate military assemblies, assemblies of tribunes of the plebeians and so forth. None were legislative bodies with the right to propose laws; assemblies merely had the right to vote as a whole, yes or no. Within them, voting blocs were given various complex percentages of the final vote, and the poorest among them in money or status had the least power in their voting bloc—hardly a democracy. This endless layering and dividing up of the vote was done to achieve two typically Roman goals—first, to keep the upper classes in power, and second, to keep any individual of those upper classes from achieving too much power. In theory the people were sovereign, but in reality the vote was more of a sop to their emotions than it was a real political power. Still, Roman citizens were very proud of having the right to vote, and justifiably so. One look at their contemporaries in the empires of Persia and the East proves that it was a big step forward. But the right to vote for a Roman had very little to do with voting rights as we understand them today.

Despite the fact that the Romans had a very complex legal system, the individual civil rights that we recognize, such as freedom of speech and the press, freedom of assembly, freedom from unwarranted search and seizure and the right to a trial by jury, were all completely unknown and utterly unimagined. Neither the Greeks nor the Romans had the rights of universal suffrage, meaning one man, with one vote. Universal suffrage—the right for each individual to vote regardless of his or her station in life—landowner, shopkeeper, nobility, gentleman, laborer—did not exist in Western society in the 1700s. There was only one place where one man did have one vote, and his was no more or less important than his rich landlord or his poor trash collector. From its inception, every Master Mason in a Masonic lodge had the same right to vote, with his vote counting no more or less than the man beside him, regardless of age, wealth, influence or rank.

The concept of representative government and majority rule were adopted in Article X of Anderson's *Constitutions*:

> The majority of every particular Lodge, when congregated, shall have the Privilege of giving Instructions to their Master and Wardens, before the three Quarterly Communications hereafter mentioned, and of Annual Grand Lodge too; because their Master and Wardens are their Representatives, and are supposed to speak their Mind.[12]

Majority rule and universal suffrage are provided for in Section 2 of Article XII as follows:

> All Matters are to be determined in the Grand Lodge by a Majority of Votes, each Member having one Vote, and the Grand Master having two Votes, unless the said Lodge leaves any particular thing to the Determination of the Grand Master for the sake of Expedition.[13]

The protection of the ballot and elections from outside influence was expressed in Article XXXIX:

> The Grand Master and his Deputy, the Grand Wardens, or the Stewards, the Secretary, the Treasurer, the Clerks, and every other person, shall withdraw, and leave the Masters and Warden of the Particular Lodges alone; in order to Consult amicably about electing a New Grand Master.[14]

Article XII sets the specific term of office of the Grand Officers at one year:

> Grand Lodge must meet Annually in order to chuse[sic] every year a new Grand Master, Deputy and Wardens.[15]

All of this was a half-century before Lexington and Concord.

To the powers-that-be of the 1700s, Article XII was the most earth-shattering thing the Freemasons were doing behind the closed doors of their lodges. They were voting for new members, for their officers, and for changes in their rules. For an overfed king, a plump pope or a comfortably entrenched parliamentarian, this was a terrifying prospect. It was heresy. It was immoral. It was probably treason, if they could just figure out how to make the charge stick.

After the Revolution there were still barriers to universal suffrage in the United States system of government—we tinker with voting rights laws even today—but by the election of 1800 the laws based on the old British way of doing things were already collapsing. Laws forbidding those without property to vote were being either openly challenged or cleverly gotten around, until at last they dropped by the wayside as relics from the past that had no respectability in the egalitarian new nation.

Confederation Congress and the Signing of the Constitution

The protracted battle to create a constitution has been well documented. The challenge was to create a national government that was strong—but not too strong—representing large and small states fairly. During the Revolutionary War, the colonies had been governed under the Articles of Confederation, and one thing everybody could agree on was that it hadn't worked very well. Because the Revolution had been fought over the tyranny of British rule, the Articles intentionally formed a flaccid central government. The colonies weren't about to shuck off a distant king just to be ruled by one closer to home, and Patrick "Give Me Liberty or Give Me Death" Henry, for one, screamed his head off every time the topic of a strong federal government came up. There was no national court system, no provision for trade between the states and no provision for raising tax money to handle pesky annoyances like paying the troops. Every individual state was allowed to print its own money and set its own exchange rate, so the simple act of carrying goods from North Carolina to New York meant passing through multiple states and dealing with different tariffs, currency, rules and regulations for every one of them. And nobody could successfully make changes in the Articles, since states weren't interested in sending delegates to the meetings, resulting in the failure to have a quorum. Winning the war had been a miraculous success; peace, however, was turning into a total disaster.

Four years after the war ended in 1783, the Confederation Congress at last agreed it was time to make some major changes. Twelve states—all but Rhode Island—convened in Philadelphia in 1787 and began to pound out a blueprint for government they could all abide by. The convention's deliberations were kept secret from the press and the rest of the country. Had they been made public, they might never have been completed. The unceasing input of the delegates was bad enough. George Washington, as president of the Constitutional Convention, stoically presided over eighty-seven miserable days of fierce debate over the document.

At one point, after a heated argument over large-state versus small-state representation, the aging Benjamin Franklin had his friend James Wilson read a message to the convention.

> We are sent here to consult, not to contend with each other; and declarations of a fixed opinion, and of determined resolution never to change it, neither enlighten nor convince us. Positiveness and warmth on one side, naturally beget their like on the other; and tend to create and augment discord and division in a great concern, wherein harmony and union are extremely necessary to give weight to our councils, and render them effectual in promoting and securing the common good.[16]

Franklin's remarks echoed one of the most important messages taught to new Master Masons in the lodge, contained in the description of the trowel. While stonemasons used the trowel for spreading cement to unite individual stones into a solid building, the Freemason is to regard its symbolic use,

> to spread the cement of Brotherly Love and Affection; that cement that unites us into one sacred band, or society of friends and brothers, among whom no contention should ever

exist, but that noble contention, or rather emulation, of who best can work or best agree.[17]

It was Roger Sherman's suggested compromise that had finally broken the impasse over representation between smaller and larger states, by suggesting a Senate with two legislators from every state, and a second chamber known as the House of Representatives that reflected the population of each state.

At last, in September, New York's Gouverneur Morris delivered the final draft, cobbled into an uninspiring legal document with an eloquent preamble ("We the people, in order to form a more perfect union . . .").

At least thirteen—and possibly nineteen—of the thirty-nine men who signed the Constitution were Freemasons:

- Gunning Bedford, Jr., first Grand Master of Delaware
- John Blair, first Grand Master of Virginia
- David Brearley, first Grand Master of New Jersey
- Jacob Broom of Delaware, who served as an officer in his lodge
- Daniel Carroll of Maryland, who would be part of the cornerstone-laying ceremony of the capitol in the new Federal City[18]
- Jonathon Dayton, Member of Temple Lodge No. 1 in Elizabethtown, New Jersey
- John Dickinson, member of a lodge in Dover, Delaware
- William Few, sometimes identified as a Mason in Georgia
- Benjamin Franklin, Grand Master of Masons in Pennsylvania
- Nicholas Gilman, member of St. John's Lodge No. 1, in Portsmouth, New Hampshire
- William Samuel Johnson, reportedly a Mason from Connecticut
- Rufus King, Member of St. John's Lodge, Newburyport, Massachusetts
- John Langdon, reportedly a Mason from New Hampshire
- James McHenry, who would become a member of Spiritual Lodge No. 23, Maryland

- Robert Morris, possibly a Mason in Pennsylvania
- William Paterson, member of Trenton Lodge No. 5 in Trenton, New Jersey
- George Read, possibly a Mason in Delaware
- Roger Sherman, reportedly a Mason from Connecticut
- George Washington, America's most famous Freemason, and president of the Congress

Franklin gave an un-rousing but honest endorsement to the U.S. Constitution before the vote recommending adoption—"because I expect no better, and because I am not sure it is not the best." Reaching an agreement had taken a long, hard session. By its own stated requirement, what remained was for at least nine of the thirteen state legislatures to adopt it before it would become the official law of the land.

Not every Freemason was in favor of the Constitution. Elbridge Gerry, who would become vice president in 1813 under James Madison, was a constant complainer.[19] Rhode Island stubbornly held out, refusing to send delegates to the convention in the first place and being the last of all thirteen states to adopt the U.S. Constitution in 1790, almost three years after it was submitted. Washington himself rode around the state rather than through it until the legislature gave in. The Constitution was officially ratified by the required two-thirds of the states on July 28, 1788.

Freemasonry and Freedom of Religion

One of the ways the Constitution was sold to members of the convention and their legislatures at home was that it wasn't finished yet. While the document itself couldn't be changed anymore, it had provisions for amendment, with the understanding that an additional Bill of Rights would be forthcoming. The U.S. Constitution was the instruction manual for physically creating a government. The Bill of Rights would say, philosophically, how it would govern.

The Bill of Rights would become the masterpiece of the U.S. Constitution. It was a simple, elegant handbook on human rights, copied almost at once by the French in their *Rights of Man*. It is still being copied to this day in darkened corners of the world reaching for the light of freedom. Arguably the centerpiece of the Bill of Rights is the First Amendment, the one that Americans hold most dear. It is, in fact, so clear and concise that it is hard to believe it was written by a lawyer.

> Congress shall make no law respecting an establishment of religion, or prohibiting the free exercise thereof; or abridging the freedom of speech, or of the press; or the right of the people peaceably to assemble, and to petition the government for a redress of grievances.

Every concept within it, nestled between some of the most important commas and semicolons in the history of mankind, is an outgrowth of the Masonic experience.

Today, separation of church and state seems natural. In the eighteenth century, however, this was a shockingly revolutionary idea that had never before been tried. After all, how was a nation to enforce civil order if the populace did not feel that the government had God on its side? The ancient Romans came the closest to having a measure of religious freedom. For the most part, the consuls and emperors of Rome did not interfere with the religions of conquered peoples, while in the city itself new deities sprang up as quickly as new fashions. Still, there was a state religion, the Rites of Jupiter and Mars. That state religion remained in place until the time of Constantine in the fourth century, and any man who was heard to disparage it might well find himself on trial for his life on a charge of profanity.

For most of the later European monarchies, the state religion was a far more powerfully entrenched ideal. The French Bourbon kings, for example, gave nearly unprecedented rights to the Catholic Church, including freedom from taxation for the Church's vast and wealthy estates and absolute control over France's educational system. All this would one day boomerang back on poor Louis XVI when the Church and her minions became the first victims of the French Revolution. Faith was literally banished from the nation along with the polite address of "Monsieur." Each man was now "Citizen" so-and-so, and the mobs fell on churches and monasteries like jungle beasts, tearing priests limb from limb. All who did not escape—priests, nuns and stubborn adherents—fell under the blade of the guillotine.

Although Great Britain never faced quite such a reactionary catastrophe, the system was not entirely dissimilar. In Britain as well as all her colonies, a law called the Test Act rejected the doctrine of transubstantiation, the part of the Catholic mass when the Eucharist literally becomes the body of Christ. In plain English, any man who aspired to a position in the military, government or any related field had to first sign a document swearing that he not only was not a Catholic but had absolute and undying faith in the Church of England (the church that, in America, would evolve first into the Anglican church, later into the Episcopalian church). For those unwilling to take such a vow, including Catholics, Jews and members of various Protestant sects, there would be little chance to rise to any position of prominence in British or colonial American society.

This was the injustice that the Founding Fathers sought to erase, and there is little doubt that the inspiration for this ideal, not as a utopian vision but as a demonstrable, workable system, was Freemasonry. Within the lodge, men had to profess a belief in God, since it was assumed that no man could take a binding oath without faith in some higher deity. But beyond this, it was forbidden to discuss religion within the confines of the lodge, and no man was allowed to question the faith of a brother. Freemasons had been functioning this way for a century, so why couldn't a nation operate under the same rule of conduct?

Much has been written and debated about the influence of Deism on our founders, as if to imply that it was an easy thing to expel the topic of religion from a lodge whose members were all atheists anyway. But although Deism was an influence of the Enlightenment on most of the thinking men of this period, this philosophy was no more a church than it was a denial of God. There were no "Our Lady of the Deistic Universe" churches. Deism was simply another approach to faith. According to its central naturalistic philosophy, God did indeed create the heaven and the earth, but that was pretty much the extent of His involvement. God was like a divine watchmaker, creating the world as a perfectly synchronized machine whose secrets could be unearthed by a study of nature through the lens of reason, the byword of Enlightenment thought. Some Founding Fathers, such as Jefferson and Tom Paine, were far more influenced by this philosophy than others. But Thomas Jefferson was hardly an atheist. In fact, he read the Bible every day for the last fifty years of his life, often in Greek or Latin. He created two edited versions of scripture, his favorite being a small volume that contained only the words of Jesus, which reveals his philosophical bent where religion was concerned.

The assertion of later critics, that godless Deism ruled the Masonic lodges, was simply not true. For example, they cite the fact that Masons often refer to God as the Grand Architect of the Universe as proof that Masonry is some sort of bizarre religion of its own, tied to Deism or some other heresy. But Masons do not teach or endorse any particular religious creed. They look for neutral terms out of courtesy and tact that embody the exhortation in Anderson's *Constitutions* to reach for that aspect of religious belief upon which all men can agree. "Grand Architect of the Universe" is a term used by Masons during prayer simply as an all-inclusive description of God that neither prejudices nor exalts any member's beliefs over another's. Such arguments are to be left outside of the door of the lodge.

Before the revolution, many colonies had in their charters and other legislation language specifically supporting Christianity in one form or another. It was that "one form or another" that was troublesome. Quakers were hanged by Puritans in Massachusetts and Virginia and went on to establish Pennsylvania as a safe haven. Maryland was the only colony friendly to Catholics, even though they had been stripped of their right to vote by the Crown in 1689. The southern colonies were more likely to be Church of England (Anglican), but Massachusetts, a stronghold of Congregationalists, adopted a state constitution that supported an official religion as late as 1780—after the Revolution had ended.

The fact is that our Founding Fathers were religious men, each in his own fashion, as it should be. Washington, Franklin, Jefferson and Paine may have all been Deists; it is hard to say, since only Paine would publicly write on the topic. Officially, Washington was an Episcopalian whose church pew is still proudly marked in Alexandria. Descriptions and paintings depict him kneeling in the snow to pray during the war, but may have simply sprung from the fervid imagination of Parson Weems and his fairy-tale book about the president. Franklin remained largely silent about his faith, as many men of that age considered it crass to discuss religion in a public forum. Although the founders differed in creed, they found a way to write into the Bill of Rights a new, simple doctrine of tolerance. They knew it would work because many of them had seen it in action—in their Masonic lodges.

Freedom of Assembly

Many years ago, I came across a small news story noting that the Chinese government had banned the right to form clubs of stamp and coin collectors. The notoriously oppressive Chinese government was not concerned with whether or not a few men wanted to collect stamps, but rather that any free assembly of men, even one formed to compare watermarks or perforation errors, might one day end up discussing politics. And so the right to free assembly was denied to the Chinese people. This sort of free assembly is protected by the First Amendment, as is the right for any group to respectfully petition the government for change. Freemasons were guaranteed freedom of speech and equality of participation in discussion in Article XXXVII of Anderson's *Constitutions:*

The Grand Master shall allow any Brother Fellowcraft, or
Apprentice to speak, directing his Discourse to his Worship; or
to make any Motion for the good of the Fraternity, which shall
be either immediately consider'd and finish'd, or else referred to
the Consideration of the Grand Lodge at their next
Communication.[20]

The right to free assembly—the right to belong to any group
one chooses—was being threatened all over Europe, especially in the
Masonic lodges. Masons were being arrested in France, Austria,
Portugal and elsewhere. Looking around them at the oppression of
their Masonic brothers all over the world was undoubtedly in the
minds of at least some of the men who voted this amendment into
law. Men like John Adams and James Madison were not Jacobins or
fire-breathing agitators. They did not intend the First Amendment
to grant the right to riot, or even to dump tea into the ocean. In fact,
most of the Founding Fathers abhorred street violence. What they
were granting was a right of *peaceable* free assembly, including the
assembly into any organization a man wished.

Even today in many parts of the United Kingdom, where
Freemasonry originated, Masons are forced to publicly declare their
membership in the lodge if they are police officers, judges or other
government officials. Freemasonry alone is singled out across
England as being sufficiently worthy of suspicion to force its members to disclose their involvement with it. It is hard to imagine what
would happen in the United Kingdom if Jews, Catholics, Muslims,
soccer fans or one-handed xylophone players were forced to register
under similar laws.

Anti-Masonic statements are common in the French and Italian
press these days as well. Respectable news magazines regularly accuse
Masons of government takeover plots or economic skullduggery. In
less toney publications, anti-Masonry is combined with anti-
Semitism. It is curious to note that despotic governments—Soviet
Russia, Franco's Spain, Mussolini's Italy, Hitler's Germany—all outlawed Freemasonry at the beginning of their rise to power. Yet today

in the former Soviet republics where freedom has been won, Freemasonry has been reborn. It seems fairly obvious that Freemasonry is no threat to liberty. In fact, it seems to be a prerequisite.

Freemasons had said it best. Anderson's *Constitutions* stated, "A Mason is a Peaceable Subject to the Civil Powers, wherever he resides or works, and is never to be concern'd in Plots and Conspiracies against the Peace and Welfare of the Nation."

CHAPTER 6

Solomon's Builders

♦♦♦

And the king commanded them, and they brought great
stones, costly stones, and hewed stones, to lay the foundation of the temple. And Solomon's builders and Hiram's
builders did hew them, and the stonesquarers; so they
prepared timber and stones to build the temple.

—I KINGS 5:17

It was a pleasant afternoon in the waning days of winter when the
procession assembled outside of John Wise's popular tavern in
Alexandria. The throng was suitably braced against the chill of the
day by a hearty meal and more than a little toasting to the occasion.
Daniel Carroll, a signer of the Declaration of Independence, and Dr.
David Stewart, another of the three city commissioners for the project at hand, were joined by the mayor and other dignitaries, along
with a large group of members of the Ancient and Honorable
Fraternity of Free and Accepted Masons. Both Caroll and Stewart
were Brothers among them.

The Freemasons assembled together at the rear of the parade,
making for an interesting sight to those who were unfamiliar with
them. Each wore white leather aprons tied around the waist, many
of which were lavishly hand-painted with strange scenes or symbols
in exquisite detail. Some also wore peculiar medals around their
necks—badges or "jewels" of office, signifying that they were officers
of their Masonic lodges.

The Tyler stood at the head of the Masons with his sword
drawn. Behind him were the Stewards, carrying their long white
staffs. Behind them came three Brothers, carrying one gold and two

silver cups. Another carried a plumb, a square and a level, the tools of architecture. The next carried a Bible, with a square and compass laying on it, the universally recognized symbols of Freemasonry. Others carried staffs, rods or other objects to be used in the ceremony they had assembled to perform.

At three o'clock the procession stepped off, joined by many local citizens. The group marched through the town of Alexandria, Virginia, to a place called Jones Point, along the bank of the Potomac River. There, a tall, narrow stone awaited them. The project's surveyor, Major Andrew Ellicott, approached to ceremonially ascertain the precise position, and the Freemasons stepped forward to put the stone in its proper resting place.

Worshipful Brother Elisha Cullen Dick, the Master of Alexandria Lodge No. 22, led his Masonic officers through the solemn ceremony. The three principal officers stepped up in turn to the granite stone. The Worshipful Master applied the square, a symbol of virtue, with which he made certain that each angle was perfectly cut. Next, the Senior Warden brought the level, a symbol of equality, and used it to ascertain that the stone was horizontally correct. And last, the Junior Warden used the plumb, an emblem of morality and rectitude, to ascertain that it was perfectly upright. The Worshipful Master proclaimed that the craftsmen had performed their duties and that the stone was indeed square, level and plumb and therefore suitable as the foundation for a dream that was about to be made reality.

Kernels of wheat were sprinkled over the stone from a golden cup as a symbol of goodness, plenty and nourishment. Wine was poured over it from a silver cup, a symbol of friendship, health and refreshment. Finally, drops of oil glistened down its sides like the sacred oil that ran down upon Aaron's beard in the Old Testament, "to the skirts of his garments; as the dew of Hermon, and as the dew that descended upon the mountains of Zion."[1] The oil symbolized joy, peace and tranquility. More than a mere blessing, the ceremony sought to place the favor and protection of God on the project for which this would be the foundation, as well as upon the men who had conceived it, those who would build it and all who would work and live within its boundaries.[2] At last the Worshipful Master took a small gavel and struck the stone three times, symbolically setting it in place. The first boundary stone for the new Federal City, which would become Washington, D.C., was officially declared "well-formed, true and trusty."

King Solomon had built his temple in Jerusalem in 1000 B.C., and the legends of the Freemasons traced their origins to the three principal Grand Masters who had overseen its construction: King Solomon of Israel, King Hiram of Tyre and Hiram Abiff, a widow's son of the tribe of Napthali and, according to Masonic ritual, the Grand Architect of the greatest temple ever erected to God. With his three taps, the Worshipful Master of Alexandria Lodge invested the stone with the spirit of those three ancient builders. And with those taps, these spiritual descendants of Solomon's builders began a new chapter in the history of the founding of the United States of America on that chilly March 15, 1791.

This was the first boundary stone of a total of forty to be placed in a perfect square, turned on edge to resemble a diamond, marking the territory that would become the new capital city of the fledgling country.

The proud participation of the Freemasons in the earliest beginnings of the Federal City has recently been interpreted by some modern critics as something sinister. An even stranger phenomenon has been the peculiar notion that the Freemasons designed occult diagrams into the street map of the city, to somehow rain down satanic blessings over the nation's capital or to "secretly" proclaim their dominion over it. All this presupposes that the Freemasons were doing more than just pouring wheat, wine and oil on a few cornerstones, an idea predicated upon the belief that the city planners were all (or mostly) Freemasons, that they could successfully hide such activities from the non-Masons involved, and that such symbols, if they existed, had a real, occult purpose.

Such accusations may sell books or make entertaining pre-dawn talk radio shows, but they have little to do with the truth. As Benjamin Franklin once pointed out, "Three may keep a secret if two are dead." Or more to the point of this discussion, three may keep a secret if they never knew about it in the first place.

◆ ◆ ◆

It couldn't have been a more horrible spot to build a city. That's the trouble with going into the wilderness and starting from scratch—it's so full of wilderness. The name of the part of Washington, D.C., called Foggy Bottom is a good indication of what the land of the district was really like. Detractors of the period used such descriptions as "howling," "pestilential" and "malarious,"[3] and it would be a long time before the place improved.

Seamen of the British Navy, who had worked blockade duty in the Chesapeake in both the Revolutionary War and the War of 1812, were convinced that the tidal basin of the Potomac was infested with noxious mists and unwholesome vapors, fog carrying particles of contagion that caused various deadly fevers, including the dreaded yellow fever or "putrid" fever. Hundreds of seamen in both wars lost their lives, not in battle, but to various malarial fevers that they believed were caused by the mysterious "miasmas" of the area, which could only be borne by American Indians, or by a proportion of the coarse and vulgar colonists who'd grown accustomed to living in such a godforsaken place. By the end of the War of 1812, Admiral Warren ordered all British ships to retire from blockade duty there in late July and August to keep his warships from becoming pesthouses.

The location of the new nation's capital was a source of tremendous partisan and regional bickering. Congress understood that no existing city could hold the title—there was too much regional pride on the one hand and mistrust on the other. New York briefly held the position of capital after the war. A year after Washington's presidential inauguration, the capital was moved back to Philadelphia,

America's most civilized city, and a strong contingent wanted it to remain there.

Article 1, Section 8, of the new Constitution passed in 1789 had empowered Congress:

> To exercise exclusive Legislation in all Cases whatsoever, over such District (not exceeding ten Miles square) as may, by Cession of particular States, and the acceptance of Congress, become the Seat of the Government of the United States . . .

In those days, Virginians thought and spoke of themselves and their state the way many Texans do today. Virginia was the biggest state in the Union, stretching into what is now western Pennsylvania, West Virginia, Ohio, Kentucky, Tennessee, Indiana and Illinois. War or no war, Virginians were Virginians first and Americans second. Three of Virginia's native sons—Washington, Madison and Jefferson—were among the most influential members of the new country's leadership. Surely they trumped the Northerners.

In pre–Civil War America, that kind of citizenship, a feeling for the home state that transcended any feeling for a far distant federal capital, was the norm. America, even in the years before the Revolution, was already dividing itself into Northern and Southern factions, a divide that Washington foresaw as early as 1792, when he cautioned against it in his farewell to his troops. This divide created a continuous tension between the New England states and the South.

Decades before the Confederates fired on Fort Sumter, the New England states made serious threats to secede from the Union over presidential bans on trade with the warring powers of England and France—embargoes that created a great economic hardship in those states. New England depended on trading for its economic health, and the great seagoing cities of that period—New York, Salem, Boston and Newburyport—were the lifeline of the Northern states. Although New Englanders were often accused by Republican Southerners of being far too chummy with England, in fact these stiff-necked Yankees were more concerned with their economic survival than with emotional ties to the mother country. Good relations with Britain meant free trade for all. As trade to the West Indies was cut off, and the military might of Great Britain at sea turned itself to the task of disrupting American shipping, the American Revolution would bankrupt these cities. New Englanders grew convinced early on that if they allowed themselves to be dragged into the ceaseless wars between England and France, they were finished.

Southerners, by contrast, were far more self-reliant and could distance themselves from the ills of Europe. Thomas Jefferson aligned himself emotionally with the French Revolution, but no matter how much innocent blood was spilled in the streets of Paris, being a Southerner he also had a deep isolationist bent and a belief that agriculture was really the only clean and honest way for a man to earn his daily bread, even though his vision of the free, self-sufficient American farmer hardly jibed with the great Southern plantations and their slaves. Yet, in the contentious battle over the location of the nation's capital, Jefferson would make it crystal clear that his Southern sympathies were more important to him than his sometimes unrealistic idealism.

The bickering over the new capital got progressively louder. The North wanted the capital to remain in Philadelphia. New York offered up Albany. New Jersey had a fondness for Trenton. The South preferred present-day Washington's location between Virginia and Maryland.

In the end, the matter was settled over dinner. This private dinner occurred in 1790 between Thomas Jefferson, George Washington's secretary of state, and Alexander Hamilton, the secretary of the treasury. The two men, who were fast becoming bitter enemies, represented the heads of the two political parties that were rapidly forming within the government, despite Washington's disdain for party politics—Hamilton for the Federalists, the party of lawyers and businessmen who wanted a strong federal government and close ties to Great Britain, and Jefferson for the Democratic-Republicans, who favored state's rights, agrarianism and an affinity with France.

Up until his death in his infamous duel with Aaron Burr, Alexander Hamilton was a political thorn in the side of Thomas Jefferson. One of the biggest bones of contention between the two men was the fact that Hamilton, as treasury secretary, wanted a federal bank, the Bank of the United States, which would assume the unpaid Revolutionary War debt held by individuals in the states. Jefferson knew that many of Hamilton's powerful friends had been quietly buying up those "worthless" bonds for pennies on the dollar. If the federal government assumed the debt, they'd make a killing.

Hamilton understood that the chaos that had nearly cost us our victory in the Revolutionary War had been caused in part by the lack of a federal bank. Embittered troops often went months without being paid, which was the province not of the federal government but of the individual states, a cumbersome and ineffectual system.

Jefferson was ideologically opposed to both the bank and the assumption of the debt. Yet, he was willing to yield on such a dearly-held principle for the sake of his Southern identity. And so the bargain was struck. Jefferson would agree to the federal bank, and Hamilton would quiet the voices in his own party who wanted the capital elsewhere. Philadelphia would remain the U.S. capital for the next ten years, pending construction of a new Federal City, which would be in the South.

The issue of the constitutionality of a Bank of the United States would plague American politics for decades to come. It does, however, serve to illuminate the depth of feeling in this line between North and South, that Jefferson was willing to cut loose one of his most cherished principles in order to have the nation's capital remain in the South.

Today, people don't really think of Washington as a "Southern" city, apart from the lovers of history. John F. Kennedy once famously quipped that Washington had all the charm of the North and all the efficiency of the South. It was a comment that would have gotten an even bigger laugh from an audience if he'd made it a century and a half before.

The wilderness that would become Washington, D.C.

In 1791, Hamilton would get his Bank of the United States. And on July 16, 1790, Congress passed the Residence Act, which allowed George Washington to pick a spot along the Potomac and select a ten-square-mile piece of property. Washington had always been something of a reluctant public servant, and if he *had* to be president, it made sense for him to choose a spot close to Mount Vernon. He was familiar with the Potomac River, and believed it could be made navigable with some work.[4] The spot he found to his liking was at the confluence of the Potomac, its eastern branch (now called the Anacostia River), and the Tiber Creek, named after the Tiber River upon whose banks ancient Rome had risen. A year later, a commission named the area the Territory of Columbia and the city itself the City of Washington. The Residence Act started the clock running on the compromise with the South: Congress agreed that the seat of government would officially be moved to the new location in just ten years.

Ten years is a short time to stake out a huge piece of property in the boondocks, clear new roads, drain swamps and, while you're at it, build a national capital from scratch, especially with a government that was still putting the finishing touches on a way to finance itself. The territorial commission and the president would need to move fast and make quick decisions that would affect the city forever. George Washington needed people he knew could work under pressure.

Andrew Ellicott, one of the most respected civil engineers in America, was a friend of both Washington and Franklin, although he was not a Freemason. Washington had entreated him to make accurate surveys of northern Pennsylvania and Lake Erie and set the borders of New York, Pennsylvania and Virginia. In later life, Ellicott went on to other government assignments to determine treaty and state boundaries. He extended the Mason-Dixon line westward from the border between Pennsylvania and Maryland, and it is a testimony to his accuracy that virtually every boundary he surveyed—from Canada in the north to Florida in the south and westward to the Mississippi—remained unchanged, and is today where he placed it. In later years, he trained Meriwether Lewis in the art of wilderness surveying before the expedition to explore the Louisiana Purchase, so that an accurate map of the journey could be re-created. But it was earlier, in 1790, that Ellicott undertook the job for which he is most remembered. He was placed in charge of surveying the property that would become Washington, D.C.

Joining him in the project were his brother Joseph and 60-year-old Benjamin Bannaker, a self-trained African-American mathematician from Ellicott's hometown of Ellicott's Mills, Maryland. Bannaker's grandmother, a freed white indentured servant from England, had purchased, freed and subsequently married a black slave named Banna Ka. His mother Mary, born free, had followed a similar path and married a former slave named Roger, who had bought his own freedom. A fascinating man, Bannaker built the first pocket watch in America—a wooden one, no less. He would later use his mathematical abilities in astronomical calculations to create a series of almanacs, which were important to a wide range of people in the period. Everyone from farmers and fishermen to surveyors and architects needed accurate ways to chart the months, track the position of the sun, predict the times of the ocean tides, and have at least some idea of what the weather might be like from one month to the next.

This is very important to understand because some authors have claimed that the designers of the Federal City had a somehow unusual or occult interest in the study of astronomy and the zodiac. In these days of Global Positioning Systems and laser-guided surveying equipment, we tend to forget that accurate surveying in the eighteenth century required a thorough understanding of astronomy. The civil engineer in the wilderness, like a navigator at sea, used a sextant. He needed to know precise positions of the sun on any given day of the year, plus the ability to reckon by the stars to determine latitude. Longitude was calculated by the accurate recording of time and the distance from a known meridian. It was a highly complex job to determine locations within a few feet in either direction. The interest in astronomy of the Ellicotts and Bannaker was shared by George Washington, who was also trained in astronomy and the art of surveying. Their interest in the stars was scarcely occult.

Both David Ovason in *The Secret Architecture of Our Nation's Capital* and Robert Lomas in *Turning the Solomon Key* try to make the connection that the study of star charts, and the ability to read them or to create them, is a *quid pro quo* that proves the casting of horoscopes with zodiacal charts was used to infuse the design of Washington, D.C., with special astrological symbolism, or in Lomas's case, special "powers." This is sheer fantasy, and given that it has become fodder for a whole brand of conspiracy theorists and fundamentalist witch hunters, it is irresponsible as well. Worse, such nonsense has been a tin can tied to the tail of the Freemasons, with wild speculations that "all of the designers" of Washington, D.C., were Masons, and implying some sort of astrology-based occult influence.

The hoary theories of so-called Masonic influence on the street layout of Washington, D.C., are filled with countless fantastic conjectures that serve no logical—or even illogical—purpose. Washington was a Mason, but the Ellicott brothers, Bannaker and Thomas Jefferson were not. Neither was the man whose initial design became the basis for all that followed. More to the point, seeing patterns in the map of Washington is little more than a colossal Rorschach test.

L'Enfant Terrible and the Plan

Pierre Charles L'Enfant was born in Paris in 1754, and after studying art under the tutelage of his father at the Royal Academy of Painting and Sculpture in Paris, he came to America with General Lafayette in 1775 as a military engineer. Wounded at Savannah in 1779, he recovered and became part of Washington's staff for the rest of the war.

Although much is made of L'Enfant being a Frenchman, he became an American citizen after the war and thereafter dropped Pierre in favor of the more American name Peter. He settled in New York, where he became known as a city planner and architect. He was commissioned to redesign and enlarge what would later be called Federal Hall in New York, where George Washington's first inauguration was held.[5]

Based upon his wartime relationship with Washington and his work in New York, L'Enfant was granted the commission to design the new Federal City in 1791. As a military engineer, L'Enfant understood how to work under pressure. But this was something altogether different. The city would last forever, so its first foundations, hurried or not, had to be right from the start. The topography of the land provided him with the locations of the two most prominent buildings of his plan. The Congress House and the Presidential Palace would sit on two hilltops within sight of each other, connected by a broad boulevard named Pennsylvania Avenue, after the cradle of American independence.

The records of the time note the name of the hill where L'Enfant located the Congress House as Jenkins Heights. Tiber Creek ran through it in those days, and L'Enfant envisioned carving a canal out of the creek and using its waters in an enormous landscaped waterfall. Echoing the origins of Tiber Creek's name, the land surrounding Jenkins Heights was called Rome. It would have seemed

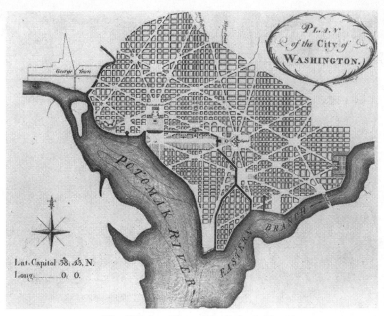

The L'Enfant Plan of the Federal City.

almost providential, if all of that Roman imagery hadn't been attached to the property as a bit of humor by former owner Francis Pope, who liked to call himself "Pope of Rome on the Tiber."[6]

Extending to the west of the Congress House and to the south of the Presidential Palace would be two wide "Grand Avenues" (known today as the National Mall), inspired by the palace at Versailles outside of Paris. They were to be lined by theaters, museums, galleries and foreign ministries. Where they intersected, an enormous equestrian statue of George Washington, the nation's hero and the city's namesake, would stand. Both Congress and the president would have a direct line of sight to his image from which to gain inspiration.

Curiously, the importance of the Supreme Court had not yet been established at this early stage. Its role would be strengthened in the coming years by Chief Justice and Freemason John Marshall. L'Enfant did not give the court a location of its own, illustrative of the ambiguity of the early Court's position in the fledgling government.[7] It was assumed from his notes that he meant it to occupy what is today known as Judiciary Square, but it was not important enough to include on the preliminary plans.

For the rest of the city, what L'Enfant envisioned was a logical grid pattern. It was increasingly common in planned American cities like New York and Savannah because it made the lots simple to package and market to real estate investors. Over the grid was laid a series of broad, diagonal tree-lined avenues, and where they intersected would be great circles, some with fountains, named for famous Americans. There would also be fifteen squares named for the fifteen states that existed in 1791.

L'Enfant epitomized the temperamental artist. He had a vision but did not always work well with others. Thomas Jefferson was something of a constant pest, passing along maps and sketches of ideas from European and ancient Greek and Roman sources. Then there were the three city commissioners. L'Enfant believed he was only answerable to George Washington, who had hired him in the first place. But the commissioners wanted to see the work in progress, and he refused even when they needed a map to begin auctioning property. There were some ten thousand lots available, and the commissioners had high hopes of selling a large number of them to raise money for construction of principal public buildings. It was not an auspicious beginning. They managed to sell just thirty-five at the first auction in October 1791.

L'Enfant had been opposed to the land auction scheme from the beginning. He had wanted the city to take shape, with the federal buildings and grand boulevards in place, before attempting to interest land speculators. Unfortunately, the reality was that there was no financing in place to build the city that was supposed to be ready for the federal government in just ten years.

Worse, L'Enfant discovered that an influential landowner in the area had started construction of a large mansion that intruded on his plan for New Jersey Avenue. Property lines had not yet been finalized, and the roads had not yet been surveyed or even approved yet, but that didn't stop L'Enfant. He had the house demolished—with explosives, according to some accounts. Unfortunately for him, the influential landowner was City Commissioner Daniel Carroll's nephew, whose farmland had made up a large portion of the real estate ceded by Maryland to become the Federal City. A little over a year after being hired, the hotheaded Frenchman was sacked by the exasperated president, who had grown sick of the complaints from all sides.

Enraged by his treatment, L'Enfant sent a bill to Congress for $95,500 for his services. Congress had a different figure in mind and paid him a mere $3,800. In later years, L'Enfant continued to petition Congress for the remainder of his bill, and they continued to ignore him. He became a strange figure in later years, roaming the streets of the capital, proclaiming that the changes made to his design had ruined the city and that the whole thing should have been plowed under and planted with tobacco. He died penniless in 1825.

Nevertheless, the design of Washington, D.C., is almost always referred to as the L'Enfant Plan. But it was actually left up to Andrew Ellicott to create a workable city from L'Enfant's drawings and notes. In fact, Ellicott arguably improved on his predecessor's design because he had a greater understanding of the area's real topography.

The President's House

An impatient Congress pressed for construction to start, so a contest was held to award the design of the President's House and the Congress House. A young architect named James Hoban won the competition over eight other entries, including one submitted anonymously by Thomas Jefferson.[8] Washington himself had recoiled at L'Enfant's designation of a "Presidential Palace," so it took on the less ostentatious name of the "President's House." (It wouldn't get the name White House until it was burned by the British in 1814 and was whitewashed to cover the scars of the fire.) Hoban based his design on Leinster House, a palace in Dublin, Ireland, but George Washington took great interest in the details and decor of the building.[9]

In fact, Washington is said to have surveyed the property and laid out the boundary stakes for the building himself.[10]

The Masonic connection between the White House, its Irish inspiration and the Freemasons is a curious one. Built in 1745, Leinster House was originally the Dublin residence of the 20th Earl of Kildare, James Fitzgerald. The earl had married well, and in 1755 King George III awarded him the title of Duke of Leinster. The duke was also the founding Grand Master of the Grand Lodge of Ireland. Curiously, there is a legend that the Knights Templar had been asked in 1204 to organize banking houses in Dublin from their commandery at Templemore on Ireland's southern coast. They had been invited by James Fitzgerald's ancestor, Maurice Fitz-Gerald.[11]

On Saturday, October 13, 1792, a procession of Masons formed at the Fountain Inn in Georgetown and marched to the site of the excavated foundation of the new President's House in the Federal City. Oddly enough, it was 485 years to the day after King Phillip IV had the Knights Templar arrested simultaneously all over France, beginning the excommunication and dissolution of the Templar order.

The barest outlines of roads were still being cleared through the dense forest when the Freemasons laid the cornerstone of the first federal building in town without much public fanfare. Hoban, himself an Irish Catholic and a member of Georgetown Lodge No. 9, took part in the ceremonial laying of the cornerstone. He became the founding Master of Federal Lodge No. 15 the following year.[12]

The cornerstone of the President's House was placed in the southwest corner of the foundation. The traditional Masonic ceremony was presided over by Maryland Lodge No. 9's Master, Peter Casanave.[13] A brass plate placed under the stone read:

> "This first stone of the President's House was laid the 12th day of October 1792, and in the 17th Year of the Independence of the United States of America."

George Washington, President
Thomas Johnson,
Doctor Stewart,
Daniel Carroll, Commissioners
James Hoban, Architect
Collen Williamson, Master Mason
Vivat Republica.

Hoban would work in the Federal City for another forty years. When the British burned the President's House in 1814, he assisted in its reconstruction. He went on to establish the first Catholic church in the city—St. Patrick's, in 1792—and in 1820 he served on the committee to erect St. Peter's Church on Capitol Hill. It was a curious dichotomy, since Pope Clement XII had issued an encyclical in 1738 threatening Catholics who became Masons with excommunication.

Washington himself was not present at the cornerstone ceremony, nor did he ever live in the house. John and Abigail Adams were the first "First Couple" to inhabit the President's House. They lived there for only four months before Thomas Jefferson took office.

The White House has seen many additions and remodelings over the last two centuries. When Thomas Jefferson moved in, he was still jealous over his own design being snubbed by the original committee, so he sent Hoban packing to another office across town and brought in his own favored architect, Freemason Benjamin Latrobe, to make changes. Latrobe altered the interior, including the addition of a wine cellar, and planned the addition of the north and south porticos. After the building was burned by British troops in 1814, it was Hoban who supervised its reconstruction, complete with Jefferson's changes.

The most radical remodeling began in 1948 under Harry Truman. The house was literally declared unsafe to inhabit as the supporting wooden structure had severely deteriorated. Everything inside of the White House was gutted, a deep basement was dug, and a steel supporting structure was erected inside of the existing exterior walls. The old place looked the same on the outside, but it was an all-new building on the inside. Former resident Eleanor Roosevelt was unimpressed. She sniffed that the new rooms looked like a Sheraton Hotel.[14]

When the crews excavated the basement and old foundation, they discovered the original cornerstone laid by the Freemasons more than 150 years before. The stone and brass plate were kept undisturbed. Harry Truman was a Freemason and a Past Grand Master of Missouri. He was also a 33° member of the Scottish Rite and the 33rd president of the United States. He was told that foundation stones had been found with "mason's marks," small inscriptions that acted as signatures of the workmen who had carved the stones when the building had been constructed. Such inscriptions play a symbolic role in the York Rite's Royal Arch degree, the Mark Master. So, Truman sent pieces of the stones to all Grand Lodges in the U.S.

The Congress House

With the President's House underway, it was time to get to work on Congress's new home. L'Enfant was supposed to have designed the building, but he coyly claimed he had it all figured out—in his head. Whether or not that was true, it went with him when Washington sacked him. Like the President's House, a contest was held in 1792 to choose the designer. Most of the designs were based on Renaissance architectural forms, but the committee was unimpressed, largely because they looked too reminiscent of the existing monarchial buildings of Europe. Every one of the seventeen proposals was rejected.

A last-minute design was entered by Dr. William Thornton, a fascinating man who was born in Tortola in the British West Indies and was raised by Quakers in England. He was trained as a physician in Scotland, but it was rare that he actually practiced his profession. Instead, he dabbled as an inventor, a painter and an architect. His proposal for the Congress House was accepted by the committee and President Washington for its "grandeur, simplicity and convenience."

Thomas Jefferson couldn't have been happier. He favored classical Greek and Roman styles, and he was also wild about domes. Thornton's original plan featured a large domed auditorium of considerably lower profile than the one that exists today. It was also a much smaller building, though still impressive. It is easy to forget that, at the time, it needed to house the senators, representatives and assorted sundry bureaucrats, lobbyists and other ne'er-do-wells from a mere fifteen states.

While the cornerstone ceremony for the White House had been hastily organized and performed with little fanfare, the city commissioners decided that the Congress House needed a bigger kickoff ceremony. On Wednesday, September 18, 1793, President Washington

The Masonic procession to the site of the Capitol, September 18, 1793.

crossed the Potomac and was escorted to the construction site of the President's House by members of Maryland's Lodge No. 9 and Virginia's Alexandria Lodge No. 22. There they were joined by the members of James Hoban's Federal Lodge No. 15, which had just received its charter from Grand Lodge six days before. The assembled Masons then marched "in the greatest solemn dignity, with music playing, drums beating, colors flying and spectators rejoicing," down the barely cleared road that would be Pennsylvania Avenue to the little hilltop clearing that would become the symbolic center of the Federal City and the nation.[15]

A trench had been dug for the foundation, and the group took their place at the southeast corner of what would be the North Wing of the Capitol. Brother Clotworthy Stephenson, Grand Marshal, presented a silver plate to the commissioners. It read:

> "This South East corner Stone, of the Capitol of the United States of America in the City of Washington, was laid on the 18th day of September 1793, in the thirteenth year of American Independence, in the first year of the second term of the Presidency of George Washington, whose virtues in the civil administration of his country have been as conspicuous and beneficial, as his Military valor and prudence have been useful in establishing her liberties, and in the year of Masonry 5793, by the Grand Lodge of Maryland, several Lodges under its jurisdiction, and Lodge No. 22, from Alexandria, Virginia."

Thomas Johnson,
David Stuart,
Daniel Carroll, Commissioners.
Joseph Clark, R.W.G.M.—P.T.[16]
James Hoban,
Stephen Hallate, Architects
Collen Williamson, Master Mason[17]

After the reading of the inscription, the cornerstone was made ready. President Washington, the Grand Master *pro tempore* Joseph Clark of Maryland, and the three attending Masters of the lodges present—Elisha Cullen Dick of Alexandria No. 22, Valentine Reintzel of Maryland Lodge No. 9, and James Hoban of Federal Lodge No. 15—took the plate and stepped down into the trench. A beautiful silver trowel and marble gavel had been crafted especially for the occasion by Brother John Duffey, a silversmith in Alexandria who was a member of the president's home lodge, Fredericksburg Lodge No. 4. The trowel had a silver blade, a silver shank and an ivory handle with a silver cap. Brother Duffey had also crafted Masonic working tools of walnut for use in the ceremony. Using the same ritual as the first boundary stone in Alexandria, the stone was ceremonially checked with the plumb, square and level. Washington placed the plate on the cornerstone, and it was consecrated in the Masonic tradition with corn, wine and oil. The silver trowel was used to spread a small amount of cement, and the marble gavel to symbolically tap the stone into place.

Non-Masons may be especially curious about the date on the cornerstone's plate—5793. One of the more confounding Masonic customs has to do with the way they date their documents. The Gregorian calendar was standardized by Pope Gregory XIII in 1582, though the non-Catholic Western world took another 200 years before they went along with the pope's idea. Since 1776, most of the world has been on the same calendar page, though Greece and Russia didn't adopt it until after World War I. Because Western Europe and America switched to the Gregorian calendar in the mid-1700s, conflicting ages are attributed to some of the notable figures of the period. Because of the confusion during the changeover, they themselves weren't always sure of their real age.

In 1658, Bishop James Ussher in Ireland believed he had determined the *exact* date of the creation of the world. Using the biblical account along with a comparison of Middle Eastern histories, Hebrew genealogy and other known events, he determined that the Earth was created on Sunday, October 23, 4004 B.C. At about the same time, John Lightfoot, vice chancellor of Cambridge University, went on to clarify that the Creation actually happened at about 9 a.m.

Ussher called his calendar *Anno Mundi*, the Year of the World. By 1700, Ussher and Lightfoot's calculations of the date and time of the Creation were accepted as fact by most Christian denominations. Beginning in 1701, new editions of the King James Bible clearly stated it right up front.

Because Ussher's Creation date was so strongly believed at the time of modern Freemasonry's origin, the Masons began dating their documents using 4004 B.C. as their beginning year . . . sort of. 4004 was an inconvenient number to remember, so Masons simply took the current year and added 4,000 to it. So, A.D. 1793 became 5793 *Anno Lucis*, or A.L., and A.D. 2007 would be 6007 A.L. *Anno Lucis* means "year of light" in Latin. Masons called it that to coincide with the Genesis passage, "And God said, 'Let there be light'; and there was light." They did this early on to lend their fraternity an air of great and solemn antiquity. If they dated their documents as being 5717 years old, they'd certainly sound more respectable and impressive than some newly formed London drinking club. Today, you will often see two dates on Masonic cornerstones—both A.D. and A.L.

Scriptures of a National Religion

James Madison had written in *Federalist No. 37*:

> It is impossible for the man of pious reflection not to perceive in it a finger of that Almighty hand which has been so frequently and signally extended to our relief in the critical stages of the revolution.[18]

In the old empires, kings, popes and archbishops ruled by divine right. God had clearly decreed that they sit on thrones, or they wouldn't have gotten the big chair with the purple cushion. But the United States would reinterpret the way that Almighty hand would influence government. Instead of God spreading his bounty on the people through the hands of a king or pope, the founders believed that God spread his beneficence directly on mankind, and it was the people's right to choose who would rule them.

This was not seen as a positive development by those selfsame kings and popes, of course. In 1884, Pope Leo XIII issued an encyclical against the Freemasons called *Humanum Genus* (Latin for "human race"). In it, he outlined the Church's position against what he called "naturalists" and the Masons.

> Then come their doctrines of politics, in which the naturalists lay down that all men have the same right, and are in every respect of equal and like condition; that each one is naturally free; that no one has the right to command another; that it is an act of violence to require men to obey any authority other than that which is obtained from themselves. According to this, therefore, all things belong to the free people; power is held by the command or permission of the people, so that, when the popular will changes, rulers may lawfully be deposed and the source of all rights and civil duties is either in the multitude or in the governing authority when this is constituted according to the latest doctrines. It is held also that the State should be without God; that in the various forms of religion there is no reason why one should have precedence of another; and that they are all to occupy the same place.[19]

Pope Leo XIII was looking back nervously on more than a century of revolutions around the world where countries and colonies cast off their kings and patterned new governments on the example they had seen in America. The pope believed that Freemasonry, not the human desire for freedom, had deprived God's handpicked sovereigns on Earth of their divine right to rule.

One of the most common modern notions about the founders is that they were overwhelmingly Deistic, and there is a sense today that the First Amendment guarantee of freedom of religion was somehow supposed to mean freedom *from* religion. Yet, once Congress took up residence in the new Capitol Building, a "variety of persons were allowed to preach in the House of Representatives." Sir Augustus Foster, secretary of the British Legation during Thomas Jefferson's term of office, sounded slightly aghast:

Though the regular Chaplain was a Presbyterian, sometimes a Methodist, a Minister of the Church of England, or a Quaker and sometimes even a woman took the Speaker's chair . . .[20]

The L'Enfant plan of the Federal City included a prominent place for a great church "intended for national purposes, such as public prayer, thanksgiving, funeral orations, etc., and assigned to the special use of no particular Sect or denomination, but equally open to all." It was to be at the intersection of 8th Street and Pennsylvania Avenue, between Congress and the President's House, where both could derive spiritual inspiration from it.

The great church of L'Enfant's plan was never constructed, at least not where he wanted it. The National Cathedral was not begun until 1907 and took nearly a century to construct. In spite of the government support that its name might imply, it is an Episcopal church, built with private donations. Its official name is the Cathedral Church of Saint Peter and Saint Paul, and it sits on Mount Alban, one of the highest spots in the northwest area of the District of Columbia. Built in the Gothic style, it has been the location for state funerals like that of Ronald Reagan's, as well as places of national

The National Cathedral.

mourning, such as the prayer service after the 9/11 attacks. It is without question a cathedral every bit as impressive, majestic and inspirational as the great cathedrals of Europe it is patterned after, and it continues to serve the sort of purpose that L'Enfant envisioned. It has even become the final resting place for Americans as diverse as Woodrow Wilson and Helen Keller, among more than 150 others.

No such place would be complete without an obligatory statue of George Washington, and in the National Cathedral it represents the completion of a full circle of Freemasonry, government and the sacred art of cathedral building. Washington stands dressed in a long coat—his Sunday best—respectfully holding his hat in his hand. On the wall behind the president are medallions depicting symbols of Freemasonry—a gavel, a square and a compass—and the morning sun bathes the scene in the dazzling colors of red and blue from the stained-glass windows nearby.

Trial by Fire

All things having been done that could be done, the federal government packed up, bid a wistful farewell to the genteel comforts of Philadelphia, and, on November 17, 1800, began moving into the bare governmental buildings along the muddy, unpaved streets of Washington City.

From the beginning, senators and congressmen were encouraged to bring their wives and families to the new capital, since everyone realized that where women and children went, civilization followed. But the city's cheap congressional row housing, thrown up by land speculators and government cronies, was so overcrowded and shabby that it was more typical for a legislator to leave his wife safely and comfortably at home. Besides, if home was a working farm or plantation, the wife needed to remain and oversee the day-to-day operations.

Of course, there were women in Washington—some wives, widows who ran boarding houses, pretty young daughters of some of the local businessmen. But for the most part it was a city filled with a very large contingent of sweaty, grumpy, lonely men who simply wanted to fulfill their obligations to the nation and then go home as quickly as possible.

Despite the mythic aspects of the new city, the weighty cornerstone ceremonies, the lofty ideology of the Baconian New Atlantis made a shining reality, there was no love lost between the city of Washington and the politicians who had to live there. In fact, by 1804, there's no denying that the nation's new capital was pretty much an unqualified flop and the butt of jokes by every humorist in America.

The situation is perhaps best summed up by historian Thomas Fleming in *Duel,* his terrific history of Hamilton and Burr:

> In the first years of Thomas Jefferson's administration, the politicians discovered that Washington, D.C., not only failed to attract land buyers and businessmen, it had a special appeal for the mentally ill, the criminal, the indigent, and the lazy; people who thought Napoleon or General Hamilton was persecuting them; who wanted pardons, reprieves, or pensions; or who connected the pursuit of happiness to a government job. In 1802, only 233 males in the local population of 4,000 [the legislators being considered "transients"] had more than $100 in cash or property to their names. Welfare, called Poor Relief in 1803, consumed 42 percent of the district's revenue. A census could only find 15 "gentlemen" in the whole city.[21]

Fleming goes on to quote one visitor having said, "Strangers, after viewing the edifices of state, are apt to enquire for the city, while they are in its very centre." The nonexistent city center was such a godawful swamp that, in that same year, a group of congressmen returning from a dinner party got lost and spent the entire night in their carriage because they couldn't find their own boarding house through all the bogs and gullies. The situation was no better a decade later, and only God could help the carriage driver who tried to maneuver the "streets" of the city in a downpour.

The turnaround in Washington's status did not come gradually. It arrived like the sudden jolt of an earthquake on the night of

August 24, 1814. Two years earlier, President Madison declared war on Great Britain over an issue that still resonates in our own age of terrorism: A nation that cannot protect its citizens outside of its borders is a nation without sovereignty. Madison's declaration of war required an almost comical level of chutzpah, although no one was laughing at the time. For over ten years, during most of which Great Britain had been at war with France, British warships routinely harassed American merchant shipping, holding vessels under the gun, searching for "contraband" (meaning anything Americans might be trading with France) and shanghaiing American seamen from their own ships, then forcing them to toil on the badly undermanned British warships, a brazenly criminal act of kidnapping that the British government referred to as "impressment." According to English law, a British citizen had no right to give up his citizenship, so any American seaman with a British accent was fair game to be snatched, flogged or even hanged, despite being an American citizen.

For two years the war dragged on, fought mostly at sea since it was a war over trade. America's worst defeats occurred in Canada and the West. Her greatest victories occurred at sea, under the command of the tactically brilliant and courageous young officers who formed the core of the fledgling United States Navy.

But in the dangerous summer of 1814, the war stopped dragging its feet. In April of that year, Napoleon was driven back to Paris by the victorious Allies. Wellington was in control of the French nation. Thousands of British soldiers, battle-hardened veterans of fifteen years of Continental warfare, could now be shipped across the Atlantic to America. Britain's navy, the most powerful in the world, was also free of the tedious blockade duty along the French coast that had taken up its time and resources. No matter the courage of the officers, no matter the superior design of the Yankee frigates, America was about to be overrun by the full military might of a very tired and testy Great Britain.

In a foul temper over American defiance, a petulant King George sent a massive, three-pronged attack across the Atlantic to take back his former colonies. A force under the combined leadership of Rear Admiral George Cockburn and Major General Robert Ross would head straight for the Chesapeake with a powerful fleet of warships under the command of the colorful British naval hero, Admiral Alexander Forrester Cochrane.

America came dangerously close to losing the War of 1812. Cockburn and Ross, their appetite whetted by their victorious rout of the Americans at the Battle of Bladensburg on the afternoon of August 24, 1814, brazenly ignored their orders to avoid going too far inland and headed for Washington, D.C. Finding the city practically deserted and the government on the run, the gentlemanly Ross was overruled and overwhelmed by the personality of the vengeful Cockburn. For two years in the Chesapeake, his weapon of choice had been the torch. On this night he used it as never before, trooping into every government building, piling flammable furniture and draperies in the center of the room, then firing Congreve rockets into the pile, setting the building ablaze with dispatch and efficiency. Adding to the inferno, the American military had sent out demolition teams all along the Eastern Branch, from the Navy Yard to the fort at Greenleaf Point, to blow up their own considerable supply of powder and arms there, to keep them from falling into the hands of British troops. The explosions could be heard for miles around, while the glow of the sky over Washington could be seen as far away as Baltimore, thirty miles distant.

Not satisfied with mere victory, Cockburn also took every opportunity on that night to mock the government, the president, the Congress and any other symbol of American freedom in sight.

The city of Washington would endure not only the hand of man but of God as well. Late into the next day, the fires were at last extinguished by a violent storm that swept in off the Atlantic. It continued through the night, and most of the burned buildings left standing would collapse under hurricane-force winds.

This night of humiliation and destruction would mark a new beginning for the United States. After the evacuation of the British troops, the fire and the storm, the dazed residents of the ruined capital knew that never again would anyone suggest abandoning the city of Washington. From that night, and for all time to come, it would be the nation's capital, pigs or no pigs, swamps or no swamps. Inadvertently, the British had given America her rallying point.

In one of the most colorful events of that remarkable two days, the Patent Office of the United States was saved from the flames by one of the city's most eccentric characters, Dr. William Thornton, curator of the Patent Office and the original designer of Congress House. Dr. Thornton's was one of the few level heads in the city after the withdrawal of the British troops; he took charge to prevent looting, setting guards to what was left of the government buildings and overseeing the wounded, both British and American.

Thornton, a product of the Age of Enlightenment, was a gentleman of many talents and interests, from poetry to taxidermy. All new inventions fascinated him. Throughout the chaotic day of the 24th, he supervised the removal of important documents before fleeing the city with the rest of the government, disheartened and worried that he'd had no time to remove the various patent models in the building. Hearing that the British were burning the public buildings, he returned to the city at daybreak hoping to retrieve a model for a new type of violin he was constructing.

He arrived just in time to find one Major Waters in the act of setting fire to the Patent Office. Brazenly he approached the major like a dachshund treeing a bear and asked for permission to enter the building to retrieve the violin. It was granted, raising his hopes that he had found a like spirit, so he proceeded to reason with the major in the most powerful of Enlightenment terms. He pleaded that the major was welcome to any public items in the building. In fact, Thornton would personally haul them out to the street and set them on fire. But the models inside the patent office were private property, and intellectual property at that. Any soldier in wartime might well have the right to destroy a building, but no man had the right to destroy an idea, certainly not one that could benefit not only America but the whole of Mankind. It was a sin as grave as the burning of the Great Library at Alexandria, one for which posterity would surely condemn them.

Deeply moved, Major Waters turned helplessly to his immediate superior Major Jones, who listened to the entire oration once again, then gave his permission for the Patent Building to be spared. At this moment in time, when the Enlightenment was coming to a close and the Romantic Age was at hand, it was surely an argument containing the best of both worlds, this plea for the sanctity of an idea.

A new Patent Office would be built in 1836, not far from where L'Enfant had wanted to build his national church. The third public building to be erected in Washington, it was designed by Freemason Robert Mills. The new nation erected on the superstructure of the Enlightenment had been born of science and reason. No better place could have been chosen as a new kind of temple than the building that housed the ideas and inventions of its citizens.

American Scriptures

In his book *Myths in Stone*, Jeffrey Meyer makes an argument for a different temple of the new nation's religion, just a block away.[22] America claimed no "divine right" to exist. It had not descended from an ageless past of conquerors, nor could it trace its creation to heroic mythology like Rome's Romulus and Remus. America's founding was not based on myth and legends. It was based on legal documents written not by the finger of God but by men. The actual parchments of the Declaration of Independence and the U.S. Constitution became the holy relics of the United States, like splinters of the true cross or the finger bones of St. Jerome. Today the documents are enshrined in as beautiful and reverent surroundings as any ancient temple or Gothic cathedral—the National Archives. A visit to the archives is supposed to inspire reverence and awe. There's more than just a hint of the Vatican's Basilica of St. Peter about the place. The viewing room's designer, Francis H. Bacon, clearly viewed the founding documents as "American scriptures."

Known today as the Rotunda for The Charters of Freedom, the room is like a shrine or a temple. Its architectural details can hold a surprise or two for Freemasons. The room is entered through two massive bronze doors that leave no doubt the treasures within are well protected. Beneath the domed ceiling, the visitor finds the documents displayed within an altar that resembles the Ark of the Covenant

The National Archives Rotunda, before its 2006 remodeling.

in Solomon's Temple. Flanking this Ark stand two columns reminiscent of the columns of the porch of Solomon's Temple, Jachin and Boaz, which represented "strength" and "establishment" in ancient times. Until its more wheelchair-friendly redesign in 2006, the altar itself stood on top of three symbolic steps, much like the three steps in the East of a Masonic lodge.

CHAPTER 7

The Mysterious Map of Washington, D.C.

✦✦✦

> The United States of America was chosen to lead the world into this kingdom of Antichrist from the beginning. The capital is Washington, D.C.
>
> In 1791, Pierre Charles L'Enfante[sic] (the designer, who was a Freemason), laid out Governmental Center of Washington, D.C., he planned more than just streets, roads, and buildings. He hid certain occultic magical symbols in the layout of U.S. Governmental Center. When these symbols are united they become one large Luciferic, or occultic, symbol. The upper four points of the Goathead represent the four elements of the world, Fire, Water, Earth, and Air. The bottom fifth point represents the spirit of Lucifer. All of which are represented in Washington, D.C. (The United States Capital) ... It demonstrates, beyond a shadow of a doubt, that our leadership has knowingly and consistently been pursuing a hidden agenda which, when fully carried out, will mean the destruction of our nation (the U.S.) as we know it today and the beginning of the Biblical Great Tribulation. Our leaders are currently calling this system the New World Order.
>
> —QUOTED VERBATIM FROM THE
> FREEMASONRY WATCH WEBSITE[1]

This paranoid view of American Freemasonry all started with one seemingly innocuous paragraph. In their 1989 book *The Temple and the Lodge*, Michael Baigent and Richard Leigh tell a fascinating story of the Knights Templar and the possibility that modern Freemasonry descended from them. On the last page of the last chapter, they write:

> Subsequently, the Capitol and the White House were each to become focal points of an elaborate geometry governing the layout of the nation's capital city. This geometry, originally devised by an architect named Pierre l'Enfant, was subsequently modified by Washington and Jefferson so as to produce specifically octagonal patterns incorporating the particular cross used as a device by Masonic Templars.[2]

Suddenly the world of esoteric researchers and conspiracy lovers alike began gazing into the geometric patterns of the map of Washington, D.C., in search of sinister or occult patterns. Soon people were "seeing" not just benign-looking octagons but Satanic pentagrams, devilish goat heads, Masonic squares and compasses, Jewish Stars of David, Baal, Moloch and pagan horned owls. Where once the world had seen a Baroque plan of broad, radial avenues, ceremonial spaces and respectful use of existing topography, they now saw only a Freemason plot—a Federal City designed to boast of the influence of its secret Masonic masters.

Unfortunately for all of these deep-thinking hysterics, Freemasons do not worship, venerate or otherwise prostrate themselves to symbols. On the contrary, Freemasonry celebrates reason, science, learning and freedom from superstition. But such trivial details never kept a good conspiracy theory down.

David Ovason's book, *The Secret Architecture of Our Nation's Capital*, was first published in 1999 under the title *The Secret Zodiacs of Washington D.C.: Was the City of Stars Planned by Masons?* In both cases, the title and packaging imply that there's something "secret" or even creepy about the building of Washington—and that the Masons must have put it there.

Ovason was not a Freemason when he wrote his book. He had not experienced its ritual ceremonies, nor had he seen or read most of the rituals of the York or Scottish Rite, the so-called "higher" degrees offered by Masonry's appendant organizations. So exactly how he developed his principal theory—that the Federal City was designed around or consecrated to the constellation of Virgo, and that Freemasons had some overt or covert connection to Virgo—is an enigma.

Ovason also spills an inordinate amount of ink obsessing over the many zodiac symbols that allegedly appear all around the city. He asserts that the multitude of Freemasons who designed the city consulted horoscopes before picking portentous dates for the laying of cornerstones and tries to make a case that Freemasons are bound inextricably with astrology. He asserts that "Freemasons" Pierre L'Enfant and Andrew Ellicott designed Pennsylvania Avenue in alignment with the setting sun's position on August 10, as seen over the White House from the steps of the Capitol Building, because the constellation of Virgo aligns to that position. Every breathless turn of the page feels as though it is rushing headlong into a revelation that will somehow change the world as we know it: ". . . this stellar maiden (Virgo) is the zodiacal ruler of Washington, D.C. . . ."[3]

There's just one problem. . . . Well, actually there are several problems, but the biggest one is that the ceremonies of Freemasonry don't involve Virgo or any other constellation. They never have. There is no astrological reference to the zodiac anywhere in Masonic ritual. Virgo, the ancient Roman goddess, isn't there, either. Unless they have been thoroughly educated in the Classics, most Masons can't remember the last time they heard of the goddess Virgo and couldn't spot her in the Milky Way on a bet. In fact, Ovason himself admits, "The zodiac appears in Masonic symbolism with surprising infrequency."[4] (Or how about not at all?) The "secret" content of Masonic rituals has been available to the public for three hundred years, but apparently Ovason had not read any of it before advancing his thesis.

The city map of Washington, D.C., designed by Pierre L'Enfant and Andrew Ellicott, is a true work of mathematical art. Anyone who has visited a very old European city knows what the new city planners were rebelling against. In his own diaries and exchanges with the bitter and embattled L'Enfant, as well as with Thomas Jefferson, Washington made it clear that he cared little about the arrangement of streets, squares and roundabouts. Washington was interested solely in the placement of the Capitol Building and the "President's House" because of their symbolic juxtaposition, each on a hill overlooking the city. A broad, panoramic street, Pennsylvania Avenue, connected them so that the Congress and the president could symbolically watch what each other were up to, while both looked out over the city.

L'Enfant and Ellicott were not Masons, so designing any sort of Masonic symbolism into the street plans of the city would have been a neat trick for them. Ovason claims L'Enfant was a Mason but admits in an endnote[5] that his alleged source material was a previously "unpublished manuscript," which has not yet been published nearly a decade later. As to Ellicott, he says, "Although I have no doubt that Ellicott was a Mason, I have not been able to discover to which lodge he belonged."[6] The book is rife with such speculation presented as fact.

After 355 pages of unsubstantiated conjecture, Ovason comes to an amazing conclusion that contradicts virtually everything else in his book: "I am not suggesting for one moment that it was 'the Masons who built Washington, D.C.,' or that Masons' Lodges ever had a coordinated, formulated plan to influence the growth of the city in any way."[7]

In 2006, popular Masonic author Robert Lomas published *Turning the Solomon Key: George Washington, the Bright Morning Star, and the Secrets of Masonic Astrology*. In it, he briefly encapsulates Ovason's Virgo theory and points out that it has nothing to do with Freemasonry. He declares that Ovason was completely wrong about George Washington and the Freemasons. The Federal City was not designed to align itself with Virgo.

According to Lomas, it was really Venus . . .

Pentagrams

One of the most common assertions concerning the design of Washington, D.C., has to do with the supposed inverted pentagram that appears in the street plan over the White House. The accusation is that the inverted pentagram was placed there by the Masonic designers of Washington, D.C., as an occult talisman to show their mysterious power over the government. Or something like that.

The pentagram, or five-pointed star, is a common symbol. It appears fifty times on the American flag, though somehow conspiracy theorists have apparently overlooked that particular occult symbol apparently placed on our flag by that pagan witch Betsy Ross and her Dark Overlord George Washington during one of their black masses or Satanic sewing bees.

The pentagram first appeared more than five thousand years ago in Mesopotamian writings and drawings. The Babylonians used it as an astrological diagram to represent the five known planets—Mercury, Mars, Jupiter and Saturn, with Venus, the Queen of Heaven, at the top point of the star. The Pythagorean Greeks used an inverted pentagram's five points to represent the classical elements of fire, water, air, earth and idea (or more properly, *Hieron*, a word meaning "divine thing"). Modern-day Wiccans and Neopagans use the symbol in a similar manner to represent the four earthbound elements and the "spirit." Depending on the variety of Wicca, the symbol may appear with the point up or down.

Early Christians used the pentagram to describe a wide range of concepts, from the five senses to the five wounds of Christ on the cross. Catholics have used it to symbolize the five "virtues of Mary" (Annunciation, Nativity, Resurrection, Ascension and the Assumption). In the fourteenth-century Arthurian tale of *Sir Gawain and the Green Knight*, it appears on Sir Gawain's shield to delineate the five virtues of knighthood: fellowship, purity, frankness, courtesy and compassion.[8]

The pentagram has occasionally appeared in the symbolism of Freemasonry, most prominently as the symbol of the Order of the

Eastern Star, part of the Masonic family of related groups known as the appendant bodies. The order was created in the 1850s by Freemason Rob Morris and his wife as a group that allowed both men and women to mix in a lodge-like setting. Men who are Masons may join, as well as women who are married or otherwise related to Masons. Morris, an inveterate lover of Masonic ritual, created a ceremony that was initiatory as in Freemasonry but was dissimilar enough so he couldn't be accused by Grand Lodges of making women into Masons.

He based his ritual on biblical sources. The degree ceremonies of the Order of the Eastern Star tell stories about five heroines of the Bible: Adah, Jephthah's daughter from the Book of Judges; Ruth, the daughter-in-law of Naomi; Esther, the brave Hebrew wife of Xerxes; Martha, Lazarus' sister from the Gospel of John; and Electa, the "elect lady" mentioned in II John.

The pentagram as used in the Order of the Eastern Star represents the Star of Bethlehem. Chapter rooms are traditionally laid out with a large floor cloth or carpet representing the pentagram and its star points. At the center of the symbol stands an altar with an open Bible upon it.

The inverted pentagram as it is used in the Order of the Eastern Star.

Apart from its use in the Order of the Eastern Star, the pentagram—right side up or inverted—does not officially appear in Masonic ritual or symbolism. Some "tracing boards," painted symbolism charts used to teach Masonic lessons, in the early 1800s contained five-pointed stars with a "G" in the center as a symbol of both God and geometry. Other researchers have suggested that it may have represented a portion of the Master Mason degree ritual, the "Five Points of Fellowship." But it was not a common symbol and has not survived in widespread use.

Freemasons, more to the point, do not venerate or worship symbols. Symbolism is primarily used in Freemasonry as a memory device or an allegory to teach a moral lesson. The inverted pentagram has never appeared as a part of regular, recognized Masonic ritual or symbolism.

So we return to the question about the supposed inverted pentagram in the capital city's streets, if it is there at all. The inverted pentacle certainly wasn't an inherently "evil" symbol when Pierre L'Enfant was alive. The first mention of pentagrams being "good" or "evil" appeared more than 60 years after L'Enfant designed the street plan for Washington, D.C., in Eliphas Lévi's book, *Dogme et rituel de la haute magie* (Doctrine and Ritual of High Magic), published in 1855. Lévi, a French student of the occult and magic, became fascinated with the subject in the mid-1800s, like much of the Western world. His book was the first known mention in print of a "good" or "bad" pentagram. He explained them as a ying-yang balance of good and evil in the universe.

A commonly reprinted drawing, allegedly created by Eliphas Lévi, shows the pentacle as a symbol of man with the head at the top and the hands and feet stretched out as the other four points. Called the Microcosmic Man, the head represents the spirit, while the hands and feet represent air, earth, water and fire. The opposite, inverted pentagram in the Lévi illustration is supposed to represent the head of Baphomet in the form of a goat's face. The beard is the bottom point, the ears the next two points, and the horns at the top.

Variously described as a demon or pagan idol of uncertain origin, Baphomet was allegedly worshipped by the Knights Templar, according to Inquisition torturers and prosecutors seeking to destroy the knightly order in the early fourteenth century. However, the symbol of Baphomet as a goat-head pentacle is really little more than one hundred years old, first appearing in the 1897 book *La clef de la magie noire* (The Key of Black Magic) by Stanislas de Guaita.[9] Unfortunately for those who continue to ascribe evil connotations to supposed pentagrams in Washington's street layouts, the Satanic connection with the pentagram did not appear until 1966, when Anton LeVey founded the Church of Satan in San Francisco. To its adherents, the inverted pentagram's upside-down three points are a parody of the Holy Trinity.

The real question is whether the pentagram actually appears in Washington's street plan at all. The answer is, sort of . . . but not really. Look at the map of the streets north of the White House. Using the White House as the bottom point, trace Connecticut Avenue to

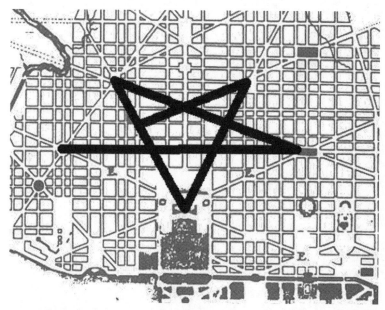

The unfinished pentagram in the streets north of the White House, from the L'Enfant Plan (1791).

DuPont Circle; Massachusetts Avenue to Mt. Vernon Square; K Street back west to the circle at 23rd Street; and then—nothing. The final leg of the pentagram is supposed to be Rhode Island Avenue, traced to Vermont Avenue and then back to the White House, the "evil" tip of the inverted point. But Rhode Island Avenue doesn't extend between 23rd Street and Connecticut Avenue, and there is no evidence that it was ever supposed to connect. As Masonic author Dr. S. Brent Morris has pointed out, if the Masons were all-powerful, wouldn't they have finished the job so this unholy talisman could achieve full potency?

Those still hunting the Devil in the roadmap might take note that in the aforementioned inverted pentagram of the satanic goat head, three roundabouts—Logan Circle, Dupont Circle and Scott Circle—make up the top three points. Each has six streets intersecting it. Therefore, "666"—the dreaded Mark of the Beast from the Book of Revelation—may indeed be found in the supposedly satanic city plan, but only by the perennially paranoid.

The Square and Compass and the Capitol

Similar claims have been made that the streets around the Capitol Building outline a Masonic square and compass. The "square" is formed by Louisiana Avenue and Washington Avenue. The "top" of the compass is the Capitol itself, with its two legs stretching down Pennsylvania Avenue to the White House and, in a broken, meandering way, along Maryland Avenue toward the Jefferson Monument. There is no Masonic significance to the Jefferson Monument, since Jefferson is not known to have been a Mason. There's also a problem with the supposed mystical symbolism of a Masonic connection between the White House and the Capitol. To the east of the White House, an obstruction to this "sacred line" was built in 1836—at the order of a Masonic president. Freemason Andrew Jackson ordered the new Treasury Building to be built next

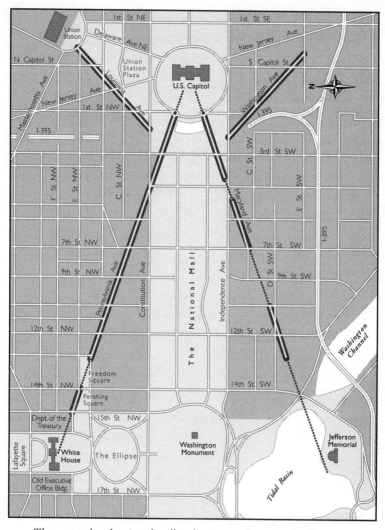

The area today showing the alleged square and compass in the streets around the Mall, Capitol and White House.

to the White House, slicing across Pennsylvania Avenue, to block his view of Congress, with whom he was at political loggerheads. As a Past Grand Master of Tennessee, perhaps Jackson should have known better, but maybe he wasn't at the lodge meeting the night his brethren discussed preserving the magic Masonic line between the White House and the Capitol.

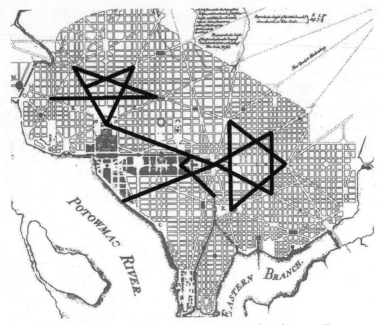

The supposed Masonic symbolism in the streets of Washington. From the L'Enfant Plan (1791).

Drawing lines all over a map of Washington is like eating popcorn. There are a half dozen pentagrams, at least two six-pointed Seals of Solomon (Star of David), and countless square and compass patterns. You get even more if you cheat with streets that don't go through, as the purveyors of these nonsensical claims do. It is a function of diagonal lines laid down over a north/south gridline.

As for Masonic All-Seeing Eyes, one item may be of interest. The lettered streets of the city include "I Street," but more than a few businesses have sought to erase the confusion between the number "1" and the letter "I" by spelling out "Eye Street." Gives you the shivers, doesn't it?

The Washington Meridian

L'Enfant designed the central area of the city in the shape of a triangle. The east/west line at the base runs from L'Enfant's proposed site for a monument to George Washington east to the Capitol Building. The hypotenuse runs from the Capitol up Pennsylvania Avenue to the White House. The vertical side of the triangle is the north/south line passing through the White House and the proposed Washington Monument site. That line, which runs straight north up 16th Street, became known over the years as the Washington Meridian. In 1793, Thomas Jefferson surveyed and marked the southwest corner of the triangle with a post, and a position one and a half miles north was marked with a stone obelisk in 1804 at the longitude of 77°2'11.56"W. Close to the location of the north stone is Meridian Hill Park, popularly referred to these days as Malcolm X Park.

L'Enfant wanted the Federal City to be the home of a new prime meridian—0° latitude, from which all others would be measured, replacing the one in Greenwich, England. If we were starting a new nation, why admit that England had any claim to being the center of longitude measurement throughout the world? L'Enfant's idea was for the new American Prime Meridian to run through the center of the Capitol Building. Today a compass rosette is set into the floor directly beneath the Capitol rotunda and dome to mark where that meridian would have passed.

The new prime meridian idea was eventually dropped, but the 16th Street meridian held on for many years, and it does make for a

Meridian Hill Park.

strong, easily seen vertical feature on the map. Conspiracy alarmists have noted there are not one but two major Masonic buildings prominently located on the 16th Street meridian: the Scottish Rite Southern Jurisdiction Supreme Council's House of the Temple and the lesser-known Scottish Rite Center for the Valley of Washington. Of course, they fail to point out that there are also no less than forty-seven churches, six synagogues and two Buddhist temples on the 16th Street meridian.

Like France's Rose Line, mentioned in Dan Brown's popular novel, *The Da Vinci Code*, the Washington Meridian fell by the wayside as a national point of pride when the world's nations agreed on Greenwich as the Prime Meridian. In 1884, at the International Meridian Conference in Washington, D.C., twenty-six countries voted to make Greenwich the meridian from which all longitude lines and time zones were measured. Only the French refused to give up their claim and continued to recognize their own Paris Observatory meridian and the Rose Line as 0° until 1911. Even then, they could not bring themselves to refer to "Greenwich Mean Time," which was clearly a plot of perfidious Albion. Until 1978, the French referred to Greenwich Mean Time as "Paris Mean Time retarded by nine minutes twenty one seconds."[10]

The Mall and the Sephiroth

One of the features that L'Enfant included in his plan of the Federal City was a large ceremonial space for parades and great national celebrations. He located it on the descending strip of land west of the Capitol Building. The mall would run along the base of the triangle discussed in the previous section. The President's House and the Capitol would face it, and the triangle would terminate in the planned location of the Washington Monument, even though the president himself felt a little squeamish about seeing it on a map. But L'Enfant's geometry was foiled by Mother Nature. The placement of the Washington Monument had to be shifted a bit south of the triangle point to avoid its being swallowed up by a swamp.

Once again, modern mapgazers have attempted to fit new symbolism—in this case, the Sephiroth—on an old blueprint. The Sephiroth concept appears in the branch of Jewish mysticism called Kabbalah as well as in occult lore. More commonly known as the *Tree of Life*, it is usually depicted as a series of ten spheres connected by twenty-two paths represented by the letters of the Hebrew alphabet. The spheres describe the ten attributes by which God can interact with Man and the Universe.

So much material exists about Kabbalah, and much of it conflicts in major and minor details. There are so many different obediences of study and opinion that it is impossible to treat the subject properly here. But for the sake of illustrating the "Tree of Life" theory of the Mall's design, it's necessary to explain a little of it.

The Sephiroth is organized into three columns. The center column is called the *Pillar of Mildness*. At the top is *Kether Elyon* (Crown), and below it are *Tifereth* (Compassion or Beauty, depending on the source), *Yesod* (Foundation) and *Malkuth* (Kingdom). The right column is the *Pillar of Mercy*, associated with the Hebrew letter *Shin*, the element of fire,

The Sephiroth, or Tree of Life, as depicted in an early work about Kabbalah, Portaelucis *(Gates of Light) by Paulus Ricius (1516).*

and is considered to be the male aspect. At the top of it is *Binah* (Intelligence), followed by *Din* (Power or Judgment) and *Hod* (Majesty or Splendor). The left pillar is the Pillar of Severity, associated with the Hebrew letter *Mem*, the element of water, and is considered to be the female side. At the top is *Chockmah* (Wisdom), followed by *Chesed* (Mercy) and *Netzach* (Lasting Endurance or Firmness). Some literature uses the Tree of Life to represent the archetypal symbol of Man. The French occultist Eliphas Lévi wrote extensively about the Sephiroth, which he related to Tarot. Another author, Albert Pike, was probably introduced to the concept through Lévi's writings in the 1870s, and it is sprinkled throughout his book *Morals and Dogma.*

Which brings us back to the Mall. The Cutting Edge Ministries ("Spiritual Insights Into The New World Order So Startling You'll Never Look At The News The Same Way Again") website[11] goes into great detail about the various features of the Mall corresponding to the Sephiroth, placing the Lincoln Monument at the Crown, the Capitol at the Kingdom, the Washington Monument at Beauty, the White House at Mercy and so on.

The allegation that the Founding Fathers were practitioners of the occult, and that they included the Sephiroth as a depiction of the archetypal man, if true, would still beg the question: So what? L'Enfant and Ellicott were not Freemasons, and there is absolutely no evidence that either man had any interest in the occult, alchemy, Rosicrucianism or Kabbalah. Nor is there any evidence whatsoever that George Washington or any other Freemason made changes to L'Enfant's plan for the Mall.

Furthermore, although the location of the Washington Monument was planned by L'Enfant, the Lincoln Memorial's location wasn't picked until 1901, and the Jefferson Memorial wasn't planned

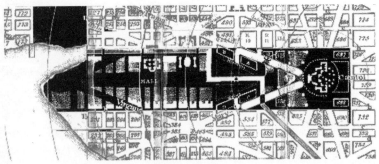

The area of the Mall as it appears in the Plan of the City of Washington dated 1833.

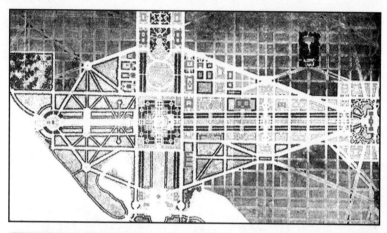

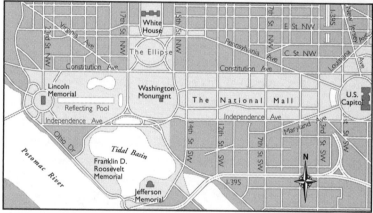

*Top: The proposed redesign of the Mall by the McMillan Commission in 1901–1902. The new shoreline of the Potomac was created by reclaiming the former swamp land at the southwest corner of the Mall, where the Lincoln Memorial would be erected. The commission was named after Senator James McMillan of Michigan, who was a Freemason. **Bottom:** The Mall as it exists today.*

until 1934. The placement of those key parts of the mysterious Sephiroth would have been impossible when L'Enfant was making his plans, since the land where they now stand was completely under the waters of the Potomac River. It took a full century of backfilling, pumping and drainage to create the new shoreline—a plan that did not exist in L'Enfant's time. Admittedly, though, President Warren G. Harding dedicated the Lincoln Memorial, and Franklin D. Roosevelt dedicated Jefferson's. You guessed it. Harding and FDR were both Freemasons.

Abraham Lincoln once said, "If you go looking for the bad in people, you will surely find it." Some people go in search of evil and some don't. Looking at the same map of Washington, D.C., I see a large crucifix formed by the Mall, the White House and the Jefferson monument. It could very well be that the planners incorporated a Christian cross into the design—a possibility far more likely than an obscure symbol of occult mysticism.

A Templar Treasure in Washington?

Readers of Dan Brown's *The Da Vinci Code* are familiar with a few of the legends surrounding Rosslyn Chapel in Roslin, Scotland, near Edinburgh. More properly called the Collegiate Chapel of St. Matthew, it was built beginning in 1446 by Sir William St. Claire, Prince of Orkney, as part of a larger cathedral that was never completed. Sir William, who died in 1484 and was buried in the chapel, is asserted by some to have secretly been a Knight Templar, and his chapel has long been the center of wild speculation, variously claimed to be connected to the Knights Templar, Freemasons, Holy Grail seekers and pop-culture pilgrims in search of Dan Brown's "Sacred Feminine" mystery. From its incredibly detailed carvings to its possible connection with Templars who may have been hiding from the Pope's wrath after their excommunication, Rosslyn is a true enigma.

Rosslyn is also the name of a neighborhood just across the Potomac on the southeast corner of Washington, D.C. Is it named after the mysterious chapel in Scotland, and does it hold some clue to the mysteries of Washington, D.C.?

According to researcher Ian Kendall, of the 1,974 communities and neighborhoods in the District of Columbia, 342 of them, or 17.3 percent, are named after Scotsmen, Scottish locations or Scottish words—one of the highest urban concentrations of Scottish place names in the United States.[12] (Nearby Baltimore has a similar con-

The paradoxical Rosslyn Chapel near Edinburgh, Scotland.

centration.) Obviously, a lot of Scotsmen roamed the banks of the Potomac in the eighteenth century. So it's entirely possible that some Midlothian Scot in the 1700s decided to name his patch of land after Rosslyn Chapel.

The mystery gets even stranger when Rosslyn, Virginia, is located on a map, just across the river from what was once known as Mason's Island (named after George Mason, who wasn't a Freemason), now called Theodore Roosevelt Island (named after a famous Freemason president), at the base of the Theodore Roosevelt Bridge. A bridge named after a Freemason passes over Mason's Island, pointing at Rosslyn in a direct line from the White House!

It is a minor footnote in Washington's history, but in 1866, there was a suggestion put forth in Congress to move the Presidential Mansion to a different location. The White House had not been expanded yet, and sewage from the city canal dumping into the near-by Potomac River, combined with the surrounding swampland, made the area less than pleasant on a hot, humid day. A commission was appointed to find a new place within the district that would pro-vide room to build a larger mansion, nestled in more pleasant sur-

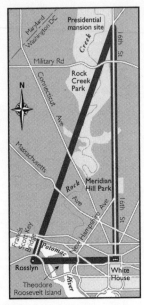

The "sacred geometry" that connects two White House locations with the new Rosslyn Chapel.

roundings. The commission, led by Major Nathaniel Michler, chose what would become Rock Creek Park. The idea of moving the White House died out quickly, but the land Michler recommended was purchased and became one of the largest city parks in America.

Now let's engage in a little "sacred geometry" of our own. Draw a line north from the White House, up the 16th Street meridian line, clear up to Rock Creek Park where the presidential mansion would have been built. Draw another line straight west from the White House, across the river, creating a right angle. The third leg of this triangle crosses diagonally over the Potomac by way of the Francis Scott Key Bridge, connecting Rock Creek Park and Rosslyn. Could the "Key" of Solomon be the Francis Scott Key Bridge, pointing the way to a modern-day Rosslyn Chapel?

There really is a temple dead center in Rosslyn, Virginia, and, as hoary legends and present-day potboilers suggest, it really does have a treasure buried in its underground vaults. The Arlington Temple United Methodist Church is at 1835 North Nash Street in Rosslyn, and if you're looking for symbolism, it rivals the original Rosslyn Chapel as one of the most peculiar churches ever constructed. The ground floor of

Arlington Temple United Methodist Church in Rosslyn.

The secret treasure of Rosslyn Chapel.

this multistory building is a Chevron station. When the church was built in the 1970s, the founders wanted it to have a reliable source of income, so the gas station was designed into the original plans. With the price of oil today hovering at record highs, I can't think of a bigger buried treasure than subterranean fuel tanks filled with $3.60 a gallon high-test.

CHAPTER 8

Occult Myths and Legends of Washington, D.C.

Freemasons, for some reason or other, always have been, and even now remain, peculiarly susceptible to the appeal of the occult ... Those who have, with worn fingers, untangled the snarl of occult symbolism, tell us that these secret cults have been teaching the doctrine of the one God, of the brotherhood of man, and of the future life of the soul; all this is good but one doesn't need to wade through jungles of weird speculations in order to come upon the teachings that one may find in any Sunday School ... Life is too short to tramp around [occultism's] endless labyrinths. Moreover, there is on the surface of Freemasonry enough truth to equip any of us for all time to come.

—A BIRD'S EYE VIEW OF MASONIC HISTORY
BY H.L. HAYWOOD

Masonic symbols and legends are misunderstood by most people who have never been members of the fraternity. Masons use symbolism largely to teach moral lessons through allegorical storytelling. The trouble with symbolism is that meanings can change over time. One culture's good luck symbol is another culture's Nazi swastika. The same is true of other symbols and legends that are familiar today but either were unknown or meant something entirely different in another time and place. Something of a cottage industry has grown up among conspiracy peddlers who seek to force upon Washington,

D.C., symbolic interpretations that did not exist when the city was built and to ascribe nefarious motives to Freemasonry as well as to men who were not even members. This chapter examines some of the more farfetched conjectures about the founders and the nation's capital.

Lucifer, Venus, Washington and the Masons

Venus is the second closest planet to the sun, and apart from the moon, it is the brightest object in the night sky. This planet plots a path through the heavens that, when the lines are connected, forms an almost perfect pentagram every eight years. Depending on the year and Venus's position relative to the Earth, it is the bright "star" that appears in the morning, just before sunrise, or the first to appear just after sunset.

The Babylonians called the planet Ishtar after their goddess of love. Because of its appearance at sunrise or sunset, depending on the year, the Egyptians and the Greeks believed it was actually two different stars. The Greeks called the morning star Phosphorus, "the bringer of light," or Eosphorus, "the bringer of the dawn," and the evening star they called Hesporus, "the star of the dusk." The Romans referred to this planet as Venus—but before that, they had another name for it. The Romans translated the Greek name "Phosphorus" as "Lucifer."

Lucifer is made up of two Latin words—*lux*, or *lucis*, meaning "light," and *ferre*, meaning "to bring" or "to bear"—so Lucifer actually means "bringer of light and knowledge." And that's where some people start to entangle Freemasons, Masonic "light" and Satan. But there is no simple way to convince people that, whatever their minister may say, Lucifer—in its original biblical connotation—does not mean Satan, the Devil, the Horned One, Old Nick, Old Scratch or Beelzebub. In Christian legend, Lucifer is a fallen archangel who rebelled against God and was cast out of heaven with one-third of the heavenly hosts. That story is told by Milton in *Paradise Lost* and by Dante in his *Divine Comedy*. But it's not in the Bible.

The following passage appears in Isaiah 14:12 of the King James Bible:

> How art thou fallen from heaven, O Lucifer, son of the morning! How art thou cut down to the ground, which didst weaken the nations!

Taken out of context, it certainly reads as if Lucifer has been cast out. Yet that's not really what it is about. The whole passage refers to a Babylonian king who has turned against his people and has brought disgrace to his country. The term "Lucifer" in this context refers to the king's once-honorable position as a "light-bringer," or bringer of knowledge to his people. The king's recent actions have disgraced him to the point that his subjects can no longer consider him a source of light.

The King James Version of the Bible came to us through a tortured path. It was first written in Hebrew, then translated into Greek and again into Latin. Different translations appeared along the way. When St. Jerome made his Latin Versio Vulgate ("Made Public") translation, there was also the complication of formal Latin versus conversational Latin dialect. Jerome's version of the Bible, published in the fifth century A.D., became the standard work upon which many subsequent translations were based. When the King James Version of the Bible was translated in the early 1600s, the source material was Jerome's Latin Vulgate version, not the original Hebrew texts.

The Hebrew word in Isaiah 14:12 is *helel*, which means "to shine brightly" as well as "to offer praise." It's the source of the word "hallelujah." King James's translators did not investigate the original source material. Thus, in the King James Bible, Lucifer became a name instead of a description. The growing popularity of the non-biblical legend of a fallen angel became confused with Isaiah's tongue-lashing for a tyrannical king.

The translation error has been corrected in later versions of the Bible. The New Revised Standard Version, for instance, translates Isaiah 14:12 to read:

How you are fallen from heaven, O Day Star, son of Dawn! How
you are cut down to the ground, you who laid the nations lo!

Lucifer has exactly nothing to do with Freemasonry, but that
hasn't stopped scores of anti-Masonic writers, Christian and Islamic
fundamentalists and conspiracy lovers from tying him to Masonry's
apron strings. They have done so because of a single passage written
by Albert Pike, who served as the Sovereign Grand Commander of
the Ancient Accepted Scottish Rite, Southern Jurisdiction.

"The Luciferian Doctrine" of Albert Pike

The Scottish Rite is a branch of Masonry open to members once
they have received the three degrees of Entered Apprentice, Fellow
Craft and Master Mason in their local lodge. Although not all Masons
go on to join the Scottish Rite, it is the largest secondary Masonic
organization in America. It offers Masons additional degrees—4°
through 32°—which are not considered superior or of higher rank
than the Master Mason. The degrees teach further moral lessons, some
of which continue the story of the building of King Solomon's Temple.
Besides the twenty-nine degrees conferred on its members, the Scottish
Rite also awards a 33° to a small percentage of members who have
distinguished themselves or performed great services to the fraternity.
These are non-voting, honorary positions. The controlling board,
known as the Supreme Council, is also made up of 33° members.

The Scottish Rite was one of the fastest-growing fraternal
organizations in the late nineteenth century, largely due to the work
of Albert Pike, who joined the group in 1853 and soon found himself frustrated with the unimpressive manner in which the degrees
were conferred. He was a self-made man of astonishing intellect—a
lawyer, poet, editor and student of ancient cultures, languages, philosophies and religions. He believed that the degrees of the Scottish Rite
held much potential for communicating important concepts, but he

felt that the existing versions had lost much of their symbolic meaning. Taking it upon himself to rewrite the degrees, he added many layers of symbolism and allegory drawn from his wealth of knowledge. He designed the degrees to be presented in a dramatic setting, like a play, which he felt would make a deeper and more lasting impression on candidates.

Pike believed that the men who had written the Scottish Rite rituals before him had hidden deeper meanings within the rituals, so, like a Kabbalist, he made it his lifelong mission to uncover these secret meanings. When he died, he left one of the largest personal libraries in America to the Scottish Rite Supreme Council. It exists today as the cornerstone of the massive Masonic library at the House of the Temple in Washington, D.C.

Pike's most famous work is his book *Morals and Dogma*, published in 1871. This ambitious volume seeks to provide insight and background into the degrees of the Scottish Rite as Pike saw them. In

Albert Pike 33°, Sovereign Grand Commander of the Ancient Accepted Scottish Rite, Southern Jurisdiction 1859–1891.

many ways it is a frustrating book, because it contains so much material about ancient mythology, religions, customs and philosophies that it almost obscures the very lessons of the degrees it purports to illustrate. Pike, a deep thinker, saw symbolism everywhere, and in the style of the Victorian Age, he rarely used two words when twenty sounded more impressively stentorian. He was also a devout Episcopalian.

In spite of critics who have called his writings un-Christian, Pike believed that fully understanding where religions came from, how they formed and what their deepest meanings were made him a better Christian. His experiences with American Indians early in his life strengthened his own feelings about the anathema of religious intolerance. As far as Pike was concerned, truth, morality, justice, charity and love were universal concepts, and any faith that espoused them was worthy of tolerance and respect. Given his philosophical background, it is surprising that he became a lightning rod for anti-Masonic authors and conspiracy lovers.

It is through the writings of Albert Pike that Freemasons became linked with Satan, or, more properly, Lucifer. On page 321 of *Morals and Dogma*, in his comments on the 19°, Pike writes:

> Lucifer, the light-bearer! Strange and mysterious name to give to the Spirit of Darkness! Lucifer, the Son of the Morning! Is it he who bears the Light, and with its splendors intolerable blinds feeble, sensual or selfish souls? Doubt it not![1]

Lucifer does not appear in the 19°, but Pike was actually making a simple point. If the original Latin word *lucifer* means "light bearer," isn't it ironic that Lucifer has come to be identified with the term "Prince of Darkness"? Yet, from that one passage, entire reams of accusations have erupted against Freemasonry connecting it with some kind of Satanic religious cult. Lucifer does not appear in any of the degrees of Freemasonry, including the first three lodge degrees, the York Rite, or in either jurisdiction of the Scottish Rite. The only connection between Lucifer and Freemasonry is this one reference in Pike's 861-page book.

The biggest and earliest purveyor of the Luciferian myth about Freemasonry was a French con artist named Gabriel Jogand-Pagès. Under the pseudonym Leo Taxil, he wrote a series of increasingly lurid pamphlets and books, starting with anti-Catholic screeds. Taxil, a rabid anti-Catholic, became further incensed when he was expelled from his Paris Masonic lodge. To exact revenge against both church and lodge, he turned his salacious mind to inventing a nonexistent order of Masonry called Palladism. To his delight, the hoax worked in both directions. He fueled anti-Masonry and made fools of churchmen, eventually including Pope Leo XIII himself, from whose name he crafted his pseudonym. He made monsters of the Freemasons, attributing sex orgies, Satanic worship, beheadings and other crimes to them, knowing they would not publicly respond. In 1889, he published the following passage and attributed it to Albert Pike:

> On July 14, 1889, Albert Pike, Sovereign Pontiff of Universal Freemasonry, addressed to the 23 Supreme Confederated Councils of the world the following instructions…
>
> "That which we must say to a crowd is—We worship a God, but it is the God that one adores without superstition. To you, Sovereign Grand Inspectors General, we stay this, that you may repeat it to the Brethren of the 32nd, 31st, and 30th degrees— The Masonic Religion should be by all of us initiates of the high degrees, maintained in the purity of the Luciferian Doctrine.
>
> If Lucifer were not God, would Adonay whose deeds prove his cruelty, perfidy and hatred of man, barbarism and repulsion for science, would Adonay and his priests, calumniate him? Yes, Lucifer is God, and unfortunately Adonay is also god. For the eternal law is that there is no light without shade, no beauty without ugliness, no white without black, for the absolute can only exist as two gods; darkness being necessary to the statue, and the brake to the locomotive.
>
> Thus, the doctrine of Satanism is a heresy; and the true and pure philosophical religion is the belief in Lucifer, the equal of Adonay; but Lucifer, God of Light and God of Good, is struggling for humanity against Adonay, the God of Darkness and Evil.[2]

Taxil had completely invented the occult-sounding statement, and in 1897 he gleefully confessed his hoax in an elaborately staged public meeting. His confession was well documented in the Paris newspapers of the period, just as Taxil intended. His object was to make fools out of the pope and the Church for believing him for so long, no matter how outlandish his stories became. He fled the theater he had rented for the event and retired quite comfortably on his ill-gotten gains.

But his quote, printed and reprinted, has since become one of the most damning and widely circulated accusations against Freemasonry. It has been repeated endlessly in a variety of books for over a century, and the Internet has given the old lie new legs. Albert Pike was not "Sovereign Pontiff of Universal Freemasonry." There is no such thing, and there never has been. There is no such thing as "Universal Freemasonry." There has never been a branch of Freemasonry called "Pallidism." Nor has there ever been a "Confederation of Supreme Councils." As for his admonition to only tell these dark secrets to the 30°, 31° and 32° Masons, every Mason who joins the American version of the Scottish Rite attains the 32° almost immediately. In the U.S., the degrees do not have to be taken in order. They are almost never presented all at one time, and many members never see all twenty-nine of the Rite's ceremonies. A 32° Mason is of no higher rank than a 3° Master Mason.

Finally, it needs to be pointed out that Albert Pike was never a Grand Master of any state's Grand Lodge. He was the Supreme Grand Commander of the Scottish Rite Southern Jurisdiction for thirty-two years, and his rituals were only performed in those states that were part of that jurisdiction, not in the Scottish Rite's Northern Masonic Jurisdiction nor in the rest of the world. He is a huge figure in Masonic history because of his tireless work and detailed writings, but his true influence needs to be kept in its proper perspective. He had no effect whatsoever on regular, recognized Craft Lodge Masonry.

Eyes, Pyramids and Trinacrias

Vittoria studied the [dollar] bill. "An eye inside a triangle."

"It's called the trinacria. Have you ever seen that eye in a triangle anywhere else?" Vittoria was silent a moment. "Actually, yes, but I'm not sure." "It's emblazoned on Masonic lodges around the world." —*Angels and Demons* by Dan Brown[3]

Everybody knows that the unfinished pyramid capped by the All-Seeing Eye on the back of the dollar bill is a Masonic symbol. In 2006 alone, at least eight different television and video documentaries about Freemasons, *The Da Vinci Code* or the Knights Templar made this assertion, and it is a common Internet claim. In the opening three minutes of the film *National Treasure*, kindly, old Grandpa Gates tells his grandson that Masons put clues to their secret treasure on the back of the dollar bill. It's common knowledge. It's a big conspiracy. Everyone knows about it. There's just one problem. It isn't true.

The pyramid, finished or unfinished, is not a Masonic symbol, at least not in regular, recognized Freemasonry as practiced in the United States, Canada and the United Kingdom. It never has been. It is not part of any of the symbolic instruction used in the ritual ceremonies of the three degrees, nor does it appear in the York Rite or Scottish Rite degrees. Yet many Masonic lodge rooms in the United States and elsewhere are decorated in Egyptian motifs. In Washington, D.C., Naval Lodge has an especially stunning room with Egyptian decor, even though Masonic ritual and origins nave nothing to do with Egypt.

In his *Constitutions*, James Anderson asserted that the Hebrew Abraham taught the Egyptians the seven liberal arts and sciences and that the Alexandrian mathematician Euclid taught the Egyptian nobility the art of geometry in the third century B.C. But it took something a lot more exciting than fanciful storytelling to turn Masons into ersatz Egyptologists.

In 1713, a French Abbot named Jean Terrasson published a three-volume romantic novel called *Sethos* about ancient Egypt. Europeans were just beginning to explore the ruins of Egypt, and everywhere they looked, they saw hieroglyphics. In those days, no one was able to decipher what the strange carvings said, which meant a clever novelist could claim they were mystic, occult symbols used by Egyptian priests to conjure up magical spells—which is exactly what Terrasson did. His trilogy tells of a prince who undergoes three trials, is initiated into the mysterious worship of the Egyptian goddess Isis, and is taught the ideals of brotherhood, truth, justice and knowledge—all of which sounds very similar to Freemasonry. The story was a hit. Appearing during the height of the Age of Enlightenment, the idea captivated many philosophers, and not all of them took it to be fiction. Lots of

Masons, as well as Rosicrucians, fell in love with the notion of the Mystery Schools of Egypt as Terrasson had described them.

In 1776, an Italian with the impressive title and name Count Alessandro di Cagliostro appeared in London and became a Freemason in Esperance Lodge No. 289. The good count had a somewhat murky background as a petty criminal. To this day, no one can definitively say exactly who he was or what his real circumstances were, but it is believed that he was, in fact, a Sicilian named Giuseppe Balsamo. Cagliostro claimed he was a magician and clairvoyant who had learned much of his art in Egypt. Almost immediately after joining the Lodge, he invented his own quasi-Masonic organization, the Mother Lodge for the Adjustment of the High Egyptian Masonry, or simply the Egyptian Rite, which he, of course, claimed was steeped in mystery and great antiquity. And he began calling himself the Great Kophta. Really.

The Egyptian Rite was a coed group, admitting both men and women, and was not recognized as Masonic by any existing regular Grand Lodge. Nevertheless, Cagliostro and his wife peddled the degrees around Europe, and he opened Egyptian Lodges in England, France, Germany and Austria. In France, he passed himself off as a "magnetic healer," and he was reportedly recommended to Benjamin Franklin to treat his gout while in Paris.

After being banished from France over a juicy scandal involving an expensive diamond necklace and Queen Marie Antoinette, Cagliostro fled to Italy. Of all the places he could have picked to start a Masonic lodge—and a decidedly pagan Egyptian version at that—under the nose of the pope was probably the worst. In 1789, he was arrested by the Inquisition. His ritual manuscript was ceremoniously burned by the public executioner, and the count was condemned to death. The pope commuted his sentence to life imprisonment, and he died after six years in prison.

A few years later, in 1789, Ignaz Von Born, a member of a lodge in Vienna, Austria, published an essay comparing Masonic ritual to similarities in Egyptian ceremonies. Never mind that no one really knew exactly what those Egyptian ceremonies were. A combination of *Sethos* and von Born's essays, along with some German fairy tales and some Masonic themes, influenced his Lodge brother Wolfgang Amadeus Mozart's opera *The Magic Flute*. Yet, most Masons today who watch or listen to *The Magic Flute* recognize nothing having to do with the Freemasonry they know.

The Rosetta Stone, discovered when Napoleon invaded Egypt in 1798, contains an identical inscription written in side-by-side Egyptian hieroglyphics (the ancient pictograms used for religious and government documents), Egyptian demotic script (a more common phonetic alphabet that developed later), and Greek. In 1822, after years of painstaking work using the Greek as a key, French Freemason Jean François Champollion translated the demotic script, and for the first time in almost two thousand years, the strange symbols of ancient Egypt could be read and understood.

With that breakthrough, Europe went barking mad for all things Egyptian. In the 1800s, two Egyptian-influenced Masonic-style degree systems—The Rite of Memphis and the Rite of Mizraim—were created in France, largely as moneymaking schemes for their promoters. Both rites had more than ninety different degrees, and in both cases, they were peddled mostly as enterprises selling spiffy diplomas with high-sounding titles for fat wads of cash. The more ancient, exotic and mysterious the rituals became, the more they were lapped up by excited initiates, and it was hard to get more ancient and exotic than the land of the pharaohs. These rites were shut down by the government of France as well as by the country's largest grand lodge, the Grand Orient of France, but they never totally died out until their inventors and hucksters passed on.

As Classical Greek styles had in the 1700s, Egyptian-influenced architecture became popular in the 1800s. Interest grew when news came to Europe of the discovery of Queen Hatshepsut's temple and several mummified pharaohs at Deir el Bahri. Egyptmania returned again in the 1920s, when Howard Carter discovered the magnificent intact tomb of King Tutankhamen. It was the major inspiration behind art deco architecture, art and design in the 1930s.

It should come as no surprise that Masonic lodge rooms built during these periods of international fascination with all things Egyptian would be decorated like Egyptian temples. So were banks, office buildings, movie theaters and gas stations. Still, Egypt has not left its visible mark on the ceremonies of Freemasonry except in the fertile imaginations of Masonic con men and their fanciful inventions. Yet even today the pyramid is commonly, though erroneously, believed to be a Masonic symbol.

One possible source of the confusion concerns an item that is often seen in photographs of lodges outside of the United States. Most people have probably seen the letter *G* depicted in the center of the Masonic square and compass and wondered why, if it is the symbol of Freemasonry, it isn't an *F* or *M* instead. The letter *G* is the initial of both geometry and God (or the Grand Architect of the Universe), and its significance dates back to the days of operative stonemasons.

The early stonemasons believed that the sacred science of geometry had been given to the Masons of the Bible by God himself. Mathematics, engineering and construction were all wrapped up together in the package of geometry, so magical that it had to have been divinely inspired and so mysterious that few could master it. In fact, during the Middle Ages, the French word *mystere* came to mean a "trade" or "craft." Like the operative guilds, modern Freemasons unite the concepts of God and geometry, fusing faith with science. In most North American lodges, the *G* appears over the Master's chair and is illuminated when the lodge is open. But in lodges in non-English-speaking countries, the words for "geometry" and "God" frequently do not begin with *G*, and in lands that use different alphabets, the letter *G* may not exist at all.

In these foreign lodges, a different solution symbol for God and geometry had to be created. The All-Seeing Eye, used to represent God, frequently appears inside an illuminated equilateral triangle representing the mathematical perfection of geometry. Its origins as a Christian symbol for God can be traced back for centuries, with the three sides representing the Christian trinity. In fact, it has appeared throughout the centuries as a symbol for many religions that have worshiped a three-part deity. It is by no means a uniquely Masonic symbol.

The first official mention of the All-Seeing Eye as a Masonic ceremonial symbol seems to be in Thomas Smith Webb's *Freemasons Monitor*, published in 1797.

> . . . although our thoughts, words and actions, may be hidden from the eyes of man, yet that All-Seeing Eye, whom the Sun, Moon and Stars obey, and under whose watchful care even comets perform their stupendous revolutions, pervades the inmost recesses of the human heart, will reward us according to our merits.

The All-Seeing Eye does appear earlier than this on hand-painted or hand-embroidered Masonic aprons, including an apron reputedly given to George Washington by Lafayette in August of 1784.

Another use of the triangle as a symbol for God makes its appearance in the York Rite and Scottish Rite degrees of Masonry. The All-Seeing Eye in these cases is replaced by the Tetragrammaton, the unspeakable, ineffable name of God in the Old Testament, set with

Embroidered Masonic apron given to George Washington by Marquis de Lafayette in August 1784. It is now on display in the museum of the Grand Lodge of Pennsylvania.

an equilateral triangle. Represented by the Hebrew letters yodh, heh, vav and heh (approximately YHWH), the Tetragrammaton was the most sacred name of God to the Hebrews, and considered unspeakable, or ineffable. The word derives from the Hebrew word meaning "to be." Moses asks the name of God at the burning bush in Exodus 3:14-15 and receives the following reply.

> And God said unto Moses, I AM THAT I AM: and he said, Thus shalt thou say unto the children of Israel, I AM hath sent me unto you.
>
> And God said moreover unto Moses, Thus shalt thou say unto the children of Israel, the LORD God of your fathers, the God of Abraham, the God of Isaac, and the God of Jacob, hath sent me unto you: this is my name forever, and this is my memorial unto all generations.

In Judaism, the name of God is considered so sacred that it is commonly replaced when reading aloud or praying with the word *Adonai*, meaning "Lord," or *HaShem*, meaning "the name." The belief that the word itself must not be spoken, and the Commandment not to take the Lord's name in vain, come from Exodus 20:7.

Its appearance within a triangle in the York Rite and Scottish Rite degrees is not unique, nor did it originate with Freemasonry's appendant organizations. Tetragrammatons in Hebrew appear in Christian art dating back to the Middle Ages.

There is also a belief within Jewish mysticism and Kabbalah that the actual name of God is 72 letters long and can be discovered by arranging the letters of the Tetragrammaton in a triangular position called a tetractys. The legend says that only the high priest could pronounce the name of God, and only on the holy day of Yom Kippur within the Sanctum Sanctorum of King Solomon's Temple. This sacred word was lost when the Temple was destroyed. It is remarkably like the Masonic legend of Hiram Abiff and the loss of the Master's Word with his death, which is the basis of several of the York Rite and Scottish Rite degrees.

As for Dan Brown's flawed reference in *Angels and Demons*, the triangle with the All-Seeing Eye is not now, nor has it ever been, called a trinicria. The trinicria is a symbol representing three bent

The trinicria as it appears on the flag of Sicily (left)
and the triskalion as it appears on the flag of the Isle of Man (right).

legs rotating around a center point, often the face of Medusa. It appears on the flag of the island of Sicily.

A similar symbol, more correctly known as a triskalion, appears on the flag of the Isle of Man in England and depicts three legs bent, clad in armor. None of these symbols are Masonic, despite Robert Langdon's claim in the novel, and the trinicria does not appear anywhere in Freemasonry.

One other possibly sinister use of the symbol occurred briefly—as a lapse of good judgment on the part of federal bureaucrats. The All-Seeing Eye has long been associated with "Big Brother," a creepy, watchful government that peers into our private lives. In the wake of the 9/11 attack on the United States, the U.S. Defense Advanced Research Projects Agency (DARPA) established a new government agency, the Information Awareness Office, in January 2002. The IAO's motto was *Scientia Est Potentia*, "Knowledge Is Power." The mission of the IAO, as stated on its website, was to:

> . . . imagine, develop, apply, integrate, demonstrate and transition information technologies, components and prototype, closed-loop, information systems that will counter asymmetric threats by achieving total information awareness useful for preemption; national security warning; and national security decision making.[4]

Their mission quickly became the subject of a public outcry and government hearings. The greatest uproar came not from the possibility that the IAO's technology might be gathering secret records in possibly illegal ways, to spy on private U.S. citizens, but from the office's choice of symbols. Their official logo depicted the Earth being watched by a pyramid capped with an All-Seeing Eye, suggesting the sort of Evil Criminal Genius's logo found in James Bond movies on the golf carts and matching jumpsuits of henchmen in secret lairs—wholly inappropriate to a real U.S. government agency.

To make matters worse, students of esoterica pointed out that the initials of the agency spelled Iao, a name for an entity that appears in some Greek and Gnostic beliefs as the Demiurge, an intermediary between God and the creation of Earth.

The short-lived logo of the U.S. Information Awareness Office.

The Iao took the cosmic energy that God had created and, from it, fashioned the material world. Plato saw the Demiurge as essentially good, while the Gnostics saw it as a source of evil because it sought to take what was divine and give it physical form, which is always flawed. Christians disliked the idea altogether because it implied a middleman between God and the Creation.

The last thing the already beleaguered IAO office needed was to be associated with an Evil God with an All-Seeing Eye. The public clamor over the logo got so bad that DARPA issued the following statement in February 2003:

> DARPA offices have traditionally designed and adopted logos. However, because the IAO logo has become a lightning rod and is needlessly diverting time and attention from the critical tasks of executing that office's mission effectively and openly, we have decided to discontinue the use of the original logo ... On an elemental level, the logo is the representation of the office acronym (IAO), the eye above the pyramid represents "I," the pyramid represents "A," and the globe represents "O."[5]

But the trouble wasn't over yet. Congress suspended the operations of the IAO in 2003 until they received a detailed report of just what the agency was really up to. The report came in May of that year, and the agency tried to dodge the issue by changing its name to the Terrorist Information Awareness Program (TIA). Fans of the MTV animated series *Aeon Flux* immediately brought to the attention of anyone who would listen that Total Information Awareness (TIA) had been used years before in an especially Orwellian manner in the sci-fi cartoon, which had also contained a character called the Demiurge, a godlike creature who needed to be removed from Earth to rid the world of its evil influence. The real TIA closed down in defeat soon after, and its mission was assumed by other agencies.

The Dollar Bill and the Great Seal

It is greatly to be regretted that the device adopted by Congress in 1782... can hardly (however artistically treated by the designer) look otherwise than as a dull emblem of a Masonic fraternity. —*Professor Charles Eliot Norton, 1883*[6]

A dozen books on the market make excruciatingly circuitous attempts to find mysterious Freemason plots to insert Masonic symbols into the Great Seal of the United States. While both sides of the official seal appear on the U.S. one-dollar bill, attention focuses on the reverse side of the seal, the one with the pyramid.

A somewhat astonishing book by Robert Hieronimus was published in 1989 as *America's Secret Destiny* and reprinted in 2005 as *Founding Fathers, Secret Societies.*[7] Among other things, it presents a unique theory that the Founding Fathers drew inspiration from the League of the Iroquois Nation for the new republic. But the bulk of the book is one of the most detailed historical accounts available about the Great Seal of the United States.

Congress appointed a committee in 1776 to design a seal for the new nation, to be used as the official "signature" of the country on documents, laws and treaties. The four men on the first committee were Benjamin Franklin, John Adams, Thomas Jefferson and the only true artist among them, Pierre du Simitière. Of the four men, only one, Franklin, was a Mason. His suggestion to the committee was that the seal depict a scene from Exodus. It would show Moses causing the parted waters of the Red Sea to destroy the oncoming chariots of Pharaoh's approaching army, while a pillar of fire reaches down from the heavens. His suggested motto was "Rebellion to Tyrants Is Obedience to God."

Thomas Jefferson's suggestions had a similar Old Testament theme. The front of his two-sided seal would show the children of Israel in the wilderness, being led to the Promised Land by a bright cloud in the day and a pillar of fire at night. The reverse of his seal would have shown Horsa and Hengist, two legendary Anglo-Saxon leaders of ancient Britain.

John Adams turned to the Greeks. He proposed an image of Hercules leaning on a large club, with the figure of Virtue on his right and Sloth on his left—the Greek equivalent of an angel on one shoulder and a devil on the other.

Du Simitière went a different route. His was a more standard European-style shield or coat of arms, divided into six sections to represent America's roots in England, Scotland, Ireland, France, Germany and Holland, surrounded by thirteen smaller shields representing the original thirteen states. On the left side of the shield

Left: Benjamin Franklin's proposal for the Great Seal of the United States, depicting Moses and the Hebrews escaping Egypt as the Red Sea swallows up Pharaoh and his army (1777). *Right:* Pierre du Simitière's proposal for the Great Seal of the United States (1777).

was a figure of Liberty, wearing armor and holding a spear in one hand. In the other was an anchor, a symbol of hope (which, by the way, does appear in Masonic symbolism with the same meaning). On the right side was a frontiersman, wearing buckskin and holding a tomahawk. Surrounding this design were the only elements from this committee that would make it to the final design. Above the shield was an All-Seeing Eye in a triangle, beaming down rays of light. Below the shield was the motto, *E Pluribus Unum* (Out of Many, One), and the Roman numerals for 1776, MDCCLXXVI. Hieronimus suggests that Du Simitière actually cribbed the motto from the title page of a contemporary London publication, *Gentleman's Magazine*.

Congress didn't think much of the committee's recommendations, so it did what congresses do best—it formed another committee. One member of the second group was Francis Hopkinson, an artist who had designed the first American flag, several official seals, and some colonial currency. Hopkinson added the idea of an unfinished pyramid based on a fifty-dollar note he had designed in 1778. It should be noted that Hopkinson was not a Mason, either.

A third committee in 1782 at last finalized the design, using elements from several different proposals, and this is the seal that appears on the back of the dollar bill today. The items most cited as being "Masonic" were explained by William Barton, an artistic consultant brought in by the committee.

> The Pyramid signified Strength and Duration: The Eye over it & the Motto allude to the many signal interpositions of providence in favor of the American cause. The date underneath is that of the Declaration of Independence and the words under it signify the beginning of the new American Era, which commences from that date.[8]

Both mottoes that appear on the reverse of the seal were contributed to the design by Charles Thompson, a member of the third committee. The Latin inscription *Annuit Coeptis* translates as "He (God) has favored our undertakings" and refers to God's assistance in the creation of the new nation. The inscription *Novus Ordo Seclorum* translates as "A new order of the ages" and signifies the new American era. It does not, as has been often incorrectly touted, mean "New World Order." Nor does it mean "Secular World Order," as fundamentalist Christians have suggested.

The reverse side of the Great Seal of the United States as it appears on the one-dollar bill.

Of all the fourteen men who had a hand in the design of the Great Seal of the United States, only Benjamin Franklin was a Mason, and not one of his design elements made it into the final version. While Elliott Norton's estimation that the reverse of the seal was "a dull emblem of a Masonic fraternity," it was nothing of the kind. Norton was most probably making a snide artistic judgment, not an anti-Masonic accusation. Nevertheless, his comment is the likely source of the notion that the back of the dollar bill contains Masonic symbols.

Forming the anagram "MASON" from the motto.

There is an unusual aspect about the symbol that most people don't know. If you don't mind defacing your hard-earned cash, take a pen and circle the *A* in *Annuit*, the *S* in *Coeptis*, the *N* in *Novus*, the *M* in *Seclorum*, and the second *O* in *Ordo*. Rearrange those letters *ASNMO* and they spell *MASON* (see illustration above right). Is it possible that

Joining the letters that make the Mason anagram with the All-Seeing Eye creates the Seal of Solomon.

Charles Thompson intended this anagram to be hidden in the mottoes he suggested, even if he wasn't a Mason himself?

Now, draw a line from the tip of the eye down to the *N*, over to the *M*, and back to the eye. Connect another line from the *A* to the *S*, down to the *O*, and back to the *A*. The lines form a hexagram, a six-pointed star better known as the Star of David or the Seal of Solomon.

Of course, the following anagrams also appear in the motto: onerous, ottoman, despots, sopranos, semiconductors, radioisotopes, uncircumcised, Micronesians, accordionists, autoeroticism and, most significantly, misconception.

Conspiracy lovers and those who get the creeps over the "occult" number thirteen may point out the thirteen rows of bricks in the pyramid. Like the thirteen stripes in the U.S. flag, there is nothing occult about their presence. They stand for the original thirteen colonies that formed the United States. Others assert that the date 1776 is there to commemorate not the signing of the Declaration of Independence but the founding in Bavaria of the Illuminati, the centerpiece organization of Dan Brown's *Angels and Demons*. The short-lived Illuminati organization used the eye within a triangle image as a symbol. To these folks, the entire image is proof that the Illuminati is alive and well and in control of the U.S. government. (It's reassuring to think that somebody is.)

The Seal of Solomon

The front side of the official seal of the United States, depicting the eagle, has been used since the beginning as the official seal on documents and treaties. The actual seal itself—the device that stamps the image into paper—has been manufactured several times since the 1780s, with slight variations, but the image on the dollar bill is an accurate depiction. It has seen its share of controversy as well, since it also contains the number thirteen, along with the Star of David. The thirteen stars at the top center above the eagle, representing the original states, are denoted by thirteen pentagrams, or five-pointed stars. At first, they appear to be clustered in a circular pattern, but it is easy to connect the dots to create a Solomon's Seal out of them.

The front of the Great Seal of the United States, as it appears on the dollar bill. The Seal of Solomon is formed by the thirteen stars above the eagle's head.

Anti-Semites often point to claim that the appearance of the Solomon Seal on the dollar is proof of a Jewish conspiracy to take over the world economy, or at least the U.S. Treasury.

The Seal of Solomon, also known as the Star of David, was named after Solomon's father, King David, who united the kingdom of Israel one thousand years before Christ. While it has become best known as a symbol of modern Israel, the ancient image has been part of Jewish, Christian, Zoroastrian and Islamic traditions. The true symbol includes the six-pointed star, made out of two inverted equilateral triangles, with an additional dot in the center. Judaism traditionally equates the symbol with the number seven, perhaps representing the "Seven Spirits of God."

A French researcher, Janik Pilet, has suggested in his book *Le sceau de Solomon, secret perdu de la Bible* (The Seal of Solomon, Lost Key of the Holy Bible), that the symbol actually represents the first chapter of Genesis, the creation of the earth in six days, while the dot in the center refers to the day when God rested.[9] Jewish Kabbalah also uses the symbol.

Some Jewish legends say that King David possessed a shield emblazoned with the symbol, which protected him from his enemies. King Solomon is said to have worn a signet ring with the symbol, giving him great powers. In the Islamic version of the tale, it allowed him to command genies, and he used the ring to imprison an especially evil one in a bottle, stamping a lead seal with the ring.

In fact, the six-pointed star probably did not exist as a real Hebrew symbol when David and Solomon ruled. It doesn't seem to have become part of mainstream Jewish culture until the fourteenth century A.D., although it did start to appear in Kabbalah in the sixth century. Given the current strife in the Middle East, it is ironic to note that in A.D. 1536, the Islamic sultan Suleiman the Magnificent, who took his name from the Arabic version of Solomon, decorated portions of the walled city and the mosque on the Temple Mount in Jerusalem with the symbol.

The name Solomon is actually a Latin translation. The Hebrew Shlomo and the Arabic Sulayman mean "peaceful" or "complete" and are related to the words *shalom* in Hebrew and *salaam* in Arabic. King Solomon was renowned for his wisdom and justice and the skill with which he ruled over a diverse kingdom. When God appeared to Solomon in a dream and granted him anything he asked for, Solomon answered (I Kings 3:9-13):

> "Give therefore thy servant an understanding heart to judge thy people, that I may discern between good and bad: for who is able to judge this thy so great a people?"
>
> And the speech pleased the Lord, that Solomon had asked this thing.
>
> And God said unto him, Because thou hast asked this thing, and hast not asked for thyself long life; neither hast asked riches for thyself, nor hast asked the life of thine enemies; but hast asked for thyself understanding to discern judgment;
>
> Behold, I have done according to thy words: lo, I have given thee a wise and an understanding heart; so that there was none like thee before thee, neither after thee shall any arise like unto thee.
>
> And I have also given thee that which thou hast not asked, both riches, and honour: so that there shall not be any among the kings like unto thee all thy days.

Franklin and Jefferson, two men who have long been accused of being irreligious Deists, both recommended biblical subjects for the Great Seal. The men of the time were well versed in biblical stories, so it is not surprising that they might include a symbolic reference to wise King Solomon as a symbol of wisdom and God's blessing on the new nation.

Those who suspect darker motives have suggested that the star's inclusion was at the behest of Haym Salomon, a Jewish financier of the Revolutionary period and a Freemason. An amazing man who spoke eight languages, his is one of the most incredible and unknown stories of the war. Salomon was a Philadelphia banker from Poland before the revolution broke out with England. Over the course of the war, he loaned the struggling new government much of his personal fortune, including $10,000 from his own pocket to pay French soldiers and keep them fighting.

Salomon negotiated most of the foreign aid that helped to rescue the United States during the war, including £3.5 million from Holland, Spain and France. A member of Philadelphia Lodge No. 2, he was a personal friend of George Washington. In 1776, he was captured by the British and sentenced to death. Using his German language skills, he talked a Hessian guard into letting him go and persuaded several of the guards to desert. A surprising number of the Hessian mercenaries stayed after the war and became U.S. citizens.

After arranging loans and financing throughout the war, Salomon fought successfully against anti-Jewish laws that barred non-Christians from holding public office in Pennsylvania. Contrary to the ugly myth of the "rich Jewish moneylender," Haym Salomon died penniless. Still, no connection between Salomon and the Seal can be proved.

To return briefly to the map of Washington, D.C., some have suggested a Seal of Solomon has been designed into the street plan as well, just east of the Capitol building, "proving" a Jewish hold on the city along with that of the Freemasons. Frivolous as the claim may be, the Seal of Solomon leads to another peculiar connection, even more obscure.

The Key of Solomon

Until the title of Dan Brown's sequel to *The Da Vinci Code* was announced as *The Solomon Key* and Brown revealed that it would be connected to the Freemasons in Washington, most fans were unaware of the connections between Masonic legends and King Solomon. The Key of Solomon has a whole series of possible connotations, and in keeping with Dan Brown's love of ciphers, a Masonic code related to Solomon's Temple has been used for several hundred years. Its origin is in the Royal Arch degrees of the York Rite. In the course of the degree, the candidate is taught about the key so he may decipher the message that is the key to the ineffable name of God, the Tetragrammaton. The code is deciphered by taking the alphabet and placing it in a tic-tac-toe pattern, then using vertical and horizontal lines and dots to replace the corresponding letters. Some confusion has occurred over the years among those who sought to decipher the code, as the keys in England differ from the ones in the United States.

Freemasons promise in their obligation as an Entered Apprentice not to "write, print, paint, stamp, stain, cut, carve, hew, mark or engrave" the secrets of the Craft—a problem for Masons who wanted to learn the rituals but couldn't write anything down. Enter the Masonic Code. For many years, "cipher books" of the rituals appeared,

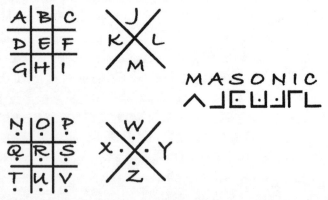

A typical Masonic cipher code. The letters within the crossed lines on the left are the key to the code. Words are written by substituting the appropriate section of the squares that correspond to the letters.

printed in this sinister-looking code. They were simply mnemonics to help masons learn their ritual ceremonies.

Another interpretation of the Key of Solomon has to do with the story told in the Master Mason degree. The Grand Architect of King Solomon's temple, Hiram Abiff, is in possession of the Master's Word. The story explains that his is only one third of the secret word and that it can only be spoken when all three Grand Masters of the Temple—King Solomon of Israel, King Hyram of Tyre and Hiram Abiff—are assembled together. When Hiram Abiff is slain, his portion of the knowledge is lost, and Solomon must substitute a word until future generations can discover the true word. In most versions of the ritual, Solomon tells the Temple's workmen to search Hiram Abiff's body to discover if any key to the word can be found on it. It is clear that the complete key requires the knowledge of all three men, and Masons are forever in search of that lost knowledge.

The most obvious reference to the Key of Solomon is the legendary book of magic, *The Key of Solomon the King*.[10] This medieval grimoire, or book of magical spells and charms, formulas for potions, astrological charts and lists of angels and demons, is the basis of much that has fallen into the folklore of wizards and magicians. While it contains many references to Judaism and Kabbalism, its alleged origin, the hand of King Solomon himself, is undoubtedly a fabrication. The earliest manuscript known is a Greek version from the 1400s.

The first modern English translation of the manuscript was done by S. Liddell MacGregor Mathers. Mathers was a curious figure in nineteenth-century England. After a brief stint in the Army, Mathers joined a Masonic lodge in Bournemouth in 1877, about the same time that he became interested in mystical and occult subjects. Mathers became bored with the lodge and, in 1882, joined Societas Rosicruciana in Anglia, an organization made up of Master Masons who had an interest in Rosicrucianism and other occult subjects. He became famous, or infamous, as a practitioner of ritual magic and in 1888 helped form the Hermetic Order of the Golden Dawn.

Mathers and the Golden Dawn members were a part of a growing group that shared an interest in magic, alchemy, Tarot, Kabbalah, Rosicrucianism, the Western mysteries and all other things occult. This was also a period of great interest in the spirit world in Europe and America, and the same names continue to cross paths as fraternal societies and orders came and went. William R. Woodman, William Wynn Westcott, Aleister Crowley, Eliphas Lévi, William B. Yeats and many others show up over a twenty-year period as alliances and schisms formed within these occult groups. Much of modern-day Wiccan literature and practice can be traced back to Mathers' writings and influence.

In 1889, Mathers translated the *Clavicula Solomonis*, or Key of Solomon, from Hebrew. It is largely confined to students of witchcraft, alchemy and other occult studies. The book has no connection to regular, recognized Freemasonry, and most Freemasons know nothing about it. While many have tried to make a direct connection between Freemasonry's origins and many of the topics that fascinated Mathers and his contemporaries, no evidence of any such relationship has ever been found. Nevertheless, with any luck it contains the proper spells and incantations to ward off onerous Ottoman despots and uncircumcised Micronesian accordionists.

CHAPTER 9

The Capitol Building

◆◆◆

When the United States Constitution was adopted, it was generally believed that the heaviest concentration of power within the government of the United States was vested in the House of Representatives and the Senate. The legislative branch was thought to be closer to the will of the people. Moreover, the two houses of Congress created the laws that would govern the nation. Therefore, the position of the Capitol building was given a prominent place in the physical design of the Federal City. The L'Enfant design placed it on Jenkin's Hill, the highest point in the city plan, both to show its predominance in the government and to symbolize that no man was above the law.

Benjamin Latrobe, the first principal architect of the Capitol building, was a Freemason. Ionic, Doric and Corinthian columns are well represented all over the Capitol building, and in Masonic ritual these "Orders of Architecture" represent Wisdom, Strength and Beauty, described as "the three great pillars of Freemasonry." Freemasonry teaches that there should be "Wisdom to contrive, Strength to support, and Beauty to adorn all great and important undertakings."[1]

Columns in the vestibule outside the Senate have detailed chapiters that depict ears of corn, a Masonic symbol of plenty used in cornerstone ceremonies. Corn also appears in the Masonic Fellow Craft degree as part of a lesson concerning the Old Testament story of Jeptha and the death of the Ephraimites (Judges 12:5, 6). Other columns contain chapiters with tobacco leaves or magnolia blossoms. Latrobe had designed these to be different from the classical forms, creating new, uniquely American columns.

The Capitol building has an enormous collection of artwork. The building itself is decorated with friezes, murals and paintings that tell the story of the United States by depicting important moments in history or abstract representations of the philosophy of our laws and principles. Statuary has been commissioned or donated over the last two centuries to commemorate heroes or the favorite sons and daughters of a moment in time from all across the country.

Masonic enthusiasts will find much in the way of the fraternity's influence on America carved in stone and marble or emblazoned on ceilings throughout the U.S. Capitol. Artwork throughout the U.S. Capitol building may be found on the Architect of the Capitol's website at www.aoc.gov/cc/art.

The Rotunda

APOTHEOSIS OF WASHINGTON

In the eye of the Capitol's rotunda dome, Constantino Brumidi's painting *Apotheosis of Washington* represents George Washington ascending into heaven. The word "apotheosis" means glorification, or raising of a person to the rank of a god. Washington is depicted between two female figures, one representing Liberty, the other Victory and Fame. Another thirteen women, symbolizing the original thirteen states, surround them in celebration.

The image was undoubtedly inspired by the over-the-top description of Washington's death and "ascension" in Parson Mason Locke Weems' notorious book, *A History of the Life and Death, Virtues and Exploits of General George Washington*, a grandiose, largely fictitious, incredibly popular book of the period:

> Swift on angel's wings the brightening saint ascended; while voices more than human were warbling through the happy regions, and hymning the great procession towards the gates of heaven. His glorious coming was seen afar off; and myriads of mighty angels hastened forth, with golden harps, to welcome the honoured stranger. High in front of the shouting hosts, were seen the beauteous forms of Franklin, Warren, Mercer, Scammel, and of him who fell at Quebec, with all the virtuous

patriots, who, on the side of Columbia, toiled or bled for liberty and truth… Their forms are of the stature of angels—their robes like morning clouds streaked with gold—the stars of heaven, like crowns, glitter on their heads—immortal youth, celestial rosy red, sits blooming on their cheeks, while infinite benignity and love beam from their eyes.[2]

The actual death of Washington was considerably quieter and less theatrical. Dr. Elisha Cullen Dick, a Freemason and Past Master of Washington's lodge in Alexandria, stood at his deathbed. When the president died, Dr. Dick went to the clock in the room and stopped its pendulum from swinging, preserving the moment forever. The clock is part of the museum collection at the George Washington Masonic National Memorial.

The painting's placement, at the top of the rotunda dome, is directly over the crypt that lies beneath the Capitol and the rotunda's floor. Before Washington's death, the plans for the Capitol included a burial vault where the president's body would be entombed forever. Washington wasn't wild about the idea himself, but the plans went ahead after he died. Washington was buried in a family crypt at Mount Vernon and, following his wishes, his family refused to allow well-meaning worshipers to move him into the Capitol when the building was finished. The room has never been used for funerary purposes. In the center of the crypt's floor is a compass rose. It marks the very center of the Federal City, the point from which all streets are numbered.

FRESCOES

The outer ring of the fresco has panels representing War, Science, Marine, Commerce, Mechanics and Agriculture. Masons should look carefully at the Science image—a teacher demonstrates the proper use of the compasses, one of the principal symbols of Freemasonry, while a group of famous American inventors look on. There is a bit of unintended irony in the group of scientists. Benjamin Franklin and Robert Fulton were both Masons; Samuel Morse, inventor of

Apotheosis of Washington *by Constantino Brumidi.*

the telegraph, was a staunch anti-Freemason. Morse looks understandably grumpy about the company he's keeping.

For curious fans of *The Da Vinci Code*, the Science panel depicts Leonardo da Vinci himself—artist, inventor, scientist and supposed past Grand Master of the Priory of Sion—holding a model of his flying machine and watching Wilbur and Orville Wright's first flight at Kitty Hawk. It is part of the Frieze of American History in the rotunda.

DECLARATION OF INDEPENDENCE

John Trumbull's famous painting of the Continental Congress is partially a Masonic portrait. It depicts the Declaration Committee presenting their document to President John Hancock while the Congress looks on. Hancock, Franklin and probably Roger Sherman were Freemasons. The painting was commissioned in 1817, and Trumbull sketched the room in Philadelphia's Independence Hall, as well as many surviving members of Congress, from life. The painting contains several men who were not actually at the reading of the Declaration The artist took intentional liberties with history to record all of the men who signed it on August 2, 1776. It contains a famous in-joke: Jefferson is stepping on John Adams' foot. The story goes that Jefferson paid the artist to include the gag. The image is

Declaration of Independence *by John Trumbull (1819).*

reproduced on the back of the modern U.S. two-dollar bill—with the offending foot "fixed."

LANDING OF COLUMBUS

In John Vanderlyn's painting of Columbus's landing at San Salvador, look carefully at the banners carried by the captains of the *Niña* and the *Pinta*. While the official notes to the painting describe them as the banner of Ferdinand and Isabella of Spain, they clearly show the cross of the Knights Templar, a motif that decorated the sails of Columbus's ships.

Columbus Landing at Guanahani, 1492 *by John Vanderlyn (1837–47).*

SURRENDER OF LORD CORNWALLIS

John Trumbull's painting of the surrender by the British at Yorktown on October 19, 1781, depicts General Benjamin Lincoln in the center, between the lines of troops. Lincoln was a member of St. Andrew's Lodge in Boston. The British commander, General Charles

Cornwallis, 1st Marquess and 2nd Earl Cornwallis, Viscount Brome, Baron Cornwallis of Eye, had been a strong defender of the American colonies as a member of the English House of Lords. Nevertheless, he was commander of the British forces from January 1, 1776, until the surrender at Yorktown. Like

Surrender of Cornwallis at Yorktown in 1781 *by John Trumbull (1819).*

George Washington, Cornwallis was also a Freemason. After the victory at Yorktown, Washington returned to New York to await the formal end of the war and celebrated the feast of St. John the Evangelist at Solomon's Lodge No. 1 in Poughkeepsie.

The Cox Corridors

The vaulted ceiling in the eastern north–south hallway of the Capitol's House of Representatives wing is decorated with murals by Allyn Cox. Beginning in 1973, Cox's paintings were grouped into different themes from the history of the United States. Many of them contain scenes of Freemasons.

THE GREAT EXPERIMENT HALL— WASHINGTON'S INAUGURATION 1789

George Washington's inauguration as the first president of the United States was dominated by Freemasons. Washington was sworn in by placing his hand on the open Bible of St. John's Lodge No.1, provided by its Master, Jacob Morton, and given the oath of office by Robert R. Livingston, Grand Master of New York.

Also on the dais that day were these other Freemasons not pictured:

- Major General Frederick William von Steuben, "drillmaster" of the Continental Army
- Major General Henry Knox, a longtime confidant and advisor to Washington, who became his secretary of war
- Morgan Lewis, Grand Marshall for the ceremony, who would later become Grand Master of New York and a major general during the War of 1812
- Frederick A. C. Muhlenberg, Speaker of the House
- Henry "Light Horse Harry" Lee, celebrated cavalry officer during the Revolution and father of Robert E. Lee[3]
- Arthur St. Clair, Scottish-born major general of the Revolution, ninth president of the Continental Congress, and governor of the Northwest Territory[4]

THE GREAT EXPERIMENT HALL—
FIRST FEDERAL CONGRESS 1789

Shown are Speaker of the House Frederick A. C. Muhlenberg and Elbridge Gerry, signer of the Declaration of Independence, governor of Massachusetts and later, vice president in the Madison administration. Both men were Masons.

THE GREAT EXPERIMENT HALL—
FIRST CAPITOL INAUGURATION, 1829

This painting shows Andrew Jackson, a Grand Master of Masons in Tennessee, being sworn in as president by fellow Mason, Chief Justice John Marshall, a Grand Master of Virginia. Jackson had defeated yet another Mason, Henry Clay, in the election.

THE GREAT EXPERIMENT HALL—
THE MONROE DOCTRINE 1823

The image shows President James Monroe, a Mason, discussing the American response to Russian territorial claims in the West. The result was the Monroe Doctrine, the policy that was designed to keep foreign powers from meddling in the Western Hemisphere. Shown with Monroe is Attorney General William Wirt, who would accept the nomination of the Anti-Masonic Party in the presidential race of 1832. The Anti-Masonic Party was the first official third party in America. Also shown is Monroe's vice president, John Quincy Adams, who would go on to write strong anti-Masonic articles, and run for Congress on the Anti-Masonic Party ticket.

THE GREAT EXPERIMENT HALL— THEODORE ROOSEVELT 1904

President Theodore Roosevelt joined Matinecock Lodge No. 806 in Oyster Bay, New York, in 1901. In 1902, Roosevelt said, "One of the things that attracted me so greatly to Masonry . . . was that it really did live up to what we, as a government, are pledged to—of treating each man on his merits as a Man."

THE HALL OF CAPITOLS—NEW YORK 1785

Part of the Capitols murals, this image depicts New York's Old City Hall (also known as Federal Hall), where Congress first convened under the new Constitution in 1785. It was here that George Washington was sworn in as the first president of the United States. In the background across the street can be seen Trinity Church. In the film *National Treasure*, this church stood on top of the subterranean vaults that held the Templar and Masonic treasure.

THE WESTWARD EXPANSION CORRIDOR— BOSTON TEA PARTY

This is a rather calm depiction of the famous raid in Boston Harbor. The badly disguised "Indians" were made up of members of the Sons of Liberty, which not coincidentally met in the Green Dragon Tavern, the meeting place of St. Andrews Lodge. The tavern was a hotbed of Revolutionary planning, and for many years Freemasons have laid claim to the raid being a Masonic "event." Unlike the stealthy scene painted by Cox, the docks along the harbor were choked with thousands of cheering onlookers as the crates of taxed tea were sent overboard. It is likely that Freemason Paul Revere, the Junior Warden of the lodge, took part in the festivities.

THE WESTWARD EXPANSION CORRIDOR—
BOONE AT CUMBERLAND GAP

The painting shows Daniel Boone leading settlers into Kentucky through the Cumberland Gap. Boone's Masonic membership has never been proved, but his son Nathan made the claim that his father was not given a Masonic funeral service simply because of the scarcity of Masons in the territory.[5]

THE WESTWARD EXPANSION CORRIDOR—
LEWIS AND CLARK

Explorers Meriwether Lewis and William Clark are shown looking out over an American Indian village during their expedition of the Louisiana Territory. After the expedition, Lewis was made governor of the Louisiana Territory. A Virginia Freemason, he belonged to Door To Virtue Lodge No. 44 in Albermarle, as well as Staunton Lodge No. 13 in Staunton, Virginia. He was later the first Master of St. Louis Lodge No. 111 in St. Louis, Missouri. William Clark joined the same lodge in 1809.

THE WESTWARD EXPANSION CORRIDOR—
LOUISIANA PURCHASE 1803

The Louisiana Purchase has gone down in history as the sweetest real estate deal ever negotiated. The mural depicts Freemasons James Monroe and Robert Livingston signing the treaty with France, whereby the United States acquired 828,000 square miles of land for $15 million—just four cents an acre. The property was nearly the size of all of France, Germany, Spain, Portugal, Italy and Great Britain combined.

THE WESTWARD EXPANSION CORRIDOR—
GOLD PROSPECTORS

Although this mural doesn't depict Freemason James W. Marshall discovering gold at Sutter's Mill in California in 1848, it shows the results of his discovery.

Statuary Hall and the Statues of the Capitol

The circular room today known as Statuary Hall was the location of the House of Representatives when the Capitol was rebuilt after the British burned it in 1814. Freemason Benjamin Latrobe had designed the original Capitol building and supervised its reconstruction until his death. The hall quickly became known for its problematic echoes from the smooth dome surface overhead, and eventually a new chamber was built for the House. This area, with its surrounding Corinthian columns (a Masonic symbol of Beauty), many doors and four fireplaces, presented a decorating challenge. At last in the 1860s, it was deemed most suitable for displaying sculpture, and each state was invited to donate up to two pieces to the growing collection. Over the years, the number of statues has grown to exceed the capacity of the hall to hold them all, so many of them are scattered throughout the Capitol. As you can imagine, many Freemasons are among the subjects. Out of the hundred statues on display, at least thirty are Masons.

STEPHEN AUSTIN (1793–1836)—HOUSE ROTUNDA

The "Founder of Texas" was born in Virginia in 1793. In 1821, Austin, a Freemason, settled three hundred Americans in Texas, under a grant from Spain. Mexico had recently won its independence from its Spanish rulers, and Austin negotiated with the new government to permit the settlements. In 1834, he returned to Mexico to again negotiate with the government over border disputes and got caught in the middle of President Santa Anna's dictatorship machinations. After a year in a Mexican jail, Austin returned to Texas, where he helped lead the revolution that would make Texas a republic. In 1836, he was nominated as a candidate for the president of Texas but lost to fellow Freemason Sam Houston.

WILLIAM HENRY HARRISON BEADLE (1838–1915)—STATUARY HALL

Beadle served as a brigadier general in the Union Army but is best known as an educator who worked to protect land for schools in the new Western Territories. In 1869, President Ulysses Grant appointed him as the surveyor-general of the Dakota Territory. He went on to serve in a wide range of educational leadership roles and influenced Congress to protect land set aside for schools. He was made a Mason in Indiana and was a strong figure in Freemasonry's long association with the promotion of funding for public education.

LEWIS CASS (1782–1866)—STATUARY HALL

Lewis Cass fought in the War of 1812, and later served as governor of the Territory of Michigan for eighteen years. The third Grand Master of Masons in Ohio, he became the first Grand Master in Michigan when its Grand Lodge was formed in 1826.

HENRY CLAY (1777–1852)—STATUARY HALL

Kentucky's most famous political figure, Freemason Henry Clay was born in Virginia. He moved to Lexington, Kentucky, in his twenties and quickly distinguished himself as the state's finest criminal lawyer. He served in the U.S. Senate for nearly fifteen years and in the U.S. House of Representatives for another thirteen, becoming Speaker of the House. He was one of the negotiators of the Treaty of Ghent, which ended the War of 1812, and served as secretary of state under the staunchly anti-Masonic President John Quincy Adams.

Clay was a member of Lexington Lodge No. 1 in Lexington, Kentucky, where he served as Master. He was the Grand Orator of the Grand Lodge of Kentucky and became Grand Master in 1820. He was an active member of a Masonic conference held in the senate chambers, Washington, D.C., on March 9, 1822—the only Masonic meeting on record ever held in that room.

His three campaigns for the presidency failed, which caused him to utter the famous sentiment, "I would rather be right than be President." He ran during the most anti-Masonic period in American history, but said, "I would not denounce and formally renounce it (Freemasonry) to be made President of the United States."[6]

GEORGE CLINTON (1739–1812)—HOUSE ROTUNDA

Clinton served both in the Continental Congress and the Continental Army. He had voted for the Declaration of Independence, but was called into military service by General Washington before being able to sign the document. Clinton refused to accept adoption of the Constitution until the Bill of Rights was added.

He became the first governor of New York in 1777, a position he held until 1795. He accompanied Washington on his ride from Virginia to New York for his inauguration as president and threw a lavish dinner for the general to celebrate of the occasion. He returned to the office of New York's governor from 1801 until 1804. He served as vice president for both Thomas Jefferson and fellow Mason James Monroe. The Master of Warren Lodge No. 17 in New York City in 1800, he was the uncle of another famous New York politician and Freemason, DeWitt Clinton.

ROBERT FULTON (1765–1815)—STATUARY HALL

Freemason Robert Fulton is best known for his design of the *Clermont*, the first American steam-powered boat in regular service, launched in New York in 1807. He had been hired five years before by Freemason Governor Robert Livingston to create a steamboat for use on the Hudson River. Fulton was a gifted inventor and engineer, who designed canals, mines, torpedoes and even submarines. Fulton is believed to have been a member of Hiram Lodge in New York. Although he is given credit for the invention of the steamboat, it was actually another Freemason, John Fitch, who predated his work.

JAMES A. GARFIELD (1831–1881)—STATUARY HALL

Freemason James Garfield was the last president born in a log cabin. He rose from poverty to become a lawyer, Union general during the Civil War, U.S. senator and the twentieth president of the United States. He was educated at Western Reserve Eclectic Institute, later called Hiram College, in Hiram, Ohio. He was initiated in Magnolia Lodge No. 20 in Columbus, Ohio, raised as a Master Mason in Columbus Lodge No. 30, served as Chaplain for Garretville Lodge No. 426, and was a member of Pentalpha Lodge No. 2 in Washington, D.C. He was a Knights Templar, and had the degrees of the Scottish Rite conferred on him by Albert Pike. He was assassinated in 1881, the second U.S. president to be murdered while in office, just sixteen years after Abraham Lincoln's death. The killer was Charles Jules Guiteau, an attorney frustrated because he had not been appointed to a government office.

JOHN GORRIE (1802–1855)—STATUARY HALL

His name is little known today, but John Gorrie's invention literally changed the way the whole world lived. In 1851, Gorrie patented a method of mechanical refrigeration, eventually making both extended food preservation and air conditioning possible. He was a doctor by profession, and his machine was designed to help keep his feverish patients cool. Gorrie was a charter member of Franklin Lodge No. 6 in Apalachicola, Florida.

NATHANAEL GREENE (1742–1786)—HALL OF COLUMNS

A distinguished general of the Revolution, Nathanael Greene was a Freemason and self-taught soldier second only to George Washington in military ability in the Continental Army. Apart from Washington, he was the only other general to serve the entire eight years of the war.

JOHN HANSON (1715–1783)—SECOND FLOOR SENATE CONNECTING CORRIDOR

Freemasons proudly claim George Washington as a Brother. But Washington was not the first Masonic president. Freemason John

Hanson of Maryland was actually the first to serve the full term as "President of the United States in Congress Assembled," under the Articles of Confederation, from 1781 to 1782. Under his brief leadership, the United States started a post office, opened a foreign consular service, began the arduous task of a national census, started the Treasury Department and a national bank with standardized coinage, appointed the first secretary of war and approved new treaties, laws and regulations. He officially ordered all foreign troops off American soil. And he established the Great Seal of the United States, which all presidents since Hanson have used on all official documents. He even declared an official date for the celebration of Thanksgiving as a national holiday. In just one year—the term limit required by the Articles—he accomplished more than most modern presidents accomplish in four, or even eight, years.

In all, there were ten presidents of the United States under the Articles of Confederation. They were:

- Samuel Huntington (1781)[7]
- Thomas McKean (1781)—Freemason[8]
- John Hanson (1781–82)—Freemason
- Elias Boudinot (1782–83)
- Thomas Mifflin (1783–84)—probable Freemason
- Richard Henry Lee (1784–85)—Freemason[9]
- John Hancock (1785–86)—Freemason
- Nathan Gorman (1786–87)
- Arthur St. Clair (1787–88)—Freemason
- Cyrus Griffin (1788–89)

An urban legend has grown up around Hanson's supposed depiction on the back of the two-dollar bill. Certain websites, most notably African-American activist Dick Gregory's, have wrongly claimed that John Hanson is shown in the engraving on the bill that is a reproduction of John Trumbull's painting, *Declaration of Independence*. They further assert that Hanson has "dark skin" in the engraving (he is supposedly the figure in the middle of the front row of seated onlookers, with his arm bent). The claim is that Hanson was, in fact, black and a Moor. A photograph of a black man usually accompanies the story, which is actually a daguerreotype taken between 1850 and 1860 of Senator John Hanson from Grand Bassa County in Liberia.

The problem with the legend is that the John Hanson of Continental Congress fame died in 1783, forty years before photography was invented and almost 75 years before the picture could have been taken. That doesn't explain the slightly darker face on the man in the front row of the two-dollar bill, but in Trumbull's original painting, that figure is actually Robert Morris of Pennsylvania. John Hanson was not present at the reading, debate or signing of the Declaration of Independence. But trifling things like facts never stopped an urban legend, and attempts to set the record straight have generally been characterized as a nefarious "cover-up."

SAMUEL HOUSTON (1793–1863)—STATUARY HALL

Born in 1793, Freemason Sam Houston lived with the Cherokee Indians for three years before joining the militia during the War of 1812, serving under fellow Mason Andrew Jackson. He became governor of Tennessee, but resigned to rejoin the Cherokees and travel throughout the Indian Territories and Texas. After the Texas Revolution, he succeeded his Masonic Brother Sam Austin as the commander-in-chief and was elected president of the Republic of Texas in 1836. When Texas joined the Union in 1845, he was elected senator. In 1859, he became governor of Texas, but he was thrown out of office for refusing to take the Confederate Oath of Allegiance when Texas seceded with the South. Houston took his Masonic degrees in Tennessee and became a member of Forrest Lodge No. 19 in Huntsville, Texas.

ANDREW JACKSON (1767–1845)—ROTUNDA

Freemason Andrew Jackson, the seventh president of the U.S., served two terms (1828–36). His statue stands in the rotunda, and can't be missed. He's the one striking the nineteenth-century Superman pose.

WILLIAM KING (1768–1852)—STATUARY HALL

Freemason William King's formal education ended at the age of thirteen, but he became a successful merchant and his state's leading ship owner. He served as a major general during the War of 1812 and, after the war, directed his energies to gaining Maine's independence from Massachusetts. In 1820, Maine's statehood was granted, and King became its first governor. He was the first Grand Master of Masons in Maine.

ROBERT LIVINGSTON (1746–1813)—CRYPT

Freemason Robert Livingston was one of the most prominent statesmen of the Revolutionary period. Serving in the Continental Congress, he was one of the five framers of the Declaration of Independence, although he was forced to return to New York before it was adopted and signed. He served for twenty-four years as chancellor, the chief judiciary official in New York, and swore in George Washington when he was inaugurated in 1789 in New York City. He was the first Grand Master of Masons in New York, and Washington took the oath of office on the Bible of St. John's Lodge No. 1. From 1801 to 1804, Livingston was the minister to France, where he negotiated the Louisiana Purchase along with fellow Mason James Monroe. While in Paris, he met Masonic brother Robert Fulton and later employed him to build a steamboat for use on the Hudson River.

OLIVER HAZARD PERRY THROCK MORTON (1823–1877) —SENATE CONNECTING CORRIDOR, FIRST FLOOR

Freemason Oliver Morton, one of the first organizers of the Republican Party, was governor of Indiana during the Civil War. He established an intelligence network to root out Confederate sympathizers in Indiana. Fiercely loyal to the Republican cause, he demonized the state's Democrats and largely ignored the Democrat-controlled legislature. He was partially paralyzed by a stroke in 1865, but went on to serve as Indiana senator from 1867 to 1877 and tried for the presidential nomination in 1867. Known both for his commanding presence and honesty, he served as a member of the Electoral Commission that investigated the contested presidential election of 1867. He died after suffering a second stroke while traveling to Oregon to investigate bribery charges against that state's newly elected senator in 1877.

JOHN PETER GABRIEL MUHLENBERG (1747–1807)— SMALL HOUSE ROTUNDA

Peter Muhlenberg's father, Dr. Henry Melchior Muhlenberg, was one of the founders of the Lutheran Church in America, and Peter followed in his father's footsteps. He was a pastor at the outbreak of the war. The story is told of him casting off his clerical robes in church to reveal his Virginia uniform, saying, "In the language of Holy Writ there is a time for all things . . . there is a time to pray and a time to fight…and that time has now come." It is said he recruited three hundred new militia members on the spot.[10] Muhlenberg was made a colonel by George Washington, and rose to the rank of major general. He later became a member of Congress and was elected senator of Pennsylvania in 1801. He was a member of Philadelphia Lodge No. 2.

WILL ROGERS (1879–1935)—HOUSE CONNECTING CORRIDOR, SECOND FLOOR

Born in Oklahoma Indian Territory and descended from American Indians, Freemason Will Rogers started in vaudeville in 1905, performing a rope act while making humorous commentary. He went on to become an author, radio commentator, newspaper columnist and the country's most popular movie star for more than a decade. His best-known phrase, "I never met a man I didn't like," was exemplified by his actions. A quiet but generous donor to charitable causes and victims of disaster, he is believed by many of his Masonic brethren to be the embodiment of the philosophy of Freemasonry. He was a member of Clairmont Lodge No. 53 in Oklahoma.

URIAH MILTON ROSE (1834–1913)—STATUARY HALL

Founder of the oldest law practice in Arkansas, the Rose Law Firm, Freemason Uriah Rose was a brilliant public speaker. During the Civil War, he opposed secession but remained loyal to Arkansas. His personal library contained more than eight thousand books in many languages, and he could speak French and German fluently. In 1907, Freemason Teddy Roosevelt appointed Judge Rose as a delegate to the Second Peace Conference in the Hague.

JOHN SEVIER (1745–1815)—STATUARY HALL

Sevier served as a militia captain under George Washington in the British Army in 1772. Later, during the Revolution, he rose to the rank of brigadier general. He briefly held the position of governor of the independent state of Franklin, which became part of North Carolina. Sevier became a state senator in North Carolina in 1789. He retired to what is now Tennessee, where, after statehood was declared, he was elected its first governor (1796–1801). He went on to become a U.S. congressman in 1811. Sevier, a Freemason, was the Worshipful Master of Tennessee Lodge No. 2 in Knoxville.

ROGER SHERMAN (1721–1793)—
SENATE NORTH–SOUTH CORRIDOR, FIRST FLOOR

Sherman was the only member of the Continental Congress who signed all four of the founding documents of the United States—the Association of 1774, the Declaration of Independence, the Articles of Confederation and the U.S. Constitution. He helped draft the Declaration of Independence with Thomas Jefferson, John Adams and Freemasons Benjamin Franklin and Robert Livingston. Patrick Henry called him one of the three greatest men of the Constitutional Convention. Sherman went on to propose the dual House and Senate system of congressional representation, which was adopted. Although researchers seem divided on the question, Sherman is believed by many to have been a Freemason, and a Masonic apron attributed to him is in Yale University's collection.

JAMES SHIELDS (1806–1879)—HALL OF COLUMNS

A prominent Illinois politician before the Civil War, Shields was born in Ireland. Over the years he served as governor of Illinois and is the only person ever to serve as a U.S. senator for three different states: Illinois, Minnesota and Missouri. He is best known for his political clash with Abraham Lincoln. A Whig at the time, Lincoln had attacked Democrat Shields in a series of increasingly insulting, if humorous, letters published in the *Sangamo Journal* in 1842. In response, Shields challenged him to a duel. Lincoln realized he had gone too far and, as the challenged party, selected cavalry sabers as the weapon of choice and a deep pit on an island as the field of honor. While he figured the ridiculous conditions would make Shields back down, he ultimately apologized. The two men became friends and political allies, and Lincoln made him a brigadier general in the Union Army during the Civil War. Shields was made a Mason in 1841 in Springfield Lodge No. 4. While living in Washington, D.C., he was the charter Master of National Lodge No. 12 in 1846.

GEORGE LAIRD SHOUP (1836–1904)—STATUARY HALL

Freemason George Shoup served as an independent scout in New Mexico, Colorado and Texas during the Civil War and was eventually made a colonel in the Union Army. After the war, he made his way to Idaho and helped found the city of Salmon. In 1889, he was appointed as governor of the Idaho Territory and became its first elected governor when statehood was declared. He was made a Mason in 1864 in Denver Lodge No. 5 in Denver, Colorado. A member of several lodges over the years, he served as Grand Master of Masons in Idaho and was a member of Almas Shrine in Washington, D.C.

JOHN STARK (1728–1822)—VESTIBULE NORTH OF THE ROTUNDA

Stark rose to the rank of major general during the Revolution and fought at Bunker Hill. He uttered his famous battle cry at Bennington: "There are your enemies, the Red Coats and the Tories. They are ours, or this night Molly Stark sleeps a widow!" He became a Mason in St. John's Lodge No. 1 in Portsmouth, New Hampshire. Stark was the last surviving general of the war when he died in 1822.

RICHARD STOCKTON (1730–1781)—VESTIBULE NORTH OF SENATE CONNECTING CORRIDOR, FIRST FLOOR

Freemason Richard Stockton was a lawyer, judge and legislator from New Jersey. At first a reluctant public servant who was opposed to independence, he changed his opinions with the passage of the Stamp Act against the colonies. He was a member of the Continental Congress and a signer of the Declaration of Independence. Shortly afterward, he was imprisoned by the British, an event that caused his health to fail. He became an invalid and died in Princeton. He was the first Master of St. John's Lodge in Princeton, New Jersey.

JONATHAN TRUMBULL (1710–1785)— HOUSE CONNECTING CORRIDOR, SECOND FLOOR

Freemason Trumbull became colonial governor of Connecticut in 1769, in spite of refusing to take an oath to enforce the Stamp Act five years earlier. He was the only colonial governor to support the Revolution. In all, he would spend fifty years in government service. His son, who was not a Mason, is the artist whose large works adorn the rotunda.

ZEBULON BAIRD VANCE (1830–1894)—STATUARY HALL

It's been said that there was a time when every home in North Carolina had a portrait of Freemason Zeb Vance on its wall. Hundreds would fill courtrooms just to hear him plead a case. As governor of the state during the Civil War, he proudly held that his would be the only state, North or South, that would not suspend the writ of habeus corpus. He was honest and passionate, and it was said that he could joke his way into anyone's heart. At the age of 28, he was the youngest congressman in the U.S. He served as a colonel in the Civil War before being elected governor and worked to end harsh conscription practices. Briefly arrested after the war, he then returned to law practice and ran for U.S. senator in 1870, but could not serve because he had not yet been pardoned. He was elected as governor again in 1877 and became a senator at last in 1879. He truly lived the philosophy of a Freemason and worked to revive industry, agriculture and public schools. His lifelong friend and Masonic brother was a Polish-born Jew, Samuel Wittkowsky, and he often traveled speaking of his admiration of the Jewish people and their achievements. He joined Mt. Herman Lodge No. 118 in Asheville, North Carolina, in 1853, and was a founding member of Excelsior Lodge No. 261 in Charlotte. During the war, a military lodge, Z.B. Vance Lodge No. 2, was chartered in his name. Nearly 10,000 people attended his funeral, including 129 Freemasons.

LEWIS WALLACE (1827–1905)—STATUARY HALL

The son of an Indiana governor, Lew Wallace briefly worked as a reporter before deciding to join the Army during the war with Mexico. In the Civil War he rose to the rank of major general and became adjutant of Indiana. He is credited with saving Cincinnati, Ohio, from being taken by the Confederates in 1863. After the war, he served as part of the court martial that tried those accused of complicity in the assassination of Lincoln. He went on to be governor of the New Mexico territory and an ambassador to Turkey. Wallace is better known as the author of *Ben-Hur*, the most popular book of the period. The biblical epic novel sold 300,000 copies in ten years. Wallace became a Mason in 1850 in Fountain Lodge No. 60 in Covington, Indiana.

A fraternal organization called the Supreme Tribe of Ben-Hur sprang up in 1893, based on Wallace's book, and received his endorsement. Like Freemasonry, it had its own initiations and secret rituals (along with its own life insurance company). At one point it had tens of thousands of members, who, as part of their ceremonies, re-enacted the famous chariot race.[11]

GEORGE WASHINGTON (1732–1799)—ROTUNDA

Washington is one of Virginia's two statues in Statuary Hall. His exploits and Masonic record are amply discussed elsewhere in this book.

JOSEPH WHEELER (1836–1906)—STATUARY HALL

"Fighting Joe" Wheeler was considered by Robert E. Lee to be one of the most outstanding cavalry commanders in the Confederate Army, and his books on military strategy are still studied today. Born in Augusta, Georgia, Wheeler served in many campaigns, including the opposition to Sherman's march on Atlanta. After the war, he became a congressman in 1881 and fought to heal the wounds between the North and South. When the Spanish-American War broke out, he volunteered for service. Fellow Freemason President William McKinley commissioned him as a major general, and placed him in charge of volunteer forces. When the war ended, he was sent to Cuba as part of the peace commission. In 1899, he again went to war, this time to command a brigade in the Philippines. He was a member of Courtland Lodge No. 47 in Courtland, Alabama, and a Knight Templar.

BRIGHAM YOUNG (1801–1877)—STATUARY HALL

Controversy has raged in both the Mormon Church and Free-masonry concerning the origins of Mormon rituals and ceremonies. Church founders Joseph and Hyrum Smith were both Masons, as was Brigham Young, their successor. Believers in the Latter-day Saints say that Prophet Joseph Smith's revelation of Mormon ceremonies derived from the story of Solomon's Temple, and it is merely a coincidence that the church and Freemasonry teach lessons with similar themes and phrases. Less charitable non-believers think that Smith simply lifted the ceremonies of the Masonic lodge and counted on secrecy of both organizations to hide his plagiarism.

Joseph Smith was killed in Nauvoo, Illinois, at the hands of an anti-Mormon mob in 1844. It is claimed that just as he was shot, he cried out the beginning of the Masonic "Grand Hailing Sign of Distress." Three years later, Brigham Young led the Mormons west to Utah, gaining the popular nickname, "The American Moses." His achievements of leadership and organization in the face of legal, social and physical adversity are truly admirable. He served as governor of the Utah Territory until President Buchanan replaced him with a non-Mormon. He was reputed to have had fifty wives and fathered fifty-seven children. He is credited with founding the University of Utah and the Mormon Tabernacle Choir, and Brigham Young University is named after him. He was truly one of the world's greatest colonizers, establishing communities throughout the West.

The Latter-day Saint's church to this day uses symbolism also found in Masonic ritual—notably the beehive, the square and compass, the "Five Points of Fellowship," secret handshakes, special garments for initiates and even aprons. Brigham Young's two homes in Utah, the Beehive House and the Lion House, both contain symbolism also found in Masonic ritual. Until the end of the twentieth century, Mormons and Freemasons in Utah were forbidden by each organization to join the other.

One other curious connection between the organizations is very strange. The infamous "Morgan Affair" in upstate New York in 1826 had touched off a national wave of anti-Masonic hysteria when "Captain" William Morgan vanished at the hands of a group of Masons. Morgan had published an exposé of Masonic ritual, and it was believed that he had been killed by Freemasons for his transgression, although no body was ever found. In spite of the belief that her husband had been murdered by members of the fraternity, Morgan's widow Lucinda went on to marry another Mason, George Harris, and they became Mormons. At some point, while still married to Harris, she entered into a polygamous marriage with Joseph Smith. In 1842, Smith received the degrees of Freemasonry, and yet somehow knew the details of the rituals before receiving them. Mormons believe he was divinely inspired. Skeptics point out that one of his wives, Lucinda, was the widow of a man who had published the most notorious exposé of Masonic ritual in America, Morgan's *Illustrations of Masonry*. It was only a few months after Smith's initiation as a Mason that he began to instruct his church leaders "in the principles of and order of the Priesthood, attending to washings, anointings, endowments, and the communication of keys pertaining to the Aaronic Priesthood, and so on to the highest order of the Melchizedek Priesthood. . . ."[12]

Doors of the Senate

The left "valve" doors of the Senate depict a scene from the laying of the Capitol cornerstone, clearly showing Washington in his Masonic apron.

Detail from the doors of the Senate depicting the Masonic cornerstone ceremony in 1793.

Cornerstone Centennial

In 1893, on the one hundredth anniversary of the laying of the Capitol cornerstone, a plaque was placed near the spot where it was believed to have originally been installed.

Beneath this tablet the corner stone of the Capitol of the
United States of America
was laid by
George Washington
First President September 18, 1793
On the Hundredth Anniversary
in the year 1893
In presence of the Congress the Executive and the Judiciary
a vast concourse of the grateful people
of the District of Columbia commemorated the event.
Grover Cleveland President of the United States

Adlai Ewing Stevenson Vice President
Charles Frederick Crisp Speaker, House of Representatives
Daniel Wolsey Hoorhees Chairman Joint Committee of Congress,
Lawrence Gardner Chairman Citizens Committee

Masonic Commemorative Cornerstone

In 1932, the bicentennial of George Washington's birth was celebrated across the nation. To mark the occasion, the Freemasons of Washington, D.C., dedicated a new stone at the Capitol building. Located at Old Supreme Court Chamber Entrance, on the First Floor, East Front, it reads:

Laid Masonically Sept. 17, 1932
in Commemoration of the Laying
of the Original Cornerstone by
George Washington

CHAPTER 10

Secrets in Stone

✦✦✦

After I'm dead I'd rather have people ask why I have no
monument than why I have one.

—CATO

The first boundary stone the Masons laid in Alexandria on March
15, 1791, became the first national monument as soon as it was
winched into place. It was one of forty that would be placed to mark
the territory that would become the District of Columbia. Today,
thirty-eight of the stones are still preserved and can be found in or
near their original positions around the perimeter of the district. The
stones placed at the north, south, east and west points of the original ten-square-mile perimeter are larger than the others. The sides of
the stones that face inward are inscribed "Jurisdiction of the United
States," while the outward sides are inscribed either "Maryland" or
"Virginia," depending on which state they are facing. The other two
sides of each stone declare the year the stone was laid and the magnetic compass point of its location.

Near the turn of the last century, the Daughters of the American Revolution took on the task of finding and preserving all of them
and erected steel fences or cages around them.[1] They are considered
the first national monuments of the United States. The first stone at
Alexandria is barely visible today, hidden in a concrete enclosure
within a seawall along the river between two modern lighthouses of
Alexandria. The city was named after the legendary city of Egypt,
whose library was the repository of all written knowledge of the
ancient world and whose fabled lighthouse was one of the seven

wonders of its time. It is fitting that the stone placed by the Freemasons is now in the shadow of the Jones Point lighthouse opened in 1856, and it is in within sight of the modern-day replica of the ancient Alexandrian lighthouse, the towering George Washington Masonic National Memorial, which stands high atop Shooter's Hill, a little over a mile away. To bring the story full circle, Alexandria Lodge No. 22 was the Masonic lodge to which George Washington himself was a member and a Past Master. Today, its meeting place is in none other than the masonic memorial.

The legendary history of the Freemasons connects them to the stone of the Earth, and even if they do not use hammer and chisel these days, Masons feel a compelling need to leave their imprint on the world in limestone, marble and granite. So it is not astonishing to find that mysteries carved in the stones of Washington, D.C.—real or imagined—are linked to them.

Albert Pike

When you become a Freemason these days, a curious dichotomy exists in the world around you. On the one hand, the vast majority of Americans haven't the slightest idea what Freemasonry is, apart from some vague connection to an old ring in the drawer that belonged to grandpa. On the other, a small knot of people chafe at the term "secret society" and go in search of unjustified, unsupported and unbelievable theories about Freemasonry and its members.

After my first couple of years in the fraternity, I thought I had heard the worst of it, and the majority of the more outlandish accusations seemed to swirl around the larger-than-life figure of Albert Pike. It seems that no thought ever passed through his mind without being committed to paper, and he filled an awful lot of it, time and time again. The problem with that much material is that there is so much to narrowly take out of context or openly criticize. More than a few have resorted to either twisting his text to their point of view or simply making up documents that never existed.

Albert Pike's statue at 3rd and D Streets NW in Judiciary Square, sculpted by Gaetano Trentanove (1901).

One day a young Marine was asking me questions about the fraternity, and out came one that I'd never heard before. "So somebody told me that the Freemasons started the Ku Klux Klan."

Thus began my search for the headwaters of this particularly foul river of untruth and, not surprisingly, once again, it led straight back to Albert Pike.

A statue at 3rd and D Streets, NW in Judiciary Square depicts a man most Americans have never heard of, unless they are Freemasons or lovers of conspiracy theories. Albert Pike was the Supreme Commander of the Ancient Accepted Scottish Rite Southern Jurisdiction for 32 years. He was a lawyer, an author, an esoteric scholar of ancient religions and philosophies, and an early champion of American Indian rights. His is the only outdoor statue within Washington, D.C., of a Confederate officer. Pike briefly served in the Confederate Army as a general, notably at the Battle of Pea Ridge, where he commanded Confederate Indian troops.

The bronze statue was sculpted by Gaetano Trentanove and was erected in 1898 by authorization of Congress. Pike is dressed, not as a Southern general, but as a civilian and a Masonic leader. A Grecian woman at the base below him holds a Scottish Rite banner, and Pike holds a copy of his book *Morals and Dogma* in his hand. The statue was moved from the triangle at 3rd and Indiana Streets in 1975 when road construction eliminated its original corner.

The reason Pike stands here is because this was the former location of the Scottish Rite's headquarters, the House of the Temple. Pike lived in the building for many years, and died there in 1891.

Today, Pike's body is actually interred in the present House of the Temple on 16th Street.

Two separate controversies have arisen over the years concerning Pike's statue. In spite of a lack of authentic evidence, it has been alleged that Albert Pike was Grand Dragon of the Arkansas Ku Klux Klan, originator of its rituals and its chief judicial officer. Despite an extensive Congressional investigation of the Klan between 1868 and 1871, Pike's name was never mentioned, and there has never been any real proof of his involvement. Still, books that were published after his death praising the Klan claim he was a member. And it is true that after the war, his writings speak of Southern "brotherhood" and a desire to keep blacks and whites separated socially.

> The disenfranchised people of the South...can find no protection for property, liberty or life, except in secret association....We would unite every white man in the South, who is opposed to negro suffrage, into one great Order of Southern Brotherhood, with an organization complete, active, vigorous, in which a few should execute the concentrated will of all, and whose very existence should be concealed from all but its members.[2]

He was a man of his own time and clearly had conflicting views on race relations. Pike was opposed to secession before the war but fought for the South. He was not pro-slavery, yet he owned slaves. Pike wrote:

> I am not one of those who believe slavery a blessing. I know it is an evil, as great cities are an evil; as the concentration of capital in a few hands, oppressing labor, is an evil; as the utter annihilation of free-will and individuality in the army and navy is an evil; as in this world everything is mixed of good and evil. Such is the rule of God's providence, and the affairs of the world. Nor do I deny the abuses of slavery.... Necessarily it gives power that may be abused. Nor will I under-rate its abuses. It involves frequent separation of families. It, here and there, prevents the development of a mind and intellect ... Marriage does not create an indissoluble bond among the slaves. It gives occasion to

prostitution. The slave toils all his life for mere clothing, shelter
and food; and the last is heard sometimes upon the plantations,
and in rare cases, cruelties punishable by the law are practiced.[3]

While he believed Prince Hall Freemasons to be as regular as
any mainstream Grand Lodge Masons, he vowed to leave the fraternity if the day came that he was forced to sit with blacks in lodge.
Yet he gave copies of his Scottish Rite rituals to his black Prince Hall
counterpart, Supreme Grand Commander of the United Supreme
Council Southern Jurisdiction PHA Thornton A. Jackson, whom he
considered a personal friend.[4]

It should also be noted that two of the leading Congressional
opponents of the Ku Klux Klan in the post–Civil War period were
Freemasons. General Benjamin Franklin Butler, as a Congressman
from Massachusetts, drafted and lobbied in favor of the first Ku Klux
Klan Act, which passed in 1871. Butler was a member of Pentucket
Lodge in Lowell, Massachusetts, and was made an honorary 33° member of the Scottish Rite, Northern Jurisdiction on March 16, 1864.[5]

John Scott, senator from Pennsylvania, formed the "Scott Senate
Committee" to investigate the actions of the Klan in 1871. His find-
ings and condemnation of the Klan led to the passage of the Ku Klux
Klan Act. Scott was a member of Lewistown Lodge No. 203 in
Lewistown, Pennsylvania.[6]

One of the most damning snips of so-called evidence used
against Pike was a book published in 1905 by Klan apologist Walter
Fleming. It was a reprint of Klan founder Captain John C. Lester's
memoirs, which had been written in 1884. Lester only mentioned
co-founder Nathan Bedford Forrest by name in his book, and notes
that the Klan was formed around Christmastime 1865 near Pulaski,
Tennessee. Unfortunately for Albert Pike's accusers, he was living in
Arkansas at the time, and there is no record of him traveling to
Tennessee until two years later. When Fleming re-published Lester's
book, there was no portion of the text that mentioned Pike. Fleming
did include Pike in a frontispiece that displayed pictures of notable
Klansmen. But he also included Daniel L. Wilson, a Presbyterian

minister who in reality was not a member of the KKK.[7] Most historians regard Fleming as a flawed source of information.

Pike may very well have been a Klan member, even though there is no proof. Certainly, many men were members of the Klan in its various forms during the immediate post–Civil War period in the South. They may have also been members of the Methodist Church, the Knights of Pythias or the Brotherhood of Locomotive Engineers. One of the biggest groups supporting the Temperance Movement in the 1920s was the Klan. Men from all walks of life belonged to it. That is not to endorse in any way the KKK's message of racial and religious hatred or the horrible violence it inflicted. It is simply to say that the Klan and Freemasonry were two separate and unrelated organizations, and whether Albert Pike put on a sheet or not, Freemasonry had nothing to do with it.

Even if Pike had been a Klansman immediately after the turmoil of the Civil War, he clearly did not participate in the KKK during the last two decades of his life, and his subsequent friendship with Thornton Jackson certainly shows a lack of race hatred. It is a ridiculous notion to believe that his outlook after the immediate defeat of the South might not have been a little bitter, especially since all his property was confiscated and he was forced to flee the country to avoid prosecution as a former Civil War general. It is likewise absurd to believe that his wisdom in so many other aspects of the world might not have tempered his later views.

The other controversy over Pike's statue has to do with those who believe that its location on federal property—in Judiciary Square, no less!—is somehow proof of a Masonic influence over the U.S. government. After the war ended, Pike was convicted in absentia of inciting the Indians to revolt against the United States. He had commanded a brigade of Cherokee, Choctaw, Chickasaw and Creek Indians at the battle of Pea Ridge, Arkansas, in March 1862. The Indians had taken scalps during the battle, then fled when the tide of the battle turned. Pike resigned his commission after the battle, both out of disgust with the actions of his own troops and over criticism of his command. In truth, he was a lousy military commander. Pike fled from Arkansas to Canada when he heard of the charges brought against him after the war, and all of his property was confiscated and sold.

President Andrew Johnson pardoned Pike in 1867. William Still's book, *New World Order*, alleges that Johnson, a Freemason, was Pike's "subordinate" in Masonry (since Pike was the Sovereign Grand Commander and a 33° Mason), and that the president was required to give Pike a pass because of the mutual Masonic obligation.[8] Still claims that Johnson pardoned Pike but waited to tell the press for nine months because of anti-Masonic fervor in the U.S. at the time. Finally, he asserts that Johnson was actually impeached by Congress in 1867 because of his special treatment of Pike.

Mr. Still has a feverish imagination. By 1867, the anti-Masonic mood of the country that had erupted almost forty years before had almost entirely vanished, and fraternalism was starting to grow by leaps and bounds. This was the dawn of the "Golden Age" of fraternalism in the U.S., so it is unlikely that Johnson hid any such thing from the press out of fear of an anti-Masonic mood swing. The president was indeed a Mason, having been raised in Greenville Lodge No. 119 in Greenville, Tennessee, in 1851. Johnson had been heavily lobbied by Masons across the country to grant leniency to Pike, and it is true that the president was later granted an honorary membership in the Scottish Rite Northern Masonic Jurisdiction—over which Pike had no authority. Andrew Johnson was impeached over far greater issues than pardoning Albert Pike.

Johnson was the target of the postwar battles over Reconstruction. A slave-owning Southern Democrat from Tennessee before the Civil War, he was picked by Lincoln as a vice-presidential running mate in 1864 specifically to draw the support of pro-war Democrats. Lincoln had professed no desire to exact revenge over the South when the war ended, but his assassination by John Wilkes Booth ended that sentiment in the radical wing of the Republican Party.

When Johnson became president, those who sought to treat the South as a conquered loser figured they had an ally in Johnson, who they hoped would go along with their plans to rewrite state lines and inflict harsh rules of occupation. Johnson subscribed to Lincoln's point of view—that the Union was indestructible and that the government's job was to stop the revolt, replace the miscreant leaders and get the country back to normal. Johnson was impeached in 1868 because he had vetoed the Civil Rights Act and the Freedman's Bureau Act and fired hawkish Secretary of War Edwin Stanton, a Lincoln appointee, in violation of the Tenure of Office Act. While his pardon of Albert Pike might well be considered an extreme act of leniency toward a Confederate general and even a Masonic brother, the radicals in Congress had far bigger issues to attack him on. Johnson escaped removal from office by just one vote. And in case anyone still believes that Johnson was bound by his Masonic oath to protect Brother Freemasons, Edwin Stanton, the man whose firing caused the final uproar in Congress, was also a Mason.[9]

Pike's writings have nothing to do with the neighborhood lodge up the street. He was the head of an appendant Masonic organization, the Scottish Rite, and only the Southern Jurisdiction. His writings were not accepted in the Scottish Rite's Northern Masonic Jurisdiction, and most Northern Masons have never even seen his books nor witnessed his version of the ritual ceremonies. Today his rituals have been substantially altered.

Kryptos

Just outside Washington, D.C., one of the world's most enigmatic sculptures resides in front of the Central Intelligence Agency's headquarters in McLean, Virginia. In 1990, artist James Sanborn erected the sculpture, entitled *Kryptos* ("hidden" in Greek), in the northwest corner of the courtyard of the CIA's new building, in the path of America's top-secret code breakers, challenging them—or anyone else—to decipher its message.

The whole sculpture is designed to be a microcosm of secret codes. As you approach the sculpture, it begins with two red granite and copper pieces that appear to be pages sprouting out of the sidewalk. These first copper "pages" are inscribed with Morse code and ancient ciphers. A magnetized lodestone with a compass rose illustration inscribed on it is embedded in the walk.

Across a reflecting pool stands the centerpiece of the work, and the conversation piece that has caused more than its share of controversy. A large column of petrified wood appears to support a tall scroll of copper made to resemble a roll of paper covered with letters in seemingly nonsensical order. The letters make up a vast code of nearly eighteen hundred figures divided into four sections.

The first two sections are a table for encrypting and deciphering code using a method developed by sixteenth-century French cryptographer Blaise de Vigenere, whose idea was to substitute letters in a message by shifting letters in the alphabet forward or backward in order, using a predetermined key. Of the four sections of messages, three have been deciphered over the years. (The spelling errors in the messages that follow are part of the decoding.) The first is a poetic message from the artist himself:

> Between subtle shading and the absence of light lies the nuance of iqlusion.

The second is a tantalizing message for treasure hunters:

> It was totally invisible. How's that possible? They used the earth's magnetic field. x The information was gathered and transmitted undergruund to an unknown location. x Does langley know about this? They should: it's buried out there somewhere. x Who knows the exact location? Only WW. This was his last message. x Thirty eight degrees fifty seven minutes six point five seconds north, seventy seven degrees eight minutes forty four seconds west. Layer two.[10]

The third section is drawn from explorer Howard Carter's diary describing the opening of King Tutankhamen's tomb in Egypt in 1922:

Slowly, desparatly slowly, the remains of passage debris that encumbered the lower part of the doorway was removed. With trembling hands I made a tiny breach in the upper left-hand corner. And then, widening the hole a little, I inserted the candle and peered in. The hot air escaping from the chamber caused the flame to flicker, but presently details of the room within emerged from the mist. x Can you see anything? q

The forth section consists of ninety-seven characters that, as of this writing, have not been broken:

OBKR
UOXOGHULBSOLIFBBWFLRVQQPRNGKSSO
TWTQSJQSSEKZZWATJKLUDIAWINFBNYP
VTTMZFPKWGDKZXTJCDIGKUHUAUEKCAR

Sanborn gave a copy of the solution to the code and the riddle it contains to then-CIA Director William Webster, and it has been passed along to each succeeding CIA director since then. It is, in fact, Webster that the line "Who knows the exact location? Only WW." refers to.

The original dust jacket of the U.S. hardback edition of Dan Brown's book, *The Da Vinci Code*, contains two references to the *Kryptos* sculpture. In the artwork depicting a tear in a piece of parchment, the words "Only WW knows." On the back cover, latitude and longitude coordinates appear vertically in red. They are the coordinates from the second section of the *Kryptos* message, with one degree digit changed. It seems to point to the opposite corner of the same courtyard where the sculpture is placed. When Brown was questioned about the text, he replied, "The discrepancy is intentional."[11]

Would-be code breakers and Washington sightseers who wish to physically see the sculpture in person will be disappointed. There is no public access to the CIA's property. The simple act of driving up to the main gate to ask questions is considered trespassing, and they are very serious about it. The CIA is aware of public interest in the sculpture and its code, and their official webpage about *Kryptos* is at https://www.cia.gov/cia/information/tour/krypt.html.

Vox Populi

When the Internal Revenue Service built its massive new headquarters in New Carrollton, Maryland, it picked a peculiar sculpture to place at its entrance, especially in light of what conspiracy theorists already think of the government in general and the IRS in particular. In the center of the entry courtyard is a black pyramid, topped with a chrome cap and inscribed with the phrase "We the People..." On either side of it, two tall, freestanding columns echo the columns of Jachin and Boaz, which stood at the entrance of King Solomon's temple and which are represented in Masonic lodges. It is not surprising that more than a few fringe authors have described the building as an "Illuminati Temple."

Here's the real story. The sculpture, called *Vox Populi* (Latin for "Voice of the People" was created in 1997 for the IRS building by artist Larry Kirkland. Between the two columns is a black marble pyramid etched with the U.S. Constitution with the words "We the People..." larger than the rest of the text.

Unlike the columns in a Masonic lodge, instead of terrestrial and celestial globes, each column is topped with a human hand. One is an index finger pointing skyward, like the symbol of a speaker giv-

Vox Populi (1997) *by Larry Kirkland, New Carrollton Federal Building.*

ing an opinion, as a symbol of argument or deliberation. The other is an open hand, representing a hand when voting or taking an oath.

Each column has a series of thirteen bands engraved with more hands and profiles of people in conversation, along with quotations from such famous people as Frederick Douglass, Ben Franklin, John Milton and many others. One from Margaret Chase Smith (R-Maine) says that Americans have the "right to criticize, the right to hold unpopular beliefs, the right to protest, the right of independent thought."[12]

Kirkland has said that the General Services Administration specifically asked that the sculpture not be about the IRS, and rumors that the hands form American Sign Language symbols for "You owe!" are not true. The pyramid was inspired by the unfinished pyramid on the back of the dollar bill, but Kirkland does not seem to be a shill for the New World Order.

To add another layer to the peculiar sculpture, it should be noted that the construction management company that supervised the building of the IRS headquarters was The Temple Group, Inc. Cue the creepy organ music. New Carrollton, site of the new IRS headquarters, was originally just named Carrollton, after Charles Carroll, a delegate to the Continental Congress and a signer of the Declaration of Independence. He is also the character in the film *National Treasure* who dies just outside of the White House while trying to deliver a Masonic message to President Andrew Jackson. Unfortunately for fans, Carroll was not actually a Mason.

The secret lies with *Charlotte*.

The Washington Statues

The hero worship of George Washington before and after his death was beyond anything modern Americans have experienced. While he was alive, he was venerated for his honor, his honesty and his leadership. After he died, more than four hundred books were published about him between 1800 and 1860, and everything from political movements and labor organizations to fraternal groups sought to ally themselves with the spotless, virtuous image of the president. It was a barren home indeed that did not have some image of him hanging on the wall in an honored place.

For a nation that wanted nothing of kings, America seemed eager to elevate its patriotic Everymen to the level of gods. This quasi-deification resulted in more than a few peculiar images of Washington in and around the Federal City. Meanwhile, the Freemasons proudly circulated images of him in Masonic regalia as he had appeared in lodge and in public.

Statues and busts of Washington exist all over the district. He is in the Library of Congress's Great Hall and on his horse in Foggy Bottom, and paintings of him are literally everywhere. Here are a few of interest for their Masonic (or more peculiar) reasons.

"THE AMERICAN ZEUS"

Thomas Jefferson referred to the men who drafted the Constitution as an "assembly of demigods," so it was hardly a surprise when Congress decided to immortalize George Washington in a similarly magisterial fashion. Greek symbolism was much admired and sought after in the Federal City, so it seemed like a scathingly good idea at the time to immortalize the president in suitably mythical fashion. In 1832, the sculptor Horatio Greenough was commissioned by Congress to create the ultimate statue of Washington. It was to be placed in the rotunda of the Capitol, underneath the Constantino Brumidi painting in the dome's ceiling, which depicted the president ascending among the clouds into heaven, surrounded by thirteen angelic spirits. Enthusiastic fans encouraged Greenough to create what they believed would be the ultimate image of the hero of the Revolution and father of the country, with just the proper amount of veneration.

What they got eight years later was a representation of George sitting with his lower extremities wrapped in a toga and his torso naked as a proverbial jaybird. Greenough patterned the image after a

classical statue of the Greek god Zeus at
Olympia, one of the Seven Wonders of the
Ancient World. The statue, installed in the
rotunda in 1842, was almost immediately
greeted with hoots of derision. No one had
ever really thought of George Washington
being naked before. In fact, Nathaniel
Hawthorne summed up the public sentiment when he said, "I imagine he was born
with his clothes on, and his hair powdered,
and made a stately bow on his first appearance in the world."[13] Others put it more
bluntly, saying it looked like the president
was emerging from a long soak in a bathtub and reaching for a towel.

American Zeus *(1840)*
by Horatio Greenough.

Equally distressing, while it was not quite as big as the original
forty-foot statue of Zeus carved by Phidias in 456 B.C., from which
it was copied, it sure weighed like it, tipping the scales at more than
twenty tons. After a year of sitting in its designated location, it was
determined to be too heavy and dangerous to the floor over the
underground crypt that had originally been designed for Washington's body, so the big, expensive embarrassment was moved to a little-
seen area outside. When the weather finally began to damage the
carving, it was hauled off to the National Museum of American
History, where it can now be seen lurking in an alcove, giving a
solemn Olympian blessing to an escalator.

Washington sits on a throne, its panels containing the image of
Helios, one of Zeus's innumerable sons, carrying the sun across the
sky on a horse-drawn chariot. It harkens back to Ben Franklin's
remarks concerning the heroic figure of Washington as he sat in a
chair at the Continental Congress. The image of the sun was carved
on the back of the general's chair.

The other side of the throne shows the image of another son of
Zeus. The baby Hercules and his twin brother Iphicles are shown in
their crib. Their mother Hera became so enraged when she discovered

Zeus had fathered Hercules by a mortal woman that she threw a snake into their crib. The infant Hercules is shown killing the snake with his bare hands. A five-pointed star—an upside-down pentagram—is shown over the head of Hercules, with the bottom point of the star touching his head.

Fringe author David Ickes has claimed that the statue of Washington bears a striking resemblance in its pose to the famous illustration of Baphomet drawn by French occultist Eliphas Lévi. In both figures, the right arm points skyward and the left points downward in the manner of the alchemical phrase, "As above, so below." Therefore, Ickes suggests, Washington's statue illustrates that he is somehow an evil

Baphomet, as illustrated by Eliphas Lévi for his book Dogme et rituel de la haute magie *(1855).*

incarnation of Lévi's satanic imagery. The drawing was made for Lévi's *Dogme et rituel de la haute magie.* Unfortunately for Ickes' theory, the book appeared in 1855, fifteen years after the Greenough statue was completed.

There is a better explanation for Washington's odd posture in this statue. The original design of the Washington Monument by Robert Mills, discussed later in this chapter, was supposed to have been a Greek-style temple, topped by a sculpture of Washington in a chariot pulled by six horses. Greenough's statue looks strikingly similar to the posture of Washington in Mills' conceptual drawing. The outstretched hand that holds a sword would have actually been holding the reins of the chariot. Greenough likely designed the statue as a demo to get the entire commission of Washington, chariot and horses for the monument. Fortunately, cooler heads prevailed, and a more monumental, if austere, design was chosen.

WASHINGTON AS A FREEMASON

The most prominent statue of George Washington as a Freemason is found, appropriately, in the George Washington Masonic National Memorial in Alexandria. Donated to the memorial by the Order of DeMolay, the statue was dedicated in 1950 by President Harry Truman. The massive bronze figure stands at the end of the majestic, colonnaded Memorial Hall, the main entry to the building. It depicts Washington dressed in full Masonic regalia—wearing an apron, sash and jewel of office, holding his hat in his left hand and a gavel in the right. The statue is said to represent him as Master of Alexandria Lodge No. 22, and it is true that he is listed in lodge records as the charter Master of the Lodge. Records show he was re-elected to a second term in the position. But there is no documentation showing that he was actually installed as Master or ever served in the position in open lodge.

George Washington in Masonic regalia. Memorial Hall, George Washington Masonic National Memorial. Sculpted by Bryant Baker.

Upstairs in the George Washington Museum stands another, smaller bronze statue of the president dressed as a Mason. Commissioned in 1959 by the Grand Lodge of Louisiana, it was presented to the museum by the Scottish Rite Southern Jurisdiction.

At the other end of the artistic spectrum is an audio-animatronic George Washington, located downstairs in Assembly Hall.

THE NATIONAL CATHEDRAL

Outside of the cathedral, at the west entrance is an equestrian statue, one of only two in the city, showing Washington riding his horse Man O' War to church.

Inside the cathedral itself is a very different Washington, not usually depicted in paintings or statues. He is dressed in his Sunday clothes, holding his hat in his hand. Sculptor Lee Lawrie was renowned for his art deco creations throughout the 1920s and '30s; perhaps his most famous work is the bronze Atlas holding the world over Rockefeller Center in New York. Yet when it came to the president, Lawrie said, "I have tried to show not the soldier, not the president, but the man Washington, coming into Christ Church, Alexandria, pausing a moment before going down the aisle to his pew." The medallions on the wall behind Washington depict the Masonic square and compass and a gavel.

The National Cathedral may well be the last Gothic cathedral ever built in the world using the medieval styles and forms. No steel was used to reinforce it, and nothing was mass produced. It is the sixth largest cathedral in the world. While visiting the cathedral, ask about the many gargoyles and grotesques that adorn its arches, spires and crevasses. (A gargoyle carries water away from the building with a channel or pipe running through its mouth, while a grotesque deflects

George Washington and his horse, Man O' War, sculpted by Herbert Haseltine (1959), near the west entrance of the National Cathedral.

water by bouncing it from its head, nose or other bulbous protuberances.) There are cats and dogs, a little girl with pigtails and the usual array of bizarre Gothic creatures. There's even a fat politician, chomping a cigar and stuffing cash into his pockets. Try to spot the malevolent grotesque of the Dark Lord of the Sith, Darth Vader. Admittedly a bizarre addition to a Christian house of worship, he was placed there as part of a children's contest. Don't worry, he's not close to the altar—you'll need your binoculars.

George Washington sculpture in the National Cathedral, by Lee Lawrie.

THE WASHINGTON MONUMENT

It must feel peculiar to approve the plans for your own memorial. In 1783, the Continental Congress proposed an equestrian statue to honor the commanding general who would become the first president of the United States. When Pierre L'Enfant drew up the plans for the area south of the President's House and west of the Capitol, with Washington's approval he included a place for "the equestrian statue of George Washington, a monument voted in 1783 by the late Continental Congress."

Washington was cold in his tomb a total of eight days before Congress lumbered into action in December of 1799. Freemason John Marshall moved that a marble monument be erected to him and that his family be requested to relocate his remains into it once completed. The president had been buried in a tomb at Mount Vernon, according to his last wishes, and with a full Masonic funeral service. The family resisted repeated attempts to have him moved, no matter how nice a crypt Congress built for him under the Capitol rotunda or how big a tomb was proposed out on the Mall.

Congress continued to do what it does best, proposing, studying and rejecting several different plans for a monument to Washington over the next three decades. A committee formed in 1800 had suggested a tomb shaped like an enormous pyramid, echoing the unfinished pyramid on the reverse of the Great Seal of the United States. Ideas continued to come in over the years, many of them incorporating pyramids or other Egyptian-themed themes. One-time mayor of the city Peter Force designed a particularly spectacular pyramid monument with an "unfinished" top and an oculus that

The Washington Monument.

emitted light down into the interior of the vault. It seemed that the gentleman farmer, general and president might now be made a pharaoh.

The nearby city of Baltimore embarrassed Congress when it erected its own Washington Monument, a two-hundred-foot-tall Doric column, to the tune of $150,000 raised from the city's citizens along with a generous contribution from the state of Maryland. If Baltimore could manage it, why couldn't the nation's capital?

Finally, a group of private citizens formed the Washington National Monument Society in 1833, to both create a design and raise money for its construction.[14] An appeal was made to every state in the nation, and donations were limited to no more than $1 a year per person to insure that they came from the hearts of all of the people and not just from deep-pocketed, fat-cat donors. A nice sentiment, but a stupid idea—the money came in at a trickle until the restriction was lifted.

The first plan submitted to the new Monument Society was by Robert Mills, a Freemason from South Carolina. Mills had been appointed in 1836 as the country's first federal architect by President Andrew Jackson, so he had an inside track on the commission. Mills' first plan was for a huge, circular temple, not unlike the current Jefferson Memorial. It was to be six hundred feet tall—forty-five feet higher than the present structure—surrounded by giant thirty-foot-tall columns and topped by an Egyptian obelisk. Mills saw the temple much like Paris' and Rome's Pantheons and

Robert Mills' plan for the Washington Monument (1836).

envisioned that it would be surrounded with statues of the Founding Fathers—signers of the Declaration of Independence and war heroes. Over the entry to the temple was to be Washington himself, facing the east, riding in a horse-drawn chariot like Helios bringing forth the dawn. Mills' design combined Greek, Roman, Egyptian and Babylonian architecture and was probably a case of over-thinking the concept. Aesthetically, it was a nightmare. Worse, Mills' proposed price tag for the thing came to $1 million in 1836 dollars, which is on the order of $17 million today. It was a little ambitious for a group that had raised only $28,000.

It took another twelve years for the society to collect $87,000, but it was enough for Congress to take them seriously and grant them the thirty-seven-acre plot of land L'Enfant had put in his plan . . . sort of. Unfortunately, the Mills design, even if reduced in size, didn't have a chance of standing there. Simply put, it was a bog. After some exploration it was determined that the land one hundred yards to the south was dry enough and sturdy enough to support the monument, so geometric symmetry gave way to practicality.

The plan was to build the obelisk first. Mills shortened it to five hundred feet to cut costs, but still called for a surrounding colonnade made up one-hundred-foot-tall columns, which would be added when the central shaft was completed.

The obelisk, a design first fashioned by the ancient Egyptians, is thought to have been inspired by the rays of the sun. Most ancient Egyptian obelisks were dedicated to the sun god Ra, and twenty-seven of them still survive today. The Romans were fascinated by them, and many of the Egyptian originals were carried off to Rome. One brought to Rome by the Emperor Caligula and re-erected fifteen centuries later by Pope Sixtus V—after an extensive exorcism—stands prominently in St. Peter's Square in front of the Vatican. Other Egyptian obelisks can be found today in London, Istanbul and New York.

The cornerstone for the monument was laid on the 4th of July in 1848, sixty-five years after Congress had first adopted the idea. The brethren of Washington Naval Lodge No. 4 helped drag the massive white marble block to the jobsite from the railroad depot four blocks away. Some twenty thousand people watched as President James K. Polk led a parade to the site of the monument.[15] Benjamin B. French, Grand Master of the Grand Lodge of Washington, D.C., approached the stone wearing George Washington's Masonic sash and apron that had been given to him by General Lafayette and used Washington's gavel to set the cornerstone. It was the same Masonic regalia and gavel the president had used to dedicate the cornerstone of the Capitol building. Curiously enough, that cornerstone has long ago been lost, buried within the fifteen-foot-thick granite walls of the monument's base.

By 1855, the obelisk had risen one hundred fifty-five feet, but then reality stepped in. To get this far had cost $300,000, and the Monument Society had run out of money. In February, they appealed to Congress, which finally stepped up and voted to partially fund the monument they had recommended seventy years before. Meanwhile, the Society sent out the word to the states again looking for help. Alabama hit upon a novel idea—the donation of a "state stone," a suitably inscribed block of stone native to its state. The idea generated enthusiastic press, and soon states, clubs, associations, labor unions, foreign nations and private citizens were contributing inscribed blocks to be used for the interior walls, where they can be seen today throughout the monument. The stone from Alaska is the most valuable. It is made of solid green jade and valued at several million dollars. At least twenty-two stones were donated by Masonic lodges and Grand Lodges across the country.[16]

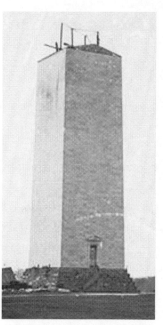

One of the stones caused a major scandal. In 1854, Pope Pius IX donated a block of marble from the Temple of Concord in Rome. During this dark period in American racial politics, the Nativist movement was growing in popularity. Nativists—American-born Protestants who had a particular dislike and distrust of Catholics—believed that new waves of Irish immigration would result in America becoming a Catholic country controlled by the Pope through his faithful surrogates. "Anti-popery" swept the nation. Pius IX had lost the control of the Papal States to the rev-

Construction stopped in 1855 at the 155-foot level.

olution that would eventually unite Italy, and his political domain was reduced from a sizeable chunk of the Mediterranean coastline to just Rome itself and ultimately to the confines of Vatican City. He had opposed liberties in the Papal States that Americans had fought hard to win in America—especially freedom of religion—and he was increasingly seen as a tyrant by Protestants. It didn't help matters that he defined the startling concepts of Immaculate Conception and the infallibility of the Holy Father when speaking on matters of faith. Protestants worldwide reacted violently to both pronouncements as heresy. So the arrival of the Pope's stone at the memorial job site was extremely bad timing.

One night, a group of ten members of the "Know-Nothing" Party broke into the construction yard and stole the Pope's stone. Rumor had it that they dumped it into the Potomac, but efforts to find it were unsuccessful. Others speculated that it was dumped into a power company job site or ground into powder and used as part of the monument's mortar mix. A replacement stone was sent and is part of the monument today.

The Know-Nothing Party was created as a secret society, and many believe it had substantial Masonic membership. As a political party, it enjoyed a brief period of popularity in the 1850s. One of the Know-Nothings' most outlandish actions was to seize the Washington Monument. Through an orchestrated stealing of the election of Monument Society members, the Know-Nothings took over the board. After four years of Know-Nothing control, nothing much was accomplished, and Congress took its $200,000 back. They would put no more money into it for another twenty years.

The Know-Nothings eventually left, but construction completely stopped in 1861, leaving the one-hundred-seventy-six-foot stump looking "like a hollow, oversized chimney," to quote Freemason Mark Twain.[17] During the Civil War, the area around the monument became a cattle yard and slaughterhouse to supply provisions for Union troops.

In 1876, with the war over and the centennial of the Declaration of Independence approaching, Congress finally appropriated $2 million to finish the job. The base was found to be insufficient for the weight of the completed structure and had to be modified before it could rise farther. And there was still that pantheon to be built.

A lawyer named George Peter Marsh finally brought everyone to their senses. As the U.S. minister to Italy, he had made a study of the art of obelisks. His recommendation was to scrap the pantheon, columns and statuary of Mills' original design and concentrate on just the elegant obelisk. Work began anew. The foundation was enlarged, hiding the cornerstone forever, and the obelisk again began to rise.

In 1851 and 1853, the original Monument Society had solicited contributions from the Freemasons nationally through the Grand Lodges, knowing the fraternity's long association with the president. The call went out again in 1874, and pledges were received from Masons all over the country, as well as from non-Masonic fraternal bodies like the Odd Fellows, Knights of Pythias, and Improved Order of Red Men. In 1875, more than two hundred Masonic lodges across the country responded to the appeal.

By 1884 the main body of the monument was completed. The difference in the age and quarry source of the marble can still be seen at the old one-hundred-fifty-five-foot level today, marked by a slight variation in color. The top of the monument was changed from Mills' flatter top to a sharper-peaked pyramidion in the 1870s re-design. To more resemble the element in the Great Seal, the pyramid was made up of thirteen rows of marble. The stonecutters dressed the final stones of the peak on the ground and hoisted it into place in one piece.

Before being delivered to Washington, the aluminum capstone was displayed in Tiffany's in New York, and patrons were given the chance to "jump over the Washington Monument." At the time, aluminum was an extremely rare metal, as expensive as silver but more durable. It was inscribed with the Latin words *Laus Deo*, meaning "Praise be to God," on one side. The other three contain details of the dates of construction and the men involved. In case there had ever been a question as to the symbol of the All-Seeing Eye atop the pyramid of the Great Seal being somehow sinister, this made it clear: The capstone of both the seal and this monument was no occult symbol but an image of God's omniscience to watch over and guide the nation.

Because the original cornerstone at the base had been buried, the aluminum capstone would become a unique replacement. It was hoisted to the top of the five-hundred-fifty-five-foot tower—in sixty mph winds—and set into place on December 6, 1884, one hundred and one years after Congress had proposed it.

Obelisks are fascinating geometric sculptures, but they are not without controversy. It doesn't take Sigmund Freud, or even Dr. Phil, very long to peg the obelisk as a phallic symbol, and there are those who suggest that the Washington Monument is an occult icon for that reason. The "Egyptian sun god" reference puts others ill at ease. Still, it must be remembered that Washington was revered for decades as a godlike character, and no amount of veneration was excessive. Connecting the general and president with a divine entity that cast the warmth of his rays on the citizenry, along with displaying five hundred fifty-five feet of virile potency, probably sounded like a laudable idea at the time. There is no mistaking the awe-inspiring vision it instills, in a way that no statue ever could, the first time you see the monument in person.

Perhaps most important is the simple timelessness of the monument's design. Robert Mills had believed that the most important part of his proposal was the pantheon of heroic figures of the nation's founding and the Greek god representation of the president himself ready to leap into the sky and race across the heavens in his chariot. Washington himself would have recoiled at such hero worship preserved forever in marble, like the world's most expensive tchotchke, with the modern-day effectiveness of a painting on black velvet. It was scarcely the "General-on-a-horse" type of thing that he, Congress and L'Enfant had envisioned. The Washington Monument succeeds as art, as a landmark, and as a symbol of the importance of his position in America, without impressing an image on us. The paintings done of him have been exposed to interminable armchair analysis. (He looks mad. He looks old. His hair looks funny. Was he wearing his "wooden teeth"?) The monument avoids that and remains ageless, devoid of false interpretations.

Four decades later, the Freemasons would break ground on a quite different kind of memorial to George Washington just across the river in nearby Alexandria. It too would have an Egyptian source. Patterned after the great lighthouse at Alexandria, its purpose would be both to preserve the physical artifacts of the president and to spread Masonic "light." We'll examine it, along with other Masonic sights of Washington, D.C., in the next chapter.

CHAPTER 11

Masonic Sites of Washington, D.C.

✦✦✦

What you leave behind is not what is engraved in stone monuments, but what is woven into the lives of others.
—PERICLES

Freemasonry does not depend on its buildings to make its way in the world. Masons have met in front parlors, stone quarries, caves, hotel ballrooms, taverns and, as the ritual says, "on high hills and low dells." Masonic temple buildings began to appear before the Revolutionary War in the United States. Of the various bursts of construction throughout the history of American Freemasonry, the most energetic was between the end of World War I and the Great Depression in 1929, a period that paralleled unprecedented construction of other American public and religious buildings. Everyone, it seemed, wanted to have their own magnificent pile in the 1920s.

When Washington, D.C., was staked out, Masonic lodges already existed in nearby Georgetown and Alexandria. The first lodge that met regularly in the District of Columbia was Federal Lodge No. 15 of Maryland, which later became Federal Lodge No. 1 under the Grand Lodge of Washington, D.C.[1] When the lodge was first chartered in 1793, it was made up largely of workmen who were constructing the Capitol building. In those days, the lodge met in a private room of a home on New Jersey Avenue, just south of the Capitol, on the present site of the Cannon House Office Building. In 1796, the lodge moved to the "Little Hotel" on F Street near 14th NW.

Columbia Lodge No. 35 was chartered in 1802 by the Grand Lodge of Maryland, made up of Treasury Department employees. Two years later, Columbia and Federal lodges jointly built the Union Lodge Room on 11th Street NW just south of Pennsylvania Avenue. They were joined by Lebanon Lodge in 1811, and the building briefly became the home to the Grand Lodge as well. In later years, Prince Hall Masons occupied it. The building was demolished near the end of the nineteenth century. The Old Post Office Pavilion, the district's first "skyscraper," now stands on the site.

Grand Lodge Buildings

The first central Masonic Hall was built in 1827 at the corner of John Marshall Place (4½ Street) and O Street NW Freemasons Hall was the location of Andrew Jackson's inaugural ball for his second term in 1833. Their second building was on southwest corner of 9th and D Streets NW from 1855 to 1870.

GRAND LODGE BUILDING (1870–1908)

901 F Street NW, Washington, DC 20004

The third Grand Lodge building was on the northwest corner of 9th and F Streets NW. For the laying of the temple's cornerstone in May 1868, President and Freemason Andrew Johnson issued an executive order giving the day off to federal employees who were Masons.

Christopher Weeks, in the *AIA Guide to the Architecture of Washington, D.C.* (Third Edition, 1994), noted:

> The polychrome stone and cast-iron veneers applied to the brick walls of this Italian Renaissance palazzo offer some of the more eye-catching façades in town. When new, the building exemplified the mixed use of space so characteristic of late-nineteenth-century, pre-zoning-code urban architecture: shops jostled one another on the ground floor, and the Masonic Hall filled the space above. President Andrew Johnson, himself a loyal Freemason, laid

Old Grand Lodge (1870–1908), now the Gallup Organization.

the cornerstone and led the gala parade that celebrated the start of construction. In its prime the hall witnessed much Gilded Age gaiety: Washingtonians feted the Prince of Wales here in 1876 at a centennial banquet, and for decades society matrons fought for the honor of having their daughter's debutante parties here.[2]

It still stands today and is the home to the Gallup Organization, just in case someone wants to try to make the claim the Masons control public opinion. Of course, it was a furniture store for a long time, which means the Masons once had the corner on the Naugahyde lounge chair market.

A century after its construction, the building fell upon hard times. It sat abandoned from 1971 until its award-winning renovation in 2000. Today, it is an outstanding example of urban restoration. The only external evidence that hints at its origin are the words "Masonic Temple" carved over the entry.

GRAND LODGE BUILDING (1908–1985)

National Museum of Women in the Arts, 1250 New York Avenue NW, Washington, DC 20005; (202) 783-5000, (800) 222-7270; www.nmwa.org

There's a certain irony that the center of Freemasonry in Washington, D.C., for seventy-five years was transformed into the National Museum of Women in the Arts in 1987. On the outside, the 1908 structure retains the Masonic symbols of its earlier owners, the Grand Lodge of Washington, D.C.

The cornerstone was laid in 1907, and the Masons were assisted by Brother Theodore Roosevelt, who was president at the time. More than two thousand Masons were accompanied by the Marine Corps Band and thousands of onlookers. When completed a year later, it had two lodge rooms, a banquet hall, a combination auditorium and ballroom, offices and a second auditorium on the top floor. It was once home to almost twenty lodges, plus York Rite and Eastern Star chapters. The law department of George Washington University was a renter at one time.

Former Grand Lodge building,
now the National Museum of Women in the Arts.

Former Grand Lodge building interior. Proscenium arch of the old stage can be seen. Stairways and balconies were added by the museum.

Little sense of the Masonic origins remains inside today. In the large open space of the museum's ground level, the proscenium arch of a theater stage can still be seen against the west wall. Property in Washington is so expensive and taxes are so high that nearly every Masonic building was originally constructed with business or rental space, or added it later, to generate income and help defray costs. This Grand Lodge building was no exception, and the ground-floor auditorium was converted to a movie house after the advent of talkies. The Masonic Theater showed movies here until the 1980s. The grand staircases and balconies that surround the old auditorium today were not original, and were added by the museum. The rest of the interior of the building has been completely converted into display and meeting space.

GRAND LODGE OF THE DISTRICT OF COLUMBIA

5428 MacArthur Boulevard NW, Washington, DC 20016; (202) 686-1811; www.dcgrandlodge.org

When the Grand Lodge built its new headquarters, a decision was made to substantially downsize. The current building is primar-

The Grand Lodge of the District of Columbia.

ily an office for the Grand Master, Grand Secretary and staff of the Grand Lodge. No lodges meet in this building, and it does not have any lodge rooms. It contains a museum and library, which are open by appointment.

MOST WORSHIPFUL PRINCE HALL GRAND LODGE OF THE DISTRICT OF COLUMBIA (AND CIVIL WAR MEMORIAL)

1000 U Street NW, Washington, DC 20001; (202) 797-8489; mwphgldc.com/grandlodge

Prince Hall Masonry started in Washington, D.C., in 1825 with the formation of Social Lodge No. 7, largely made up of free blacks who had been made Masons in England and Philadelphia. The Union Grand Lodge of the District of Columbia was formed in 1848, and Social Lodge became No. 1.

The large Prince Hall Grand Lodge building includes offices for the Grand Master and other officers

The Most Worshipful Prince Hall Grand Lodge of the District of Columbia.

and staff, as well as those of other Prince Hall Masonic groups in Washington, D.C., such as the Eastern Star and the Royal Arch. It also contains lodge rooms, and other rooms large enough to hold Grand Lodge sessions and banquets. At one time, there was even a bowling

alley in the basement. The neoclassical building, designed by African-American architect Albert I. Cassell, was built between 1922 and 1930, and is a centerpiece of the historic U Street Corridor. Up until the 1960s, U Street was Washington's "Black Broadway" and the heart of African-American business and culture.

Next to the Grand Lodge building is the African American Civil War Memorial, dedicated to the black soldiers who fought to save the Union

The adjacent African American Civil War Memorial.

during the Civil War. A nearby museum contains exhibits about the indispensable role of African-American soldiers during the war.

NAVAL MASONIC HALL

330 Pennsylvania Avenue SE, Washington, DC 20003; (202) 543-1349; www.naval-lodge.org

When Washington Naval Lodge No. 41 of Maryland (later No. 4 under the Grand Lodge of Washington, D.C.) first opened, its members rented space at 1129 7th Street SE near the gates of the Navy Yard. The upper floor was the lodge room, and the downstairs was a school. In 1820, Naval Lodge and Union No. 6 jointly built a lodge building on the northwest corner of 5th Street and Virginia Avenue SE.

In 1848, the members of Naval Lodge helped drag the cornerstone from the city railroad depot to the Washington Monument worksite and later placed their own commemorative stone within the monument itself.

Naval Masonic Hall (left) and its signature Egyptian decor (right).

Because of their association with the Egyptian-style monument, when they built their new building in 1894 the lodge room
was decorated in a brightly colored Egyptian motif. It is truly one of
the most unique and beautiful lodge rooms in the Washington, D.C.,
area, as well as the oldest lodge building still in use in the District of
Columbia.

Lodges that meet in the current building are Naval Lodge No.
4, Washington Daylight Lodge No. 14, Lafayette-Dupont Lodge No.
19 and Alianza Fraternal Americana Lodge No. 92.

ALMAS SHRINE CENTER

1315 K Street NW, Washington, DC 20005; (202) 898-1688;
www.almasshriners.org

The Ancient Arabic Nobles of the Mystic Shrine, an appendant
body to Freemasonry, originated in the 1870s as a high-spirited,
hard-drinking alternative to the teetotaling Masonic lodges. Almost
from the beginning, Shriners, readily identified by their distinctive
red fezzes, quickly became identified as professional party animals.
They are world-renowned as much for their little cars and marching

units in parades as for their philanthropy. The Shriners Hospitals comprise 23 orthopedic and burn hospitals across North America that provide care for children at no charge to families.

The Almas Shrine building, located in the business area of Washington, D.C., looks strangely out of place on Franklin Square with its distinctive Arabic façade. Built on the eve of the Great Depression in 1929, it would be easily mistaken for a mosque, with its pointed arches and its beautiful terracotta tile work. It houses offices for the Potentate and other officers of the local Shrine. It contains one of the city's most impressive ballrooms and can accommodate four hundred guests. The Sphinx Club, with its characteristic vaulted arches, is a true hidden treasure in the district. There is also an auditorium and smaller rooms where the Shrine and some of its groups hold meetings. The Lodge of the Nine Muses No. 1776, named after the famous

Almas Shrine Center.

Paris lodge of Franklin and Voltaire, meets here.

Famed "March King" John Philip Sousa, a member of Almas, was the honorary director of their Shrine Band until his death in 1932. He composed the march Nobles of the Mystic Shrine in 1923.

The biggest secret of the Almas Shrine is that it was not built at this location. At one time, the Shrine owned the entire block now dominated by the Franklin Square office complex. In 1987, to make way for the new office building, its façade was dismantled brick by brick into thirty-five thousand pieces, numbered, catalogued, moved and reassembled in its present spot. The meeting rooms, auditorium and dining space are all new construction.

Georgetown Masonic Hall.

GEORGETOWN MASONIC HALL

1212 Wisconsin Avenue NW, Washington, DC 20007; (202) 337-9709; www.potomac5.org

Six lodges, including Potomac Lodge No. 5, and Benjamin B. French Lodge No. 15, meet in this hall. The original lodge building was constructed in 1859, and the first floor was leased to W. T. Weaver & Sons Hardware Store. In 1963 a spectacular five-alarm fire totally destroyed the Masonic Hall, and a new building was erected here the following year. Today, the venerable Weaver's, a Georgetown institution for more than a century, is gone, and the downstairs is inhabited by Abercrombie & Fitch.

TAKOMA MASONIC CENTER

115 Carroll Street NW, Washington, DC 20012; (202) 829-7790; www.ht10.com

Ten different lodges meet in this building in the northwest part of the

Takoma Masonic Center.

District, including Hiram-Takoma Lodge No. 10. It's hard to miss at night with the large backlit square and compasses against its brick façade. The Takoma Center has recently been redecorated on the inside and contains one of the most beautiful painted cloud pattern ceilings anywhere, ranging from darkness to sunrise.

Anacostia Masonic Hall.

ANACOSTIA MASONIC HALL

2010 Martin Luther King Jr. Avenue SE, Washington, DC 20003; (202) 678-6546; www.anacostialodge.org

The Anacostia section of Washington has been a working-class neighborhood since the 1850s, largely providing homes for workers at the nearby Naval Yard across the river. Frederick Douglass, Marvin Gaye, Ezra Pound, Marion Barry and Roy Clark have all called Anacostia home, but there's no denying that the suburb has seen better days.

The lodge was chartered in 1868. Like so many other lodge buildings in Washington and other cities, Anacostia Lodge No. 21 constructed their current home with a source of income downstairs. Built in 1940, the only visible sign of a Masonic presence is a door at the east end of the storefront. The commercial space is presently home to a large furniture store.

Singleton Masonic Hall.

SINGLETON MASONIC HALL

4441 Wisconsin Avenue NW, Washington, DC 20016; (202) 364-9409

Seven lodges meet in the mint-green Singleton Masonic Hall, including William R. Singleton–Hope–Lebanon

Lodge No. 7, whose hyphenated name evinces several consolidations over the years. It is also home to Justice–Columbia Lodge No. 3, one of the oldest lodges in the city.

Other Masonic Buildings in Washington, D.C.

SCOTTISH RITE CENTER

2800 16th Street NW, Washington, DC 20009; (202) 232-8155; www.dcsr.org

The first home of the Scottish Rite in the District of Columbia was on the southwest corner of 7th and D Streets NW in 1875. The first Scottish Rite Cathedral was built at 1007 G Street NW in 1886 and lasted until 1910.

Today's Scottish Rite Center for the Orient of the District of Columbia and the Valley of Washington sits just a few short blocks up 16th Street from the Supreme Council's headquarters, the House

Scottish Rite Center, Orient of the District of Columbia and the Valley of Washington.

of the Temple. The Scottish Rite Center, while certainly smaller and less grandiose than its cousin down the street, is still a beautiful building.

Scottish Rite degrees are presented to large classes or convocations of members, and they are done in a theatrical setting. The Rite's degrees are dramatized as theatrical plays, complete with elaborate sets, props, costumes and lighting. They are large, complex affairs, and staging them requires a hundred or more men onstage and off.

As a result, Scottish Rite facilities are generally large structures, and the Washington, D.C., center is no exception. It contains a large and impressive auditorium and a massive banquet hall and kitchen, along with lodge rooms used by area Masonic lodges. The building is home to Federal No. 1, the first lodge chartered in the district just one day before the laying of the White House cornerstone.

THE HOUSE OF THE TEMPLE

The Supreme Council, 33°, 1733 16th Street NW, Washington, DC 20009; (202) 232-3579; www.scottishrite.org

The House of the Temple on 16th Street NW is the headquarters of the Ancient Accepted Scottish Rite, Southern Jurisdiction.[3]

The Scottish Rite, an appendant body of Freemasonry, offers additional degree experiences to 3° Master Masons. Many have likened it to "continuing education." The Rite confers its fourth through thirty-second degrees on men who have already received their Master Mason (3°) degree in their local lodge. The belief that 32° members of the Scottish Rite are somehow more important or exalted than a 3° Master Mason is false, as is the notion that only a certain rarified group attains the 32°, making them so-called "high-ranking" Freemasons. Once a man attends his first Scottish Rite convocation to receive his degrees, no matter what other degrees may be conferred on him, he will, in most cases, become a 32° Mason. This is not true outside of the United States, where it may take many years to slowly advance through the degrees. But in the U.S., joining the Scottish Rite almost always makes you a 32° Mason.

The House of the Temple, headquarters of the Ancient Accepted Scottish Rite, Southern Jurisdiction, Supreme Council 33°.

There is also a 33° conferred by the Scottish Rite. It is an honorary position bestowed on several hundred men every year who have served the Rite, Masonic fraternity or society in an extraordinary way. The governing board of the Rite, the Supreme Council, is made up entirely of 33° Scottish Rite Masons. Their authority only extends to the business of the Scottish Rite, and they have no say-so over other Masonic organizations, including the state Grand Lodges. As big and imposing as the House of the Temple may be, and as impressive as the name may sound, the Supreme Council 33° only governs the Scottish Rite in thirty-five states of the U.S.

The House of the Temple is without equal in the world of modern Masonic architecture. It even looks like what you'd expect the headquarters of a secret society to look like. Its imposing façade, guarded by two sphinxes, does indeed conceal magnificent treasures. Completed in 1916, the building and much of its interior decoration were designed by architect John Russell Pope, whose other accomplishments include the Jefferson Memorial. For decades, the House of the Temple has been revered and praised by the architectural community as one of the top examples in the world of the Classical style.

The design is based on the legendary Mausoleum at Halicarnassus in Persia, one of the Seven Wonders of the Ancient World. The original mausoleum was built as the burial place for King Mausollos of Caria in about 350 B.C. in southwestern Turkey on the Aegean Sea, in the city of what is today known as Bodrum. The House of the Temple is related to the ancient mausoleum in more than just architectural detail. It's filled with libraries, museums and even a tomb.

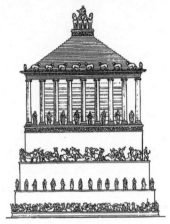

The Mausoleum at Halicarnassus, inspiration for the House of the Temple's design.

The Scottish Rite draws upon many ancient cultures and religions for its ritual ceremonies and moral teachings. As you explore the building, you'll see details with Greek, Egyptian and Persian origins. Symbolism is in every crevice. There's even a manhole cover behind the rear entrance inlaid with glass in the shape of a Seal of Solomon. As you approach the entrance, two massive seventeen-ton sphinxes guard the steps. The sphinx on the right, its eyes closed in contemplation, symbolizes Wisdom, and the one on the left, its eyes wide open, symbolizes Power. Look up and you'll see thirty-three Greek Ionic columns (themselves a Masonic symbol of Wisdom) supporting the upper tier, capped by what resembles a stepped pyramid. Some comparing the "unfinished pyramid" on the top of the House of the Temple to the unfinished pyramid in the Great Seal of the United States have attempted to make a symbolic connection, but the design is actually taken from a description of the mausoleum by the Roman author Pliny in his work *Natural History*, written almost two thousand years ago.[4] On the top of the flat portion of the pyramid of King Mausollos's original was a sculpture of four horses and a marble chariot.

Albert Pike lived in the romantic Victorian period, when the public had an endless fascination with Egyptian, Assyrian, Hebrew, Greek and Roman imagery, and he injected it into his rewritten ceremonies for the Rite. As a result, the House of the Temple combines those same influences architecturally. Passing through the bronze doors, you enter a lavish hall lined by deep green marble Doric columns, ending with a grand staircase. Greek, Egyptian and Assyrian statues, carvings and details fill the room, lit by tall brass sconces.

The grand staircase leads to the stunning Temple Room, the ceremonial meeting place of the 33° Supreme Commanders of the Scottish Rite Southern Jurisdiction. Each stained-glass window is adorned with a brass sculpture celebrating illumination, the symbol for knowledge. The symbol of the order, the double-headed eagle, is frequently represented in an elongated, Egyptian style, as in the panels around the skylight.

The Temple room is actually used for only a few ceremonies, such as the meeting of the 33° Supreme Council. For their regular, non-ceremonial meetings, they gather in the Executive Chamber, a smaller and slightly cozier room that contains just thirty-three seats, one for each member of the council.

There are museum rooms dedicated to famous Scottish Rite Masons from Burl Ives to J. Edgar Hoover. The temple is also home to the largest Masonic library in the United States, which includes Albert Pike's private collection. Many of Pike's personal effects are here as well. The Robert Burns Library is one of the finest and most complete collections of Scotland and Freemasonry's bard. Other specialized holding include private collections of Abraham Lincoln material, esoteric literature and the works of Johann Wolfgang Goethe. The temple's library is the oldest library open to the public in the District of Columbia, and today contains more than 250,000 volumes.

The building houses a warren of offices, meeting rooms, display areas and storage vaults. The House of the Temple is a modern-day national treasure. Including its contents, its worth has been estimated at between $350 and $400 million.[5]

Even the address of the building, 1733, is not the proper address. It was created with the help of the U.S. Post Office to interject the symbolism of thirty-three. The number thirty-three was not selected at random by the originators of the Scottish Rite. It has long been considered sacred within Christianity for several reasons. It is the multiple use of three, signifying the Holy Trinity. Christ was thirty-three years old when he ascended into heaven, and the gospels list thirty-three miracles performed by Christ. Many Christian obediences use the number of three or thirty-three in their symbolism. Thirty-three also appears in the Old Testament and other Jewish writings. Jacob had thirty-three children; Mosaic Law required that a women purify herself for thirty-three days after her male child was circumcised; the holy day of Lag B'Omer occurs thirty-three days after the start of Passover; and the Seal of Solomon, or Star of David, made up of two intersecting triangles, is considered a graphic representation of 3+3. It also plays a prominent role in Kabbalah. The religions of Islam, Zoroastrianism, Buddhism and Hinduism all associate sacred meanings with the number thirty-three. Therefore, it appears in the Scottish Rite as a symbol of the fraternity's universality as well as the perfection that every man should aspire to achieve in his soul.

Albert Pike, the sage of the Scottish Rite's Southern Jurisdiction and its Sovereign Commander for thirty-two years, is actually buried within the building itself. Although he had instructed that his body be cremated and his ashes strewn around the roots of two acacia trees in front of the Supreme Council's original home, he was buried in Oak Hill Cemetery instead. When the new building was finished, his remains were moved to a vault in a beautiful stained-glass light well under the main staircase.

One other curious connection with Freemasonry exists with the inspiration of the House of the Temple's design. The ancient Mausoleum at Halicarnassus was partially damaged by an earthquake after standing strong for almost sixteen centuries. Then the Turks invaded the region and destroyed what was left. The Knights of St. John of Malta invaded the area and built an enormous fortified castle in 1496. They dismantled the mausoleum to get the stones for their construction project, and today there is nothing left of the original ancient structure apart from a few foundation stones. The Knights of Malta today appear as a part of the chivalric orders of the York Rite of Freemasonry.

ORDER OF THE EASTERN STAR NATIONAL HEADQUARTERS

1618 New Hampshire Avenue NW, Washington, DC 20009; (202) 667-4737; www.easternstar.org

The Order of the Eastern Star is an appendant organization of Freemasonry that allows female spouses and relatives of Freemasons to participate. It does not confer the degrees of Freemasonry on its members but has its own ceremonies and degrees, called "star points." Although it is considered to be non-denominational, its symbolism is based on the Old and New Testaments, relating the tales of five heroines of the Bible and their virtues. The predominant symbol of

Order of the Eastern Star National Headquarters.

the order is the inverted pentagram, representing the Star of Bethlehem rising in the East and pointing down to the birthplace of Christ.

The national headquarters of the Order of the Eastern Star is in a magnificent mansion built on a triangular lot on New Hampshire Avenue NW. Built between 1906 and 1909 by Perry and Jessie Belmont, it was part of Washington high society's party circuit for sixteen years.

The home was sold to the Grand Chapter of the Order of the Eastern Star in 1935. As part of the agreement with the Belmont family, it must remain in use as a residence, so besides being the headquarters of the order, it is the home of the Grand Secretary. The carefully preserved residence contains paintings and antique furnishings collected by the Perrys. *National Treasure* fans take note: The mansion contains both a "gold room" and a "treasure room."

GEORGE WASHINGTON MASONIC NATIONAL MEMORIAL
101 Callahan Drive, Alexandria, VA 22301; (703) 683-2007;
www.gwmemorial.org

In 1911, a meeting took place at Alexandria-Washington Lodge No. 22 in Alexandria, Virginia, in a room over City Hall. The lodge was in possession of artifacts from President Washington's life, especially from the moment of his death at Mount Vernon. These were priceless relics, and the lodge wanted to create a museum to both display and protect them.

On May 22, 1932, the George Washington Masonic National Memorial was dedicated. It was grander than anything the men who assembled in 1911 had ever dreamed. In spite of the individual sovereignty of the Grand Lodges in each state, this remains the only national project built with the participation of all of them. Unlike the more famous monument in Washington, D.C., this one was erected in just ten years, entirely from the contributions of American Freemasons.

It is three hundred thirty-three feet tall—considerably shorter than its more famous cousin across the Potomac. It is built on the highest point in Alexandria, Shooter's Hill, the site of a seventeenth-century plantation, an eighteenth-century home and a Union fort during the Civil War.

Like the legendary lighthouse that adorned the harbor of Alexandria in ancient Egypt, this modern-day "lighthouse" holds cherished relics and knowledge of the fraternity. The centerpieces of the memorial include the bronze statue of Washington in the colonnaded Memorial Hall and murals depicting the cornerstone ceremony of the Capitol and General Washington with his officers at Christ Church in Philadelphia during a St. John's Day Observance on December 28, 1788. There is an extensive museum filled with artifacts relating to Washington, sponsored by the Southern and Northern Masonic Jurisdictions of the Scottish Rite. The Memorial's library contains over twenty thousand volumes of Masonic and related works.

The George Washington Masonic National Memorial in Alexandria.

The Memorial is home to two lodges that meet regularly, plus a lodge of research and at least seven other Masonic groups. Alexandria-Washington Lodge No. 22 has a recreated lodge room from the period during which Washington was a member. It is a replica of the room in Old Town Alexandria where the lodge met for many years. The lodge today meets in a separate lodge room in the Memorial. Andrew Jackson Lodge No. 120 meets in the North Lodge Room, a differently styled chamber with Gothic details.

The various affiliated organizations of Freemasonry contributed to the memorial as well, and several floors are designed and dedicated to them. The top floor, which also serves as an observation deck, contains a representation of the interior of King Solomon's Temple and Solomon's throne room, presented by the Tall Cedars of Lebanon.

The York Rite's Knights Templar sponsor a medieval chapel. The other two York Rite groups, the Royal Arch Masons and the Cryptic Masons, present scenes from the building of the Temple, the Ark of the Covenant, and the secret crypts said to have been excavated beneath the Temple during the time of Enoch. The Ancient Arabic Nobles of the Mystic Shrine, the fez-wearing Shriners, have a large display area promoting their charitable works and their twenty-two children's hospitals throughout North America. Likewise, the Mystic Order of Veiled Prophets of the Enchanted Realm, better known as the Grottos, has a floor dedicated to its social and charitable mission. Other members of the Masonic family are represented, including the National Sojourners, other York Rite bodies and the youth groups like De Molay.

✦ ✦ ✦

GADSBY'S TAVERN MUSEUM AND RESTAURANT

134 North Royal Street, Alexandria, VA 22314; (703) 838-4242; http://oha.alexandriava.gov/gadsby

Alexandria represents a return to the beginning of Freemasonry's connection to the founding of Washington, D.C. Tavern

Gadsby's Tavern Museum and Restaurant in Alexandria.

The lighthouse at Jones Point

proprietor John Wise's establishment on Royal Street is where the Masonic procession drank, dined and set off for the ceremonial laying of the first boundary marker for the Federal District in 1791. It survives today as Gadsby's Tavern Museum and Restaurant. The museum side has been restored to its Revolutionary War period appearance, and the restaurant serves appropriately authentic fare. Unlike so many other places that have made the fanciful claim over the years, George Washington really did eat here, along with many notable political figures of the period. In the late 1700s, it was the center of political and social life.

JONES POINT LIGHT

Jones Point Park, Alexandria, VA

Today, the site of Washington, D.C.'s origin is all but forgotten. A public park exists at Jones Point, accessible only by a bicycle path, and in the shadow of the Woodrow Wilson Bridge that carries the busy Capital Beltway traffic overhead.

Alexandria eventually turned its back on the Federal City. By the 1840s, local merchants were less than enthusiastic over the lackluster financial rewards of being on the southern bank of the Potomac,

Where it all began: the first boundary marker of the Federal City, in its hidden location under the Jones Point lighthouse.

since most development was happening on the Maryland side where L'Enfant's plan was centered. In addition, pro-abolitionist sentiments were growing within the Federal District, which would shut area Virginians out of the lucrative slave trade. And they had much the same complaint over a lack of representation and self-government that Washington's modern citizens still have today. After four decades of complaining, the portion of the District of Columbia south and west of the Potomac, including Arlington, Alexandria and Jones Point, was "retroceded" back to Virginia in 1847.

A lighthouse was built on the Point in 1855, and the stone sea-wall along the shore was constructed several years later, burying the first boundary marker of the Federal City. In 1912, the marker was excavated from its hiding place. It turned out to be a replacement stone erected in 1794. There is no record of what happened to the original stone from the Masonic ceremony just three years before.

When the lighthouse was restored by the Daughters of the American Revolution in the 1920s, an abscess was created in the seawall, and a steel door and grate were installed to protect the boundary stone. There is no historical plaque or any other evidence that this is where the city of Washington, D.C., began with so much fanfare and hope. Even the inscriptions on the marker have deteriorated badly and cannot be read. The intrepid explorer who knows what to look for can still find it today, buried in its ignominious cell, anonymous and all but hidden from view under the Jones Point lighthouse.

CHAPTER 12

'Tis Well

✦✦✦

To enlarge the sphere of social happiness is worthy [of]
the benevolent design of the Masonic Institution; and it is
most fervently to be wished, that the conduct of every
member of the fraternity, as well as those publications
which discover the principles which actuate them may tend
to convince Mankind that the grand object of Masonry is
to promote the happiness of the human race . . . I sincere-
ly pray that the Great Architect of the Universe may bless
you and receive you hereafter into his immortal Temple.
—GEORGE WASHINGTON[1]

On Thursday, December 12, 1799, George Washington rode out to
inspect portions of his five farms, as he had nearly every day since the
end of his presidency. Unfortunately on this particular day, he was
caught in the rain, wind and sleet of a terrible winter storm. When
he returned that afternoon, his hair caked with snow, he was quite
wet in spite of his woolen greatcoat.

The next day, he went out into three inches of new snow and
freezing weather and insisted on marking trees he wanted cut down.
His throat was sore, and he became hoarse as the day progressed. By
late evening, it was clear that he was having trouble breathing.

On Saturday morning, he had a severe fever and could hardly
speak. He asked his personal secretary, Tobias Lear, to send for his
family physician, Dr. James Craik, who had served with the general
during the French and Indian War and all through the Revolution.
Washington's wife Martha also sent for Dr. Gustavus Brown, who
was living across the river from Mount Vernon in Maryland, in case
Craik was otherwise detained.

Washington anticipated that Dr. Craik would prescribe "bleeding" to draw off the "bad blood" that was believed to cause fever and illness, so he also had Lear send for Albin Rawlins, one of Washington's overseers from his nearby Union Farm, a veterinarian who was also proficient in the practice of bloodletting. The general wanted him to get an early start, even if the doctors hadn't yet arrived. Martha was alarmed over the amount of blood that Rawlins drained from her husband, even though Washington kept encouraging him to draw "More! More!"

Dr. Craik arrived shortly thereafter and concurred that bleeding was the proper treatment, especially since the general couldn't manage to swallow any throat-soothing mixtures that were offered. One attempt to gargle nearly choked him to death. Craik drew more blood, but he desperately wanted another opinion. Since Dr. Brown had not yet arrived, he sent for Dr. Elisha Cullen Dick, a resident of Alexandria and Master of Alexandria Lodge No. 22, where Washington was a member.

Eventually, all three doctors were in attendance and attempted to diagnose Washington's deteriorating condition. Brown and Craik decided it was "quinsy," an inflammation related to tonsillitis. Dr. Dick was considerably younger than the other two physicians, and his education was more recent and better informed in new methods of diagnosis. He believed that Washington's throat membranes had swollen shut. The general was literally choking to death, and he recommended an immediate tracheotomy. Such a radical procedure had never been done in the United States at that time, and Brown and Craik rejected both the diagnosis and Dick's recommendation. The two older doctors continued to bleed him over the protests of both Martha and Dick, eventually drawing nearly five pints of blood from the dying man—almost half his body's blood supply. Unbeknownst to them, his larynx had swollen shut and he was dying of asphyxia aggravated by dehydration and the loss of blood.

A few minutes before ten o'clock on Saturday night, as the helpless doctors looked on, Washington whispered his final words to Lear.

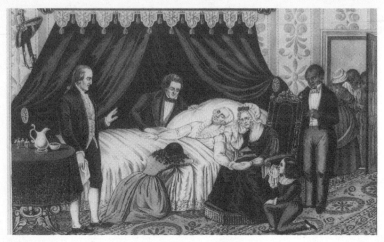

The death of George Washington.

"I am just going; Have me decently buried; and do not let my body be put into the vault in less than three days after I am dead. Do you understand?" Lear promised he would do as Washington asked. The general nodded slightly, and said, "'Tis well."[2]

For a moment, his breathing became less labored, less ragged. A short time later, he felt for his own pulse and then died. The father of the nation, its greatest war hero, its first president, quietly slipped away into history. His friend, his doctor and his Masonic brother, Dr. Elisha Dick, turned away from the scene, knowing that he might very well have saved him had he been allowed to do what he knew was right. Doctor Craik would later admit with great sorrow that Dr. Dick had been correct and that their friend might have survived if they had listened to him.

Brother Dick walked across the general's bedroom to the clock that sat on the fireplace mantel. He reached into his pocket for his folding knife, opened the back of the clock, and sliced through the catgut string that operated its mechanism. The ticking stopped, and the hands froze at 10:20, where they remain to this day in the George Washington Masonic National Memorial's museum.

News traveled slowly in those days. Congress was in session in Philadelphia, and they would not know of Washington's death until the day of the funeral. Martha Washington followed the general's wishes for his burial. He would never be placed in the crypt being prepared under the rotunda of the Capitol House, which was being built across the river in the new city that would bear his name. Nor would he be enshrined in a new monument that would eventually be erected in geometric alignment with the Congress House and the President's House. He was, first and foremost, the master of Mount Vernon, a Virginia farmer, and there he would remain.

Washington's body had been placed on a bed in Mount Vernon's front drawing room. So that the cold would preserve him, no fires were lit. On December 17, the lead-lined mahogany casket arrived.

The next day, Wednesday, December 18, the procession began to form outside Mount Vernon's mansion. Servants had cleared the snow between the house and the crypt, and mourners began to gather just before noon. The Virginia Militia was delayed, so the gathering was given a last opportunity to view the body. At 3 p.m., the procession at last lined up and made its way to the place of burial. As it went, a schooner anchored out in the Potomac fired its cannon in salute.

The Freemasons of Alexandria Lodge No. 22 assembled to perform their final duty to their fallen brother, sending him on to the celestial lodge above. His friend and brother, Dr. Elisha Dick, performed the Masonic funeral service, and the Reverend James Muir assisted with the prayers and Bible readings.

The Reverend Thomas Davis read the Episcopal Prayer Book's funeral service and praised Washington's character and virtues in the sermon that followed. Then, as is still the practice today, the Masons stepped forward to conduct the final ceremony due a Master Mason. Worshipful Master Dick stood at the head of the casket and Reverend Muir at its foot, and they recited the service from memory.

"From time immemorial," Dr. Dick intoned, "it has been the custom among the fraternity of free and accepted Masons, at the request of a brother upon his death-bed, to accompany his corpse to its place of interment, and there to deposit his remains with the usual formalities."

He spoke the same words used for all men of the fraternity—dustmen, cobblers, bankers, doctors, blacksmiths and presidents, "whose memory we revere, and whose loss we now deplore." In death as in life, all Masons meet upon the level, act upon the plumb, and part upon the square, and the loss of one brother weakens the chain by which all Masons are united.

Finally, Dr. Dick approached the body of Washington and deposited within the coffin his Masonic apron—an emblem of innocence and the badge of a Mason. It was followed by a sprig of evergreen representing the acacia plant, a Masonic symbol of immortality and rebirth. When they finished, the lead seal was laid in place, then the casket lid. The wooden box was closed, and a black cloth pall was laid over the top.

Washington's remains were carried into the vault, and its door was closed. The artillery and infantry assembled nearby simultaneously fired three volleys, the traditional symbolic military ritual marking the end of the battle of life. The funeral party returned to the mansion and, after some light refreshments, sadly went their separate ways.

Several years later, the simple brick crypt was deemed too small for George and Martha's remains, and perhaps a little too simple. After three decades, a new crypt was built nearby. The gates were flanked with two matching Egyptian-style obelisks, foreshadowing the Washington Monument years before it would be constructed.

Washington's will is fascinating to read. Apart from the many specific pieces of property he designated to family, friends and servants, he made remarkable provisions for a man of the period. He freed his slaves upon the death of his wife Martha and saw to it that those who could not make their own way in the world would be provided for. He left money to start a "free school" for orphans. He established a university.

But one seemingly small passage especially caught my eye as I looked over the carefully handwritten document. In it, he left his military swords to each of his nephews,

... accompanied with an injunction not to unsheath them for the purpose of shedding blood, except it be for self defence, or in defence of their Country and its rights; and in the latter case, to keep them unsheathed, and prefer falling with them in their hands, to the relinquishment thereof.[3]

Honor remained his watchword, even as he contemplated his own death. Moreover, it was a lesson he insisted be passed on to the next generation. In short, Brother George Washington was in death as he was in life, a living example of Masonic principles of truth, honor, faith, hope and charity.

✦ ✦ ✦

There is a secret room in the Library of Congress. Well . . . not exactly a secret, but the public doesn't usually get to see it. It is the private reading room reserved for the members of Congress itself. On the ceiling of that room are seven round ceiling panels, painted by the artist Carl Gutherz, and they represent a unique idea. Gutherz took the colors of the spectrum that go together to make up white light one step farther. Each panel is painted in a different hue—red, orange, yellow, green, blue, indigo and violet. The panels also depict the spectrum of intelligence and achievement: faith in God; excellence through progress; truth destroying ignorance; learning through research; science harnessing nature; literature and poetry; and, finally, liberty, suffrage, justice and equality placed in the care of the state. The symbols are there to inspire the men who govern us, who make our laws, who affect our lives every day, whether they have ever gazed up at them over their copies of Roll Call or not.

Like these images, the symbolism that appears in the philosophy of Freemasonry is there to inspire the individual Mason to think higher thoughts, perform nobler deeds and attain greater achievements. Freemasonry is not a religion. It is not a plan for worldwide domination. It is an institution that inspires its members simply to be better men, better citizens, better sons and fathers. And like Carl Gutherz's paintings, it does so by encouraging them to pursue "light" in all of its spiritual and intellectual forms. Freemasonry, like any other institution on earth, is neither saintly nor demonic. It is an institution that encourages Masons to be the best possible men they can be to their families, their communities and their Creator. By their hard work and example, perhaps the world may become a better place. To suggest anything more diabolical is a despicable accusation that is bred of ignorance and is a gross insult to the millions of men who have been Freemasons the world over.

Masonic "secrecy" is an overrated myth, and has become an all-purpose bogeyman. The new Freemason, the Entered Apprentice, is taught "secrecy" as a lesson in keeping his word. It goes hand-in-hand with honor. If he cannot keep a promise not to show his non-Masonic buddies a funny handshake or tell them a password—even if it has been published in books and available to the public for three centuries—how can his word be trusted? What does it say of his character? If Freemasonry were truly teaching its members something dangerous, scandalous, unscrupulous, seditious, treasonable or Satanic, would millions of men have joined, encouraged their children to join, and proudly proclaimed their own membership? Wouldn't thousands, and even hundreds of thousands, of men walk away in disgust, especially from a group that has no punishment or threat over those who simply stop paying their annual dues, apart from expulsion?

Most importantly, would men like George Washington have remained Masons all their lives if what they had found within its lodge rooms was evil? Would men as diverse as Benjamin Franklin, Paul Revere, John Hancock and John Dickinson have joined and remained Masons if the institution itself were dishonorable? Would fourteen U.S. presidents on all sides of the political spectrum have remained members of the fraternity if they had found themselves pawns of an evil, occult organization? For that matter, what of the literally thousands of ministers, rabbis, priests, imams and other religious leaders who have been Masons over the centuries? Were they all agreeable to participate in a Satanic ritual and too frightened to stop paying dues and walk away?

Of course not.

Solomon's Builders still construct temples on Earth today, but they do not need to hew stones or erect marble edifices. They do not need to hide cryptic messages in street maps or conceal strange symbols in the dentils and modillions of public buildings. The temples they build are in their own hearts—spiritual buildings, not made with hands. And the monuments they leave behind are far more eternal than any limestone obelisk.

That is the true secret of Freemasonry.

Appendix

The Masonic Presidents of the United States

The following are the generally accepted, known U.S. presidents who were members of the Masonic fraternity.

GEORGE WASHINGTON, 1ST PRESIDENT, 1789–1797

Commanding general during American Revolution, made a Master Mason August 4, 1753, in Fredericksburg Lodge (now No. 4), A.F. & A.M., Fredericksburg, Virginia.

JAMES MONROE, 5TH PRESIDENT, 1817–1825

Made a Master Mason November 9, 1775, in Williamsburg Lodge (now No. 6), A.F. & A.M., Williamsburg, Virginia.

ANDREW JACKSON, 7TH PRESIDENT, 1829–1837

Harmony Lodge No. 1, Nashville, Tennessee, an Honorary Member of Federal Lodge No. 1, F. & A.M., Washington, D.C., and Jackson Lodge No. 1, F. & A.M., Tallahassee, Florida. In 1822 and 1823 he served as the Grand Master of Masons in Tennessee.

JAMES KNOX POLK, 11TH PRESIDENT, 1845–1849

Made a Master Mason September 4, 1820, in Columbia Lodge No. 31, F. & A.M., Columbia, Tennessee.

JAMES BUCHANAN, 15TH PRESIDENT, 1857–1861

Made a Master Mason January 24, 1817, in Lodge No. 43, F. & A.M., Lancaster, Pennsylvania.

ANDREW JOHNSON, 17TH PRESIDENT, 1865–1869

Made a Master Mason in May 1851, in Greeneville Lodge No. 119 (now No. 3), F. & A.M., Greeneville, Tennessee.

JAMES ABRAM GARFIELD, 20TH PRESIDENT, 1881

Made a Mason November 22, 1864, in Columbus Lodge No. 30, F. & A.M., Columbus, Ohio.

WILLIAM MCKINLEY, 25TH PRESIDENT, 1897–1901

Made a Master Mason May 3, 1865, in Hiram Lodge No. 21, A.F. & A.M., Winchester, Virginia.

THEODORE ROOSEVELT, 26TH PRESIDENT, 1901–1909

Made a Master Mason April 24, 1901, in Matinecock Lodge No. 806, F. & A.M., Oyster Bay, New York.

WILLIAM HOWARD TAFT, 27TH PRESIDENT, 1909–1913

Chief Justice Supreme Court 1921–1930; made a "Mason at Sight" in an "Occasional Lodge" called for that purpose on February 18, 1909, in the Scottish Rite Cathedral, Cincinnati, Ohio, by Charles S. Hoskinson, Grand Master of Masons in Ohio.

WARREN GAMALIEL HARDING, 29TH PRESIDENT, 1921–1923

Made a Master Mason August 27, 1920, in Marion Lodge No. 70, F. & A.M., Marion, Ohio.

FRANKLIN DELANO ROOSEVELT, 32ND PRESIDENT, 1933–1945

Made a Master Mason November 28, 1911, in Holland Lodge No. 8, F. & A.M., New York, New York, the same Lodge in which George Washington, the first U.S. president, held Honorary membership.

HARRY S TRUMAN, 33RD PRESIDENT, 1945–1951

Made a Master Mason March 18, 1909, in Belton Lodge No. 450, A.F. & A.M., Belton, Missouri. Served as Grand Master of Missouri in 1940. In 1911, several Members of Belton Lodge separated to establish Grandview Lodge No. 618, Grandview, Missouri, and Brother Truman served as its first Worshipful Master. Served as Grand Master of Missouri in 1940–41. Was made a Sovereign Grand

Inspector General, 33º, and Honorary Member, Supreme Council on October 19, 1945, at the Supreme Council A.A.S.R. Southern Jurisdiction Headquarters in Washington, D.C., upon which occasion he served as Exemplar (Representative) for his Class. Elected an Honorary Grand Master of the International Supreme Council, Order of DeMolay. On May 18, 1959, Truman was presented with a fifty-year award, the only U.S. president to reach that golden anniversary in Freemasonry.

GERALD R. FORD, JR., 38TH PRESIDENT, 1974–1977

He was raised to the Sublime degree of Master Mason on May 18, 1951, in Columbia Lodge No. 3, F. & A.M., of Washington, D.C., as a courtesy for Malta Lodge No. 465, F. & A.M., of Grand Rapids, Michigan.

James Madison is strongly believed to have been a Mason, but his membership has never been conclusively proved.

Thomas Jefferson was also long considered to have been a Mason, but no definitive proof has ever been found.

Lyndon Baines Johnson took the Entered Apprentice degree in Johnson City Lodge No. 561, Johnson City, Texas, on October 30, 1937, but never advanced.

William Jefferson Clinton joined the Masonic youth group DeMolay in the ninth grade. While he wrote favorably about DeMolay and Freemasonry, he never went on to join a lodge.

Endnotes

◆ ◆ ◆

INTRODUCTION

1. Richard Brookhiser, *Founding Father: Rediscovering George Washington* (New York: Free Press Publishing, 1997), p. 149.

CHAPTER 1: A KNOCK AT THE DOOR

1. Sources conflict as to the meeting place of Fredericksburg Lodge during this period. The earliest written records date to September of 1752. It is believed that the lodge met in Freemason Charles Julian's Tavern on the northeast corner of Amelia and Caroline streets in Fredericksburg. It has also been rumored that the lodge met for a time in Charles Washington's Rising Sun Tavern, but that has been largely discounted. It is possible that the lodge met in the Market House, the large brick city hall building, at this time, which it certainly did after 1762. Unfortunately, lodge records rarely mentioned where meetings actually took place in those days. For details, see Jeffrey Garth Edmunds, *250 Years of Freemasonry in Fredericksburg* (Central Rappahannock Regional Library, May 31, 2003), www.historypoint.org/columns2.asp?column_id=529&column_type=hpfeature.

2. There is no written version of the ritual used at Washington's Masonic degrees, but this account is taken from Samuel Pritchard's *Jachin and Boaz: An Authentic Key to the Door of Freemasonry* (1762: Facsimile edition by Kessinger Publishing). Pritchard published several exposés of Masonic ritual in London, beginning with *Masonry Dissected* in 1730. *Jachin and Boaz* was published just ten years after Washington's initiation, and it is remarkably close to the most commonly used Masonic rituals in the United States today. Confusingly, it is divided into two sections that seem to describe the Entered Apprentice degree in two completely different ways—presumably because of the growing schism between the Ancient and Modern lodges brewing in both England and the colonies during this period. I have chosen the section that more closely parallels the modern format, believing it is probably the version most commonly in use during the mid-1700s in the

American colonies. It closely parallels the form and words that Thomas Smith Webb based his *Freemason's Monitor* on in 1818.

3. "The Lodge of Fredericksburg" would later become Fredericksburg Lodge No. 4 after the Revolution under the Grand Lodge of Virginia, and it still exists today.

4. "The Character of a Freemason," in *The Farmer's Almanack*, ed. Robert B. Thomas (Boston: J.H.A. Frost, 1823).

5. The account of King Athelstan's role in originating the first guild of Freemasons appears in the earliest known Masonic document, the Regius Poem, also known as the Halliwell manuscript, written in approximately A.D. 1390, and located in the British Museum. It is believed by most scholars to have been copied from an even earlier source.

6. See in particular David Stevenson's *The Origins of Freemasonry: Scotland's Century 1590–1710* (Cambridge, MA: Cambridge University Press, 1988).

7. See John J. Robinson's *Born in Blood: The Lost Secrets of Freemasonry* (M. Evans & Company, 1990). See also Michael Baigent and Richard Leigh's *The Temple and the Lodge* (New York: Arcade Publishing, 1989).

8. Tobias Churton's *The Golden Builders* (York Beach, ME: Red Wheel/Weiser, 2005) is an excellent examination of the Hermetic, Greek and Rosicrucian theories of Freemasonry's origins, and the original students of Rosicrucianism who may have influenced modern Freemasonry.

9. The biblical account of the building of Solomon's Temple can be found in I Kings Chapter 6, and II Chronicles Chapter 3.

10. Samuel Eliot Morison, *The Young Man Washington* (Cambridge, MA: Harvard University Press, 1932).

11. John J. Lanier, *Washington: The Great American Mason* (New York: Macoy Publishing, 1922), pp. 24–25.

12. Pritchard, p. 27.

CHAPTER 2: FROM DARKNESS TO LIGHT

1. Alf J. Mapp, *The Golden Dragon: Alfred the Great and His Times* (Lanham, MD: Madison Books, 1974), p. 94.

2. Marc Bloch, "Vassal and Lord," in *Feudal Society Vol. 1*, trans. L.A. Manyon (Chicago: University of Chicago Press, 1961).

3. David C. Lindberg, *The Beginnings of Western Science* (Chicago: University of Chicago Press, 1992), p. 287.

4. Thomas B. Costain, *The Conquering Family* (Garden City, NY: Doubleday and Company, 1949), pp. 277–332.

5. Alister McGrath, *In the Beginning* (New York: Anchor Books, 2001), pp. 12–13.

6. *Encyclopedia Britannica Macropaedia*, 15th ed., s.v., "Biblical Literature."

7. Richard Erdoes, *A.D. 1000: Living on the Brink of Apocalypse* (New York: Barnes and Noble Books, 1995).

8. Michael Farquhar, *Royal Scandals* (New York: Penguin Press, 2001), p. 223.

9. Paul Johnson, *A History of Christianity* (New York: Atheneum Press, 1976), p. 219.

10. Jasper Ridley, *Bloody Mary's Martyrs: The Story of England's Terror* (New York: Carroll & Graf, 2001).

11. Jean V. Matthews, *Toward a New Society: American Thought and Culture 1800–1830* (Boston: Twayne, 1991), p. 102.

12. Margaret Jacob, *Living the Enlightenment* (New York: Oxford University Press, 1991), p. 4.

13. It has often been asserted that Napoleon was a Freemason. There is no proof of it, although many of his military officers, members of his Grand Council for the Empire, and 22 out of the 30 Marshals of France and his four brothers were. Napoleon's wife, the Empress Josephine, was admitted into a French female lodge in 1804. Of the Masons, Napoleon once called them "a set of imbeciles who meet for a good meal." See Jasper Ridley, *The Freemasons* (New York: Arcade, 2001), p. 152. See also "Bonaparte," in *Coil's Masonic Encyclopedia*, ed. Henry Wilson Coil (Richmond, VA: Macoy Publishing, 1961, rev. ed. 1996).

CHAPTER 3: FREEMASONRY BEFORE THE REVOLUTION

1. Correspondence from George Washington to Massachusetts Grand Lodge of Masons, December 27, 1792, reprinted in *A Treasury of Masonic Thought,* ed. Carl Glick (New York: Vail-Ballou Press, Inc., 1959), p. 204.

2. George Unwin, *Guilds and Companies of London* (London: Methuen & Co., 1908), pp. 6–7.

3. James Davis Carter, *Masonry in U.S. History—Through 1846* (Waco, TX: Grand Lodge of Texas, A.F. & A.M., 1955), p. 120.

4. John Anderson, "Article II: Of the Civil Magistrate, Supreme and Subordinate," *The Constitutions of the Freemasons* (London: 1728).

5. Ibid.

6. For a detailed account, see *The Masonic Stone of 1606,* by R.W. Bro. Reginald V. Harris, Grand Historian, Grand Lodge of Nova Scotia; *The Builder Magazine*, Vol. X, No. 10, October 1924.

7. Even today, multiple Grand Lodges coexist outside of the United States, even if they do not permit their members to visit each others' lodges. Freemasons who have grown up within the very rigid Grand Lodge system in place in the United States may seem perplexed at the proliferation of multiple Grand Lodges and chaotic lack of sovereignty between jurisdictions. From about 1800 until the 1990s, the system in the United States had been strictly one Grand Lodge per state recognized as being in authority by its neighbors. The exclusive territorial rights of each Grand Lodge were not changed until the gradual joint recognition of predominantly African-American Prince Hall Grand Lodges beginning in the 1990s. The Prince Hall Grand Lodges had developed as a separate organization, complete with their own lodges, rules and governing bodies. The vestiges of racial segregation, and later organizational stubbornness, had kept the two groups laboring in isolation from each other since the 1780s.

8. The Junto would later become the American Philosophical Society.

9. "Benjamin Franklin, Freemason," *Short Talk Bulletin,* Vol. XI, No. 10 (Masonic Service Association), October 1933.

10. Michael Baigent and Richard Leigh, *The Temple and the Lodge* (New York: Arcade Publishing Inc., 1989), p. 211.

11. Henry Wilson Coil, *Coil's Masonic Encyclopedia*: Knights Templar (Masonic), p. 349.

12. Phillip A. Roth, *Masonry in the Formation of Our Government 1761–1799* (A facsimile of the first edition. Whitefish, MT: Kessinger Publishing, 1927), p. 18.

13. Ibid, p. 17.

14. Steven Bullock, *Revolutionary Brotherhood* (Chapel Hill, NC: University of North Carolina Press, 1996), p. 62. The judge of the Vice-Admiralty Court was a Mason, as was the solicitor to the Board of Customs Commissioners. The Crown Advocate was Jeremy Gridley, also a member of First Lodge, along with Otis. Gridley was the Provincial Grand Master for portions of the American colonies. Yet Jeremy Gridley's own brother Richard was a member of Boston's Second Lodge, and would go on to join the Continental Army and command the Boston defenses that would eventually drive the British out.

15. Sidney Morse, *Freemasonry in the Revolution* (A facsimile of the first edition. New York: Kessinger Publishing, 1924).

16. The Boston Tea Party Ships and Museum, "*December 16, 1773,*" www.bostonteapartyship.com/history.asp.

17. A. Cerza, "The Boston Tea Party and Freemasonry," *Ars Quatuor Coronatorum,* Vol. XCVIII (1985), p. 207.

CHAPTER 4: WAR AMONG BROTHERS

1. Thomas Fleming, *Liberty!* (New York: Viking Press, 1997), p. 88.

2. John Dickinson was a member of Lodge No. 18, Dover, Delaware. See William R. Denslow and Harry S Truman, *10,000 Famous Freemasons* (N.p.: Missouri Lodge of Research and William R. Denslow, 1957), p. 315.

3. John Jay's Masonic membership has never been ascertained, but he has long been believed to have been one. In a letter to George Washington, he made certain Masonic references that infer his familiarity with the fraternity.

4. Denslow, p. 264.

5. Charles S. Lobingier, "Freemasons in the American Revolution," *The Builder,* Vol. IV, No. 3, March 8, 1918.

6. Ibid.

7. Letter from Samuel Parsons, quoted in *Freemasonry in the Thirteen Colonies,* J. Hugo Tatsch (New York: Macoy Publishing, 1933), p. 213.

8. Paul M. Bessel, "George Washington's Generals and Freemasonry," http://bessel.org/gwgenmas.htm.

9. Harlow Giles Unger, *Lafayette* (New York: John Wiley & Sons, 2002), p. 15 and p. 389 note 41.

10. The events of the battle and the massacre that followed were portrayed in James Fennimore Cooper's novel, *The Last of the Mohicans* (1826).

11. The State Society of the Cincinnati of Pennsylvania website, www.pasoci etyofthecincinnati.org/Cinnweb/SOC/1-1-1main.asp (accessed September 1, 2006).

12. Steven Bullock, *Revolutionary Brotherhood* (Chapel Hill, NC: University of North Carolina Press, 1996), p. 130 and p. 360 note 60.

13. "Prince Hall Revisited" by Tony Pope, presented March 26, 2004, Victorian Lodge of Research, Melbourne, Australia; Pietre-Stones Review of Freemasonry, "Tony Pope Masonic papers," www.freemasons-free masonry.com/popefr.html (accessed August 25, 2006). This collection of papers, including in particular "Our Segregated Brethren, Prince Hall Freemasons Part I," includes a painstaking examination of all available documentation of the foundation of African Lodge, especially letters written by Hall to the Grand Lodge of England (Moderns). The seemingly obsessive concerns by researchers over the origins and "legality" of African lodge and its subsequent transformation from a mere Masonic lodge into a Grand Lodge is important to Prince Hall Masons. However, the mainstream and predominantly white Grand Lodges in the United States have used questions of regularity for two centuries to justify their refusal to recognize African-American Masonry as legitimate.

14. See *Official History of Free Masonry Among the Coloured People in North America* by William H. Grimshaw (Past Grand Master, 1907, of the Prince Hall Grand Lodge of Washington, District of Columbia), published in 1903. Despite its title, it is scarcely the "official history," and large parts of the book—about, in particular, Hall's early life—have long been discredited as pure invention.

15. In later years, St. Andrew's Lodge would be more enlightened. At least nine black Masons were initiated, passed and raised in St. Andrew's in the mid-1800s, and in 1871, eight of them petitioned the Grand Lodge of Massachusetts to charter a new lodge. The application was denied. See *Negro Masonry in the United States* by H. V. B. Voorhis (1940), p. 108.

16. "Prince Hall Revisited," see note 13.

CHAPTER 5: HOW THE FREEMASONS INVENTED AMERICA

1. Margaret Jacob, *Living the Enlightenment* (New York: Oxford University Press, 1991), p. 22.

2. John Jay's Masonic membership has been disputed, but letters he wrote indicated, through his use of Masonic terminology in them, that he was a Freemason.

3. James Anderson, "Charges of a Freemason, Article I," *The Constitutions of the Freemasons* (London: 1723).

4. Ibid., "Article VI, of Behaviour, Viz," etc.

5. I am deeply indebted to James Davis Carter and his paper *Masonry in U.S. History—through 1846* (Waco, TX: Grand Lodge of Texas, A.F. & A.M., 1955) for his careful enumeration of the many similarities between Anderson's *Constitutions* and the U.S. Constitution and Bill of Rights.

6. Anderson, "General Regulations, Article XXXIX."

7. Ibid., "General Regulations, Article X."

8. Ibid., "General Regulations, Article XXVIII."

9. Ibid., "General Regulations, Article XXIX."

10. Ibid., "General Regulations, Article XIV."

11. Ibid., "General Regulations, Article XXVIII."

12. Ibid., "General Regulations, Article X."

13. Ibid., "General Regulations, Article XII."

14. Ibid., "General Regulations, Article XXXIX."

15. Ibid., "General Regulations, Article XII."

16. Catherine Drinker Bowen, *Miracle at Philadelphia* (Boston: Little Brown and Company, 1966, 1986 edition), p. 96.

17. Thomas Smith Webb, *The Freemason's Monitor or Illustrations of Freemasonry* (1818), p. 65.

18. Not to be confused with Charles Carroll, who had signed the Declaration of Independence. He was a Catholic, and not a Freemason, as he is mistakenly identified in the 2004 film *National Treasure*. A story is told that after Charles Carroll signed the Declaration, an anti-Catholic political enemy rose and protested that Carroll's signature on the treasonous document was no risk. Certainly the countryside was rife with men named Charles Carroll, and the king's men would have no proof of just who had really signed it. Carroll rose again and stepped up to John Hancock's desk to amend his signature. If you look at the document today, you will see that it says, "Charles Carroll of Carrollton."

19. Gerry's Masonic membership has not been confirmed, but his descendants have always contended he was a Mason.

20. Anderson, "General Regulations, Article XXXVIII."

CHAPTER 6: SOLOMON'S BUILDERS

1. Psalm 133:1. This is commonly the biblical passage read during the Entered Apprentice degree of Freemasonry in U.S. lodges.

2. While there is no written record of the actual ceremony performed at the laying of the first boundary stone of the Federal District, this description is based on the ceremonies typical of the day used by Masonic lodges to lay cornerstones or foundation stones. See William Preston's *Preston's Masonry* (1792) and Thomas Smith Webb's *Freemason's Monitor or Illustrations of Masonry* (1818). However, the procession itself is described in detail in Dunlop's *American Daily Advertisor* [sic], Philadelphia, April 28, 1791.

3. Thomas Nelson Page. *Washington and Its Romance* (New York: Doubleday, Page & Co., 1923).

4. Washington had his own selfish motives besides mere convenience to home. After the Revolution he became obsessed with the notion of building a canal that would connect the Potomac with the Ohio River, to increase commerce along the river and surrounding areas. In fact, he became something of a notorious pest about the canal topic, managing to work it into almost any unrelated conversation during social events at Mount Vernon.

5. The building at 26 Wall Street in New York today is called Federal Hall, but only to commemorate the original building. L'Enfant's structure was

demolished in 1812 and replaced by the current building, the first U.S. Customs House. The name was changed to Federal Hall to commemorate the location of the first Capitol of the United States under the new Constitution. A statue of Washington stands on the spot where he took the first oath of office.

6. "Washington." *The Catholic Encyclopedia* (1914), www.catholicity.com/encyclopedia/w/washington.dc.html (accessed September 1, 2006).

7. The Supreme Court was the redheaded stepchild of the city plan for many years. When it moved to Washington, D.C., in 1801, a building was planned, but the funding was not. Consequently, the Court was housed in the Capitol building, eventually moving into the basement in 1810. It is a magnificent room even today and is known as the Old Supreme Court Room. It later moved upstairs into the Old Senate Chamber, where it remained until occupying its present building in 1935.

8. S. Brent Morris, *Cornerstones of Freedom* (Washington, DC: The Supreme Council, 1993), p. 30.

9. Leinster House in Dublin has served as the parliament building of the Republic of Ireland since 1922.

10. Robert Lomas, *Turning the Solomon Key* (Gloucester, MA: Fair Winds Press, 2006).

11. Charles Addison, *The History of the Knights Templar* (1842).

12. It would later become Federal Lodge No. 1 when the Grand Lodge of the District of Columbia was formed.

13. Maryland Lodge No. 9 would become Potomac Lodge No. 5 under the Grand Lodge of the District of Columbia.

14. William P. O'Brian, "Reality and Illusion—The White House and Harry Truman," *White House History Journal*, The White House Historical Society website, www.whitehousehistory.org/08/subs/08_b05.html (accessed September 10, 2006).

15. *The Columbian Mirror* and *Alexandria Gazette*, September 25, 1793.

16. "Right Worshipful Grand Master, *pro tempore*."

17. *Columbian Mirror*

18. James Madison, *The Federalist No. 37—Concerning the Difficulties of the Convention in Devising a Proper Form of Government* (1788).

19. "Humanum Genus," *Encyclical of Pope Leo XIII on Freemasonry*, April 20, 1884. Papal Encyclicals Online, www.papalencyclicals.net/Leo13/l13human.htm (accessed September 8, 2006).

20. Page, *Washington and Its Romance*, p. 182.

21. Thomas Fleming, *Duel* (New York; Basic Books, 1999), p. 151.

22. Jeffrey E. Meyer, *Myths in Stone: Religious Dimensions of Washington, D.C.* (Berkeley, CA: University of California Press, 2001).

CHAPTER 7: THE MYSTERIOUS MAP OF WASHINGTON, D.C.

1. "Freemasonry and Washington D.C.'s Street Layout," http://freemasonry watch.org/washington.html (accessed July 1, 2006).

2. Michael Baigent and Richard Leigh, *The Temple and the Lodge* (New York: Arcade Publishing Inc., 1989), p. 262.

3. David Ovason. *The Secret Architecture of Our Nation's Capital* [originally published as *The Secret Zodiacs of Washington, D.C., Was the City of Stars Planned by Masons?* (London: Random House UK, 1999], p. 170.

4. Ibid., p. 171.

5. Ibid., p. 459 note 59.

6. Ibid.

7. Ibid., p. 355.

8. J. R. R. Tolkien, trans., *Sir Gawain and the Green Knight, Pearl, and Sir Orfeo* (New York: Ballantine Books, 1975).

9. Stephen Dafoe, *Baphomet: The Pentagram Connection,* www.templarhistory. com/pentagram.html (accessed June 28, 2006).

10. Jay Griffiths, "The Tyranny of Clocks and Calendars," *The Guardian,* August 28, 1999, www.guardian.co.uk/comment/story/0,,266761,00.html (accessed August 25, 2006).

11. Cutting Edge Ministries, "Former Satanist Informs Us That Government Mall in Washington D.C. Was Originally Conceived as a Satanic Sephiroth Tree of Life!" www.cuttingedge.org/news/n1399.cfm (accessed August 25, 2006).

12. Ian Kendall, "*Scottish Place Names—Washington, D.C.,*" www.rampant scotland.com/placenames/placename_washington.htm (accessed August 15, 2006).

CHAPTER 8: OCCULT MYTHS AND LEGENDS OF WASHINGTON, D.C.

1. Albert Pike, *Morals and Dogma* (Washington, DC: The Supreme Council of the Southern Jurisdiction A.A.S.R.U.S.A., 1871, revised edition 1950), p. 321.

2. A. C. DeLa Rive, "La Femme et l'Enfant dans la Franc Maconnerie Universelle?" (1894). Cited in *Is It True What They Say about Freemasonry?* by Arturo de Hoyos and S. Brent Morris (New York: M. Evans and Company, 2004).

3. Dan Brown, *Angels and Demons* (New York: Pocket Books, 2000), pp. 111–112.

4. Information Awareness Office Home Page, as archived by The Memory Hole at www.thememoryhole.org/policestate/iao/iao-original.htm. Accessed 7/31/2006.

5. Statement of the Information Awareness Office regarding the meaning and use of the IAO logo. Source: Question 15 in the IAO Frequently Asked Questions document dated February 2003, at www.information-retrieval. info/docs/IAO-logo-stmt.html (accessed July 31, 2006).

6. Robert Hieronimus, with Laura Cortner, *Founding Fathers, Secret Societies* (Rochester, VT: Destiny Books, 2006; originally published as *America's Secret Destiny*, 1989), p. 102.

7. Ibid.

8. H.S. Wycoff, "The Great American Seal," *The Mystic Light, the Rosicrucian Magazine*, pp. 56–62.

9. www.janik.online.co.ma (accessed July 15, 2006).

10. S. L. MacGregor Mathers, *The Key of Solomon the King* (Clavicula Salomonis), R. A. Gilbert [Foreword] (Weiser Books, 2000).

CHAPTER 9: THE CAPITOL BUILDING

1. Ralph P. Lester, *Look to the East: A Ritual of the First Degrees of Masonry* (Harwood Heights, IL: Charles T. Powner Co., 1982), p. 52. While there are many local variations between each Grand Lodge's individually approved rituals, most jurisdictions—with the notable exception of the Grand Lodge of Pennsylvania—use ceremony rituals that are similar to this work.

2. Mason Locke Weems, *A History of the Life and Death, Virtues and Exploits of General George Washington*, 1809.

3. According to Charles Callahan, Past Grand Master of Virginia, in his book, *Washington: The Man and the Mason* (Gibson Bros. Press, 1915), Henry Lee was a member of Hiram Lodge No. 59, Westmoreland County, Virginia.

4. Arthur St. Clair was descended from Sir William St. Clair, builder of the famous fifteenth-century Rosslyn Chapel in Roslin, Scotland. The chapel has long been thought to have both Templar and Masonic significance.

5. Neal O. Hammon, ed., *My Father, Daniel Boone—The Draper Interviews with Nathan Boone* (Lexington, KY: University Press of Kentucky, 1999), p. 139.

6. Christopher L. Murphy, "Henry Clay: A Proud American and a Proud Mason," *Virginia Masonic Herald*, April 1989.

7. Samuel Huntington was not a Mason, but his son would join the fraternity, and became a Grand Master of Masons in Ohio.

8. Thomas McKean was noted as a frequent visitor to Perseverance Lodge No. 21, Harrisburg, Pennsylvania, although his own Masonic record is not known.

9. Richard Henry Lee has been associated with Hiram Lodge No. 59, Westmoreland County, Virginia, but his membership has never been confirmed.

10. George W. Baird, "Great American Masons," *Little Masonic Library Book IV* (Masonic Service Association of the United States, 1924), p. 116.

11. Arthur M. Schlesinger, "Biography of a Nation of Joiners," *American Historical Review 50* (October 1944), pp. 2, 15.

12. *History of the Church*, May 4, 1842, vol. 5, p. 1.

CHAPTER 10: SECRETS IN STONE

1. The boundary stones continue to be cared for by the Daughters of the American Revolution, and the detailed location of each one can be found on their website at www.dcdar.org/BoundaryStoneLocations.htm.

2. Editorial, *Memphis Daily Appeal*, April 16, 1868.

3. Fred W. Allsopp, "Letters to the People of the Northern States," *Albert Pike, A Biography* (Little Rock, AR: Parke-Harper Company, 1928), p 181.

4. Wayne Craig Wade, *The Fiery Cross, The Ku Klux Klan in America* (New York: Simon and Schuster, Inc., 1987), p. 58.

5. Grand Lodge of British Columbia and Yukon website, Albert Pike Did Not Found The Ku Klux Klan, http://freemasonry.bcy.ca/anti-masonry/kkk.html (accessed June 20, 2006).

6. Ibid.

7. "It is proper to say that the writer of the paper is an active minister in the Southern Presbyterian Church. We may state also that he has no personal knowledge of the Ku Klux, although he has had abundant opportunity to know as much of the inside history of the Klan as if he had been a leading member; he has had access, besides, to authentic private documents." New Light on the Ku Klux Klan (editorial), *Topics of the Times, The Century*, Volume 28, Issue 3, July 1884.

8. William Still, *New World Order* (Lafayette, LA: Huntington House Publishers, 1990), p. 123.

9. Edwin Stanton was a member of Steubenville Lodge No. 45 in Steubenville, Ohio. He became a charter member of Washington Lodge No. 253 in Pittsburgh, Pennsylvania.

10. Until recently, the last line of this section had been translated to say "ID by rows." In April of 2006, the artist came forward with a sheepish admission: that the fourth section of the message actually contained a typo. On the sculpture, Sanborn had left an "x" out of the text, which wound up changing the last line of a decoded portion of the message significantly. The properly decoded line reads, "Layer two." See *Wired News*, "Typo Confounds Kryptos Sleuths," www.wired.com/news/technology/0,70701-0.html?tw=wn_story_page_prev2, April 20, 2006.

11. Elonka Dunin. *The Mammoth Book of Secret Codes and Cryptograms* (New York: Carroll & Graf, 2006).

12. *Washington Post,* "John Kelly's Washington," June 20, 2005.

13. William Alfred Bryan, *George Washington in American Literature 1775–1865* (Westport, CT: Greenwood Press, 1979), p. 84.

14. The entire history of the Washington Monument is told in great detail in *A History of the Washington Monument 1844–1968* by George J. Olszewski (Washington, DC: Office of History and Historic Architecture, United States Department of the Interior, National Park Service, 1971).

15. Polk was a Freemason. He was a member of Columbia Lodge No. 31 in Columbia, Tennessee. See Denslow/Truman, p. 353.

16. National Parks Service, "List of Memorial Stones with Inscriptions," www.nps.gov/archive/wamo/history/appd.htm, August 23, 2006.

17. National Parks Service, "A History of the Washington Monument," www.nps.gov/archive/wamo/history/chap3.htm, August 25, 2006.

CHAPTER 11: MASONIC SITES OF WASHINGTON, D.C.

1. For an exhaustive history of Freemasonry in the District, see *History of the Grand Lodge and of Freemasonry in the District of Columbia* by Kenton N. Harper (Washington, DC: R. Beresford, 1911).

2. Christopher Weeks, *AIA Guide to the Architecture of Washington, D.C.* (Baltimore, MD: Johns Hopkins University Press, 3rd edition, 1994).

3. The A.A.S.R. Northern Masonic Jurisdiction (NMJ) is composed of the fifteen states east of the Mississippi and north of the Mason–Dixon line: Connecticut, Delaware, Illinois, Indiana, Maine, Massachusetts, New Hampshire, New Jersey, New York, Ohio, Pennsylvania, Rhode Island,

Vermont and Wisconsin. The NMJ's headquarters are in Lexington, Massachusetts. All other states are governed by the Supreme Council Southern Jurisdiction in Washington, D.C.

4. There is no shortage of other non-Masonic buildings based on this same design. Some of them include: Grant's Tomb in New York City, the spire of St. George's Church Bloomsbury in London; the Indiana War Memorial in Indianapolis, Indiana; and the Shrine of Remembrance in Melbourne, Australia.

5. Margaret Hair, "Masonic house of the temple a not-so-secret marvel," *Mercury News*, July 24, 2006, www.mercurynews.com/mld/mercury news/living/travel/15109705.htm (accessed July 30, 2006).

CHAPTER 12: 'TIS WELL

1. *The Writings of George Washington from the Original Manuscript Sources, 1745–1799*, United States George Washington Bicentennial Commission and published by authority of Congress; John C. Fitzpatrick, editor. (Washington DC: U.S. Government Printing Office; 1931–44), Vol. 36.

2. Charles Callahan, *Washington: The Man and the Mason* (Washington, DC: Gibson Bros. Press, 1915), p. 191.

3. Ibid., "Appendix: The Will of George Washington."

Bibliography

✦✦✦

Allsopp, Fred W. *Albert Pike, A Biography*. Little Rock, AR: Parke-Harper Company, 1928.

Anderson, James. *The Constitutions of the Freemasons*. London, 1723.

Baigent, Michael, and Richard Leigh. *The Temple and the Lodge*. New York: Arcade Publishing Inc., 1989.

Baird, George W. "Great American Masons," in *Little Masonic Library Book IV* (Masonic Service Association of the United States, 1924).

Bloch, Marc. "Vassal and Lord," *Feudal Society Vol. 1*. Chicago: University of Chicago Press, 1961.

Brookhiser, Richard. *Founding Father: Rediscovering George Washington*. New York: Free Press Publishing, 1997.

Brøndsted, Johannes. *The Vikings*. Translated by Kalle Skov. London: Penguin Books, 1965.

Bryan, William Alfred. *George Washington in American Literature 1775–1865*. Westport, CT: Greenwood Press, 1979.

Bullock, Steven. *Revolutionary Brotherhood*. Chapel Hill, NC: University of North Carolina Press, 1996.

Callahan, Charles. *Washington: The Man and the Mason*. Washington, DC: Gibson Bros. Press, 1915.

Carter, James Davis. *Masonry in U.S. History—Through 1846*. Waco, TX: Grand Lodge of Texas, A.F. & A.M., 1955.

Churton, Tobias. *The Golden Builders*. York Beach, ME: Red Wheel/Weiser, 2005.

Coil, Henry W., ed. *Coil's Masonic Encyclopedia.* 1961. Reprint, Richmond, VA: Macoy Publishing Company, 1996.

Costain, Thomas B. *The Conquering Family.* Garden City, NY: Doubleday and Company, 1949.

Coxe, Daniel. *Description of the English Province of Carolana...1722.* A facsimile of the first edition. Gainesville, FL: University of Florida, 1976.

Darnton, Robert. *The Forbidden Best-Sellers of Pre-Revolutionary France.* London: Fontana Press, 1996.

De Hoyos, Arturo and S. Brent Morris. *Is It True What They Say about Freemasonry?* New York: M. Evans and Company, 2004.

Denslow, William R. and Harry S Truman. *10,000 Famous Freemasons.* N.p.: Missouri Lodge of Research and William R. Denslow, 1957.

Drinker Bowen, Catherine. *Miracle at Philadelphia.* 1966. Reprint, Boston: Little Brown and Company, 1986.

Duckett, Eleanor Shipley. *Alfred the Great: The King and His England.* Chicago: University of Chicago Press, 1956.

Dunin, Elonka. *The Mammoth Book of Secret Codes and Cryptograms.* New York: Carroll & Graf, 2006.

Durant, Will and Ariel Durant. *The Age of Napoleon.* New York: MJF Books, 1975.

Ehrman, Bart D. *Truth and Fiction in The Da Vinci Code.* New York: Oxford University Press, 2004.

Erdoes, Richard. *A.D. 1000: Living on the Brink of Apocalypse.* New York: Barnes and Noble Books, 1995.

Farquhar, Michael. *Royal Scandals.* New York: Penguin Press, 2001.

Farrah, George. *The Temples at Jerusalem and Their Masonic Connections.* Hinckley, Leicestershire, England: Central Regalia Ltd., 2003.

Fleming, Thomas. *Duel.* New York: Basic Books, 1999.

Fleming, Thomas. *Liberty!* New York: Viking Press, 1997.

Hammon, Neal O., ed. *My Father, Daniel Boone—The Draper Interviews with Nathan Boone.* Lexington, KY: University Press of Kentucky, 1999.

Harper, Kenton N. *History of the Grand Lodge and of Freemasonry in the District of Columbia.* Washington, DC: R. Beresford, 1911.

Holmes, David L. *Faiths of the Founding Fathers.* New York: Oxford University Press, 2006.

Jacob, Margaret. *Living the Enlightenment.* New York: Oxford University Press, 1991.

Jacob, Margaret. *The Origins of Freemasonry.* Philadelphia, PA: University of Pennsylvania Press, 2006.

Johnson, Paul. *A History of Christianity.* New York: Atheneum Press, 1976.

Lanier, John J. *Washington: The Great American Mason.* New York: Macoy Publishing, 1922.

Lester, Ralph P. *Look to the East: A Ritual of the First Degrees of Masonry.* Harwood Heights, IL: Charles T. Powner Co., 1982.

Lindberg, David C. *The Beginnings of Western Science.* Chicago: University of Chicago Press, 1992.

Lomas, Robert. *Turning the Solomon Key.* Gloucester, MA: Fair Winds Press, 2006.

Loomis, Stanley. *Paris in the Terror.* Philadelphia, PA: J.P. Lippencott, 1964.

Mapp, Alf. J., Jr. *The Golden Dragon: Alfred the Great and His Times.* Lanham, MD: Madison Books, 1974.

Matthews, Jean V. *Toward a New Society: American Thought and Culture 1800–1830.* Boston: Twayne, 1991.

McGrath, Alister. *In the Beginning.* New York: Anchor Books, 2001.

Meyer, Jeffrey E. *Myths in Stone: Religious Dimensions of Washington, D.C.* Berkeley, CA: University of California Press, 2001.

Morison, Samuel Eliot. *The Young Man Washington.* Cambridge, MA: Harvard University Press, 1932.

Morris, S. Brent. *Cornerstones of Freedom*. Washington, DC: The Supreme Council, 1993.

Morse, Sidney. *Freemasonry in the Revolution*. A facsimile of the first edition. New York: Kessinger Publishing, 1924.

Murphy, Christopher L. "Henry Clay: A Proud American and a Proud Mason," *Virginia Masonic Herald*, April 1989.

Ovason, David. *The Secret Architecture of Our Nation's Capital* (originally published as *The Secret Zodiacs of Washington, D.C., Was the City of Stars Planned by Masons?*). London: Random House UK, 1999.

Page, Thomas Nelson. *Washington and Its Romance*. New York: Doubleday, Page & Co., 1923.

Ridley, Jasper. *Bloody Mary's Martyrs: The Story of England's Terror*. New York: Carroll & Graf, 2001.

Ridley, Jasper. *The Freemasons*. New York: Arcade, 2001.

Robinson, John J. *Born in Blood: The Lost Secrets of Freemasonry*. N.p.: M. Evans & Company, 1990.

Roth, Philip A. *Masonry in the Formation of Our Government 1761–1799*. A facsimile of the first edition. Whitefish, MT: Kessinger Publishing, 1927.

Scarre, Chris. *Chronicle of the Roman Emperors*. London: Thames and Hudson Ltd., 1995.

Schlesinger, Arthur M. "Biography of a Nation of Joiners," *American Historical Review 50*, October 1944.

Stevenson, David. *The Origins of Freemasonry: Scotland's Century 1590–1710*. Cambridge, MA: Cambridge University Press, 1988.

Still, William. *New World Order*. Lafayette, LA: Huntington House Publishers, 1990.

Tatsch, J. Hugo. *Freemasonry in the Thirteen Colonies*. New York: Macoy Publishing, 1933.

Unger, Harlow Giles. *Lafayette*. New York: John Wiley & Sons, 2002.

Unwin, George. *Guilds and Companies of London*. London: Methuen & Co., 1908.

Wade, Wayne Craig. *The Fiery Cross: The Ku Klux Klan in America*. New York: Simon and Schuster, Inc., 1987.

Walker, J. Travis. *A History of Fredericksburg Lodge No. 4, A.F.& A.M. 1752–2002*. Fredericksburg, VA: Sheridan Books, 2002.

Webb, Thomas Smith. *The Freemason's Monitor or Illustrations of Freemasonry*. 1818.

Weeks, Christopher. *AIA Guide to the Architecture of Washington, D.C.* Baltimore, MD: Johns Hopkins University Press, 3rd edition, 1994.

Weems, Mason Locke. *A History of the Life and Death, Virtues and Exploits of General George Washington*. 1809.

Wood, Gordon S. *Radicalism of the American Revolution*. New York: Vintage Books, 1991.

Artwork credits

Index

❖ ❖ ❖

About the Author

Christopher Hodapp is a Freemason and a Past Master of two Masonic lodges. His first book, *Freemasons for Dummies,* has quickly become the most popular modern guide to the ancient and accepted fraternity of Freemasonry. He has written for the *Indiana Freemason, Masonic Magazine* and *Templar History Magazine,* and he is a monthly columnist for the *Texas Home Gardener.* Hodapp has spent more than twenty years in advertising as a commercial filmmaker. He and his wife Alice live in Indianapolis.